Polar Research

To the Present,
And the Future

AAAS Selected Symposia Series

Published by Westview Press
5500 Central Avenue, Boulder, Colorado

for the

American Association for the Advancement of Science
1776 Massachusetts Ave., N.W., Washington, D.C.

Polar Research

To the Present,
And the Future

Edited by Mary A. McWhinnie

AAAS Selected Symposium **7**

AAAS Selected Symposia Series

Published in 1978 in the United States of America by

Westview Press, Inc.
5500 Central Avenue
Boulder, Colorado 80301
Frederick A. Praeger, Publisher and Editorial Director

Library of Congress Catalog Card Number: 78-52068
ISBN: 0-89158-435-8

Printed and bound in the United States of America

About the Book

Highlighting twenty years of U.S. scientific research conducted since the International Geophysical Year (IGY) of 1957-58, this volume marks a turning point in the history of polar investigations and provides a lucid summary of the contributions of many distinguished scientists. The authors provide an overview of major polar research programs, past and present; explore concepts derived from highly interrelated aspects of physical and life sciences; and seek to offer a glimpse of future polar science and polar development.

The introduction briefly describes major physical, biological, and interdisciplinary research programs, as well as the magnitude, extent, and international character of contemporary polar science. Twenty years of polar biological investigations are then reviewed, and subsequent chapters address principles and advances in meteorology, physical oceanography, glaciology, and the geological evidence that bears on the origin of Antarctica. These physical sciences delineate a matrix for the polar biospheres and provide a background for understanding the major categories of structure and dynamic functioning of the marine ecosystem, polar marine mammals, adaptational physiology, and terrestrial biotic adaptations.

Contents

List of Figures

Chapter 2, continued

Chapter 3

Chapter 4

Chapter 10

List of Tables

xvii

Foreword

The *AAAS Selected Symposia Series* was begun in 1977 to
provide a means for more permanently recording and more
widely disseminating some of the valuable material which is
discussed at the AAAS Annual National Meetings. The volumes
in this *Series* are based on symposia held at the Meetings
which address topics of current and continuing significance,
both within and among the sciences, and in the areas in which
science and technology impact on public policy. The *Series*
format is designed to provide for rapid dissemination of information, so the papers are not typeset but are reproduced
directly from the camera copy submitted by the authors, without copy editing. The papers are reviewed and edited by
the symposia organizers who then become the editors of the
various volumes. Most papers published in this *Series* are
original contributions which have not been previously published, although in some cases additional papers from other
sources have been added by an editor to provide a more comprehensive view of a particular topic. Symposia may be reports of new research or reviews of established work, particularly work of an interdisciplinary nature, since the AAAS
Annual Meeting typically embraces the full range of the
sciences and their societal implications.

WILLIAM D. CAREY
Executive Officer
American Association for
the Advancement of Science

Preface

    This volume assembles a collection of inter-disciplinary research reports of natural phenomena characteristic of polar regions. It represents the results of countless years of effort in field research in those forbidding and beautiful high latitudes. The physical endurance of scientists and technicians has been sustained by the challenge to understand the environmental forces and their syntheses for the interpretation of natural phenomena which are impossible to study elsewhere.

    It has been twenty years since the International Geophysical Year of 1957-1958 and it is appropriate to bring together many of the prominent scientists who have been engaged in polar research since that time. The historical balance of twenty years of study makes it possible to measure our progress in the closely related fields of physical and life sciences. We hope to present in this volume a review of selected categories of biological research as each has emerged through years of intense scientific studies and investigations. We can now point to the future, so far as evident trends, our experience, and our insights will permit.

    The symposium on which this volume is based was sponsored by the Biological Sciences Section of the American Association for the Advancement of Science. The organizer of the program deemed it essential to recognize the relationships between the environment and biota of the polar regions. A careful study of Antarctica's history senses the

moving spirit of the exciting stages of discovery.
We are optimistic about the continent's future.

The contributions contained in this volume
have been made by scientists who are deeply involved in polar research. They include studies on
meteorology, physical oceanography, geology, and
descriptions of operative biological elements and
systems. Some of the papers examine the problems
of biological research in marine ecosystem structures, the dynamic functions of marine mammals
and their ability to adapt to the harsh conditions
under which they survive. All of these studies
provide fertile grounds for the exchange of ideas
and delineate specific areas for further investigation. If this symposium has stimulated more
intensive research in any of these fields of study,
some of its objectives will have been achieved.

As arranger of the symposium and editor of
this volume, I acknowledge with gratitude the un-
common cooperation of the authors who have con-
tributed to it. In addition, I must acknowledge
the many polar scientists who have assisted
Duwayne M. Anderson and me in the development of a
view of contemporary research in high latitudes.
In particular, we acknowledge the assistance of,
D. James Baker, Jr. and Richard S. Greenfield
(GARP; Polar Sub-Experiment), Charles R. Bentley,
Terence J. Hughes, Ian M. Whillans, Kendall N.
Moulton, Robert H. Thomas and Richard L. Cameron
(RIGGS; IAGP; WISP), John W. Clough and John F.
Splettstösser (RISP), Curtis A. Collins and Victor
T. Neal (ISOS), Ian W. D. Dalziel and Mortimer D.
Turner (Scotia Arc-Antarctic Peninsula Tectonics
Program), Sayed Z. El-Sayed (BIOMASS), Theodore D.
Foster (IWSOE; Weddell Gyre), Benson T. Fogle,
Robert A. Helliwell and L. J. Lanzerotti (Solar-
Terrestrial Physics), Donald W. Hood (PROBES),
Charles J. Jonkel and Bart O'Gara (Arctic Mammal
Program), Chester C. Langway, Jr. (GISP), George
A. Llano (RATE; Man in the Arctic Program; Tundra
Biome), Lyle D. McGinnis (DVDP), Troy L. Pewe
(Permafrost) and Norbert Untersteiner (AIDJEX;
POLEX; NDS).

As Editor I owe a personal debt to many but I
must identify Horace D. Porter for his generous
editorial advice and assistance; Edward W.

Londregan who greatly improved our Introduction;
Gerald Pagano who contributed much to the historical accuracy; Lloyd G. Blanchard for his continued
help through all phases of this undertaking;
Walter R. Sellig for his creative and gently
underspoken design on page xxx of this volume,
and Vivina I. Ortner and Eleanor C. Swiatly whose
skill and patience with manuscript details and
preparation brought development of this volume to
a finished state. Not least among the foregoing,
I am grateful also to the American Association for
the Advancement of Science for publication of this
volume.

September, 1977   M. A. McWhinnie
                                   De Paul University

About the Editor

Mary A. McWhinnie *is a professor in the Department of Biological Sciences at De Paul University. Her research has focused on comparative physiology, particularly the metabolic basis of low temperature adaptation in cold-blooded animals and the life cycle of* **Euphausia superba** *(krill) and she has published widely on these subjects. She was the first American woman scientist to work in Antarctica, to winter-over at McMurdo Station, and to serve as station scientific leader. She has participated in seven cruises on the antarctic research ship USNS* **Eltanin** *and was chief scientist in 1972. She chaired the Advisory Committee for Processes and Resources of the Bering Sea (PROBES) and is a member of the Polar Research Board of the National Academy of Sciences and of many other national and international groups concerned with polar activities.*

About the Authors

*Duwayne M. Anderson is chief scientist with the Division
of Polar Programs at the National Science Foundation; his
work has focused on geology, soil chemistry, physical chemistry, physical chemistry and plant physiology. His former
positions include principal investigator of the Viking (Mars
Lander) Team and chief of the Earth Sciences Branch of the
U.S. Army Cold Regions Research and Engineering Laboratory.
He is coeditor of* Geotechnical Engineering for Cold Regions
(in press).

*Campbell Craddock, professor of geology at the University
of Wisconsin-Madison, has directed numerous field programs in
Antarctica and Alaska. He was co-chief scientist of the Deep
Sea Drilling Project, Leg 35, in Antarctica and is U.S. dele-
gate and chairman of the Scientific Committee on Antarctic
Research (SCAR) Working Group on Geology. He has compiled
geologic maps of Antarctica and was awarded the U.S. Antarctic
Service Medal (1968) and the Bellingshausen-Lazarev Medal
from the Soviet Academy of Sciences (1970).*

*Arthur L. DeVries is assistant professor in the Depart-
ment of Physiology and Biophysics at the University of Illinois at Urbana. He has conducted extensive investigations of
the physiological and biochemical basis of freezing resistance
in antarctic fishes, and was the discoverer of a unique glycopeptide antifreeze compound which protects fish swimming in
ice-laden seawater.*

*L. Lee Eberhardt is staff scientist at Battelle-North-
west, Richland, Washington, and affiliate professor at the
Center for Quantitative Science in Fisheries at the University
of Washington. His areas of specialization are wildlife
management and biostatistics, and he has conducted research
projects in Antarctica, New Zealand, and Australia. He is a
Fellow of the American Association for the Advancement of
Science.*

Sayed Z. El-Sayed, professor of biological oceanography at Texas A&M University, has participated in many antarctic expeditions and has been chief scientist on several **Eltanin** *cruises. His areas of interest are marine phytoplankton, primary productivity, marine ecosystems and living resources, and population dynamics of marine fisheries.*

Joseph O. Fletcher, deputy director of the Environmental Research Laboratories at the National Oceanic and Atmospheric Administration, has worked extensively in arctic research, specifically climatic variation and fluctuation. In 1952 he led an expedition which established a research station on Fletcher's Ice Island, a massive chunk of drifting ice in the Arctic Ocean. He was formerly head of the National Science Foundation's Office of Polar Programs, and is current chairman of the U.S.-Soviet Joint Working Group of Experts on Large-Scale Ocean Atmosphere Interaction.

Theodore D. Foster, associate research oceanographer at Scripps Institution of Oceanography, University of California, San Diego, has conducted studies and published numerous articles concerning physical oceanography in the polar regions. He was scientific leader of the International Weddell Sea Oceanographic Expedition to the Southern Ocean for three seasons.

Laurence M. Gould, professor of geosciences at the University of Arizona, specializes in Antarctic glaciology and geology. He was second in command and senior scientist of the Byrd Antarctic Expedition (1928-1930), director of the U.S. International Geophysical Year Antarctic Program, chairman of the Committee on Polar Research at the National Academy of Sciences, and president of SCAR.

John J. Kelley is director of the Naval Arctic Research Laboratory and assistant professor, Institute of Marine Science, University of Alaska. He has engaged in research on the causes of variations and exchange of atmospheric CO_2 in polar marine and terrestrial systems and has published over 50 articles and monographs on gas exchange and polar microclimate. He is former co-principal investigator with the Tundra Biome, U.S. International Biological Programme.

George A. Llano, program manager in the Division of Polar Programs at the National Science Foundation, specializes in lichenology and polar ecology. He has worked in Alaska and Antarctica and was chief scientist on five oceanographic cruises. He has published numerous articles and five books, most recently the **SCAR Symposium of Antarctic Biology, Third: Proceedings of Adaptations with Antarctic Ecosystems** *(Gulf, 1977).*

Bruce C. Parker *is a professor of botany at Virginia Polytechnic Institute and State University specializing in psychology and microbial ecology. He directed preparation of the first Environmental Impact Assessment in Antarctica. He has published three books, most recently* Conservation Problems in Antarctica *(University Press of Virginia, 1977).*

Robert H. Rutford, *vice-chancellor for research and graduate studies at the University of Nebraska-Lincoln, specializes in glacial geomorphology and has conducted extensive research in Antarctica. He is former director of the Ross Ice Shelf Progject and former division director of Polar Programs at the National Science Foundation.*

Donald B. Siniff, *professor in the Department of Ecology and Behavioral Biology at the University of Minnesota, is currently principal investigator in studies on Antarctic seal population dynamics, biota of the Antarctic pack ice and related biotelemetry and data analysis. He is presently Commissioner of the Marine Mammal Commission. His specialty is vertebrate ecology and he has published over 40 articles and monographs, most recently* Ecology of the Red Fox *(with A.B. Sargent and D.W. Warner, in press.*

Ian Stirling, *research scientist with the Canadian Wildlife Service at Environment Canada, is also chairman of the Marine Mammal Committee of the American Society of Mammalogists and chairman of the Canadian Federal-Provincial Technical Committee for Polar Bear Research and Management. His main areas of interest are population ecology and seal and polar bear behavior; he has published extensively in these fields.*

Gene C. Valentine *is public affairs officer, U.S. Navy Support Force, Antarctica. He is a psychologist by training and has served for 3 years with the United States Antarctic Program, Operation Deep Freeze.*

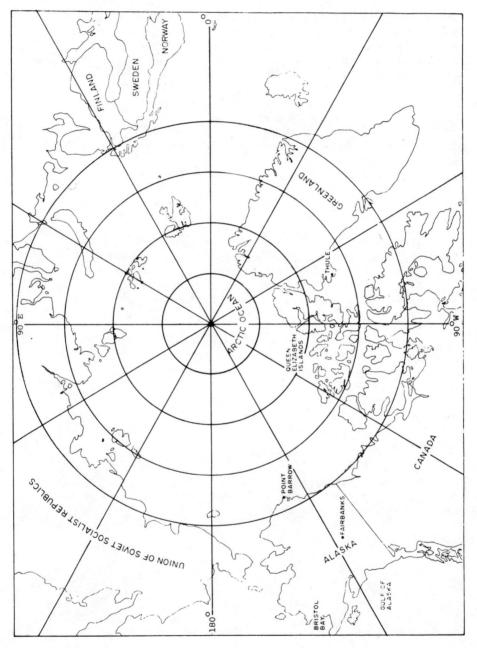

ARCTIC

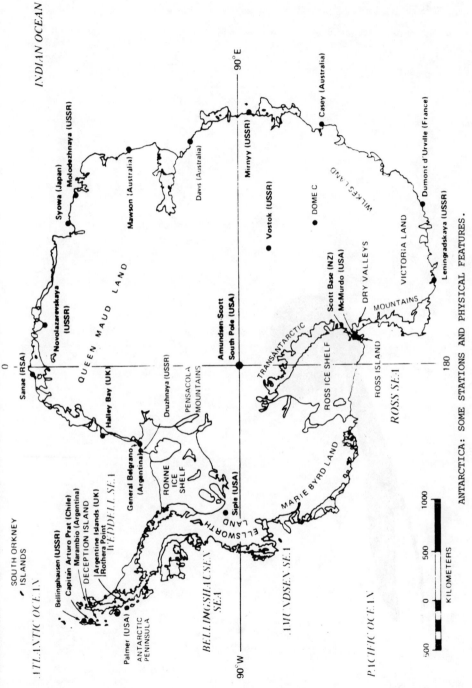

ANTARCTICA: SOME STATIONS AND PHYSICAL FEATURES.

Drawing by Walter R. Sellig

Introduction

Mary A. McWhinnie and Duwayne M. Anderson

Mankind's history in the polar regions has
passed through three phases: the heroic period,
the courageous exploratory period, and the technological period. We have now entered an inevitable fourth, or scientific era. The scientific era
can be most easily identified as starting with the
International Geophysical Year (IGY) of 1957-58.
In its original concept, the IGY was to be the
third International Polar Year, following the
first of 1882-83 and the second of 1932-33. However, the inclusion of physical phenomena of the
entire earth so broadened its scope that the des-
ignation became the International Geophysical
Year. The multi-national IGY was organized as a
broad based multi-national program of physical
science. Significantly, for the polar regions, it
provided the impetus to transform the technological period of polar investigations into the present
scientific era. None of its work was directed
toward exploitation or political goals. Advances
on the frontiers of all disciplines of the natural
sciences have been made since the beginning of
that 18-month year. It is particularly timely
that the Section on Biological Sciences of the
American Association for the Advancement of Science
should have arranged for its 143rd annual meeting
this interdisciplinary Symposium on polar research
in 1977.

This Symposium honors the past 20 years of
scientific effort that followed the IGY, and all
the scientists who conceived, structured, and participated in that effort and its successes. However, this volume cannot be construed as a complete
historical representation of the scope and depth of

the new understandings which have been developed
through these years by hundreds of scientists of
diverse disciplines whose contributions can be
found in numerous scientific reports and periodi-
cals. That task must remain an ambitious chal-
lenge for the future. The advances through these
two decades have been unequaled in rate and scope,
and we have yet to synthesize the whole of the
status of human knowledge of all natural phenomena
as discovered in these once considered impenetrable
polar regions.

The objective of this Symposium was to present
the status of selected categories of biological
investigations as they are coupled to the severe
physical environment which directs and permits diverse levels of biotic activity. This central
theme arose from the realization that nowhere on
this planet is the interweave of the physical environment with its resident biota more explicit
and still unaltered by human activity than in
polar regions.

It was felt that the historical setting and
present status could be developed properly only
by Laurence M. Gould, the distinguished scientific
leader of the IGY for the United States (Chapter
2), and by Robert H. Rutford, the recent Director
of U.S. activities in polar regions (Chapter 12).
It was likewise felt that a summary of polar
biological investigations through these years
could best be presented by the renowned biologist,
George A. Llano, whose guidance and vigorous efforts on behalf of the U.S. programs in biology and
medicine were begun immediately after the IGY and
continue to the present day (Chapter 3).

These considerations set the spirit of the
Symposium. It is our hope that readers of this
volume will discover the broad characteristics and
the importance of polar research not only to develop a better understanding of physical phenomena
on local and global scales but also the adaptational capabilities and ecological relationships
of living systems at high latitudes.

The polar regions of earth belong to no nation,
in a sense of sovereignty, and therefore they have
served as a scientific frontier for investigators
of all nations. There is strong evidence that men

of common spirit, inspiration, and goals have
brought the level of understanding of polar regions
to a plane not yet achieved at all regions of lower latitudes.

With a new perspective, we study now the successful colonization of polar regions by flora and
fauna once thought to be unable to survive in such
harsh physical conditions. The evolutionary origin
of fauna, unique in kind and adaptability, are under investigation, as are the behavior, communications, and many aspects of physiology among the
higher fauna: the fish, birds, and mammals. The
physical and chemical base supporting the production of marine phytoplankton have been and continue to be areas of essential investigation in
both polar regions. Additionally, the biota, although sparse in the fresh-water lakes that are
often under a permanent ice-cover, is being
studied in both polar regions. The migrations,
feeding ecology, and population dynamics of birds
have been a significant part of polar biological
study since before IGY, and they remain so today.
The terrestrial biota have been systematically
cataloged, although survival mechanisms and environmental limits of tolerance remain to be ex-
plained. Soils and microbial ecology have been
studied and, with other studies of biotic communities, will provide an index of environmental
change with activities of field operations and
polar development.

Study of the habitat and food chains of high
arctic mammals, the polar bears, seals, and lesser
species, is in progress. These animals are at the
top of the north polar food chain utilizing both
terrestrial and marine food sources. They can
therefore be expected to serve as indicators of the
status of the arctic environment and its ultimate
change with time. With the beginning of development of the Arctic Basin such study is essential
to monitor the consequence of regional and territorial pressures and changes, as well as to provide
biological understanding of nutritional efficiency,
adaptational physiology, and species productivity.
Because of the circumpolar habitat of these animals,
this is an international program being conducted by
scientists of the United States, Canada, Norway,
Denmark, and the Soviet Union. This comprehensive
study follows closely upon the U.S. Tundra Biome

program of the International Biological Program
(IBP), which was initiated in 1969.

The Tundra Biome Program sought to discover and
describe mechanisms and processes within terrestrial ecosystems of high latitude and high altitude.
More specifically its objectives were to develop a
detailed understanding of the wet coastal tundra of
northern Alaska and to obtain a data-base for the
cold-dominated ecosystem types within the United
States. Mathematical modeling and simulation were
prominent activities to make possible comparison
with results from other circumpolar countries.
This will greatly aid in bringing basic environmental knowledge to bear on problems of degradation, maintenance, and restoration of the tempera-
ture-sensitive and cold-dominated tundra-taiga
ecosystems. Few programs have been so far-sighted
and timely relative to the onset of human developments in remote regions. Several internationally
coordinated volumes have been published, and
others are in preparation. These will constitute
a comprehensive synthesis of the knowledge
presently available.

A program to continue and extend studies of the
tundra biome, Research on Arctic Tundra Environments (RATE), was initiated in 1974. Investigations of the influence of grazing on the arctic
tundra ecosystem at Meade River near Atkasook,
Alaska, extends terrestrial studies, while an
aquatic ecosystem study of Toolik Lake focuses on
predation and grazing effects on the structure of
lower-level communities. In both programs, all
levels of these ecosystems, from primary production to final consumers in the food-web, are
being studied. Again, an important objective is
to develop a model to describe and predict grazing
effects on physiological characteristics and
survival, and on growth and reproduction of ecosystem components.

Following resource discovery and development
in a technologically poised civilization, human
societies will inevitably be influenced and
changed. The changes in the U.S. arctic and subarctic regions will influence indigenous people
in ways for which there are few precedents in human
history. The consequences of thrusting modern
civilization, upon culturally distinct peoples,

whose habits of survival are through utilization
of the resources of land and sea, are poorly understood and cannot be predicted with confidence. It
is already tumultuous. It is most desirable that
public and private institutions be capable of
intelligent balanced action designed to mitigate
the powerful forces of conflict and change resulting from hydrocarbon resource development, environmental conservation aims, land reallocation, and
tenacious efforts to preserve the cultural complex
of the society of indigenous arctic peoples. It
is inevitable that development of the Alaskan North
Slope will open that rural area. Diverse activities undoubtedly will accelerate the process of
cultural change and intensify its attendant
problems.

A project to study imminent changes, the Man
in the Arctic Program, is being conducted by research scientists and specialists in economics,
demography, anthropology, political science,
psychology, wildlife management, transportation,
engineering, and community and regional planning.
The benefits of this and similar cross-disciplinary
research programs will, in time, enrich the fund
of knowledge of human societies and their internal
and external interactions. The sparseness of the
Alaskan population (native and immigrant), and the
related simplicity of its institutional economic
structure, allow analyses and generalizations no
longer possible in metropolitan areas which are
characterized by highly complex institutions and
systems. Moreover, on a small scale, patterns of
human interaction, with competitions and complementarity between different ethnic groups, are
more discernible and susceptible to broad-scale
conceptualization while retaining the manage-
ability required in scientific research. Under the
Man in the Arctic Program, Alaska has become the
laboratory in which institutions, conditions, and
processes of society are identified and their
interactions are studied.

Implicit in polar development is the need to
understand its frozen substrate, permafrost, upon
which the structures and material developments of
polar societies rest, (permafrost is defined as
ground below 0°C for at least two years). The
science of permafrost is developing rapidly through
the work of North American and Russian scientists;

construction engineering has advanced to a considerable degree. There is need to gain a better
understanding of offshore permafrost. Seismic and
reflection surveys, coupled with drilling and
coring, to provide a basis for interpretation of
seismic data are needed. Such studies will also
extend information on the quaternary history and
geology of polar marine coastal areas. Frozen
marine sediments are known to exist in inshore
areas to a depth of four meters and extending,
with variation, some 900 meters from the Siberian
coastline. However, little is known of the thickness, continuity, and ice-content of offshore
permafrost even where its presence is firmly established. When they are developed, models of the
offshore premafrost regime will permit prediction
of developmental perturbations in the permafrost
environment as they include thermal, chemical,
hydrological, and electrical properties.

In the polar marine environment, long-term
biological studies include the internal interactions of benthic communities and shifts in population structure with time and disturbance. Study
of the physiology and biochemistry of organisms
and cells has led to increased understanding of
mechanisms of adaptation to low temperature and
has provided a basis for the well known high lipid
content and slow growth rates which characterize
organisms living continuously at, or near, zero
degrees centigrade. Animals in the pelagic realm
of polar waters have been investigated systematically with regard to diversity, seasonal variation,
and biomass. Currently, the pelagic south circumpolar euphausiid, Euphausia superba (krill) is
under increased investigation to establish, with
certitude, feeding rates, growth rates, age at
maturity, biomass, and longevity; all aspects which
are critical to conservative utilization of this
species as a non-conventional protein resource.

Comprehensive investigations of the northern
polar marine basin (Arctic Ocean) and south circumpolar waters have resulted in an understanding
of broad-outlines of their extent and their interrelations with world oceanic circulations. Their
role in influencing, if not determining, the distribution, diversity, longevity and success of
the biota is increasingly apparent. The geomorphology of the sea floor strongly influences oceanic

circulation in the polar regions. Together with
investigations of physical oceanography future work
will be directed toward our understanding of the
interdependence of ocean currents and biotic
distributions.

Past histories of climate can be deduced from
the stratigraphic record which has been locked in
the extensive polar ice sheets, both north
(Greenland) and south (Antarctica). Glaciological,
as well as sub-ice sheet studies hold promise to
help uncover the earth's history from a physical
and climatological point of view.

Contemporary seasonal changes in ice can be
followed, with a convenience and a scope impossible
only a few years ago, by means of satellites whose
orbits permit a view of land and sea nearly up to
both poles. These orbiting instrumented space
vehicles also provide repetitive imagery disclosing
such features and events as annual pulsations and
other changes in sea-ice, as well as characteristics unique to particular oceanic regions (i.e.,
polynas in the Weddell Sea, Baffin Bay, etc.).
Study of the annual variations, when coupled in
analysis with marine and atmospheric currents,
will allow better access to the antarctic continent and the Arctic Ocean for research investigations than has been previously feasible. A new
level of precision in cartographic data is also an
important reality as a result of the availability
of these and other planned research satellites
(Seasat I, Nimbus G, etc.).

The contents of this volume present the physical features and phenomena of a south polar land
mass; its increasing discovery through time and
its probable origin, polar climates and oceanic
environments (Chapters 2 and 4 to 6). With this
background, the over-all history of biological
research, the polar marine ecosystem, marine mammals and organismic adaptations to the marine and
terrestrial environments are discussed in Chapters
3 and 7 to 10. Chapter 11 discloses the magnitude
of logistic support, while Chapter 12 points to
the future. The last Chapter (13) summarizes contemporary international programs, the objectives
and scope of their investigations and completes the
theme of this Symposium as it briefly describes in

broad outlines 20 years of polar science since the International Geophysical Year.

1

The Emergence of Antarctica

Laurence M. Gould

Introduction

Man's conception of Antarctica divides
itself into three stages which parallel his own intellectual development. In the classical ages it
was a myth. Then it evolved as a hypothetical continent up to the 20th century. The first third of
the 20th century is commonly referred to as The
Heroic Age and was characterized by the exploits of
Nordenskjöld, Scott, Shackleton, Amundsen, Mawson,
Byrd and others. Then came the modern age in which
Antarctica has emerged as the world's greatest
natural laboratory.

The two most distinctive achievements of the
International Geophysical Year were the development
of the space science program and the uncovering of
Antarctica. When we consider the highly developed
methods of transportation and communication by the
middle of the twentieth century it is in some ways
a source of wonder that a continent as large as the
United States and Europe combined should have remained so little known so long. The major part of
the continent had not yet been seen by man at the
inception of the IGY on July 1, 1957.

The difficulty of access due to its "halo" of
pack ice and icebergs, together with the severity
of its climate helped to preserve Antarctica's
secrets, especially from shipboard explorers.

Even with the development of world wide use of
aircraft by our midtwentieth century air age
Antarctica was largely by-passed until the Inter-

national Geophysical Year.   There was no economic
motive for its exploration.   Most of the earth's
most highly developed and, except for India and
China, most populous regions lie about the Arctic.
Ninety percent of the world's people live north of
the equator, and the world's traffic continues to
be largely between points in the Northern Hemisphere.   The major air routes connecting the world's
centers of population lie north of the equator, and
many of them cross parts of the Arctic.   True, in a
great-circle route from Argentina or Chile to
Australia one would fly over a part of Antarctica,
but the commercial prospects for such a flight are
slight.

     The existence of a southern continent was one
of geography's most ancient assumptions.   During
the sixth century B.C. Pythagoras postulated a
spherical earth.   With the Greek's love of symmetry
this persuaded his followers to assume that there
would be large masses of land in the southern hemisphere to balance those which formed the inhabited
earth.

     The most noted geographer of antiquity, the
Roman Claudius Ptolemaeus or Ptolemy, who lived in
Alexandria during the second century A.D., drew an
immense southern landmass which he called "Terra
Incognita" connecting Africa with the Malay Peninsula on the east, making the Indian Ocean a closed
sea.   This conception was not disproved until nearly the end of the fifteenth century.

     The idea of a spherical earth was not compati-
ble with early Christendom's dedication to a flat
saucer-shaped planet.   Ptolemy's ideas languished
for a long time but the idea of a spherical earth
and the likelihood of reaching India by sailing
west from Spain was kept alive by monastic scholars.
Then in the late fifteenth century stirrings of the
Renaissance began.   In addition to its greatness in
art and science the Renaissance was man's first
space age.   Here was sparked the greatest era of
geographical exploration in man's history -- a
period of exploration during which the size of the
known world was doubled and which was not equaled
until the International Geophysical Year.   Ptolemy's
geography was revived and during the late fifteenth
century many maps appeared in Europe based on his
concepts, with his "Terra Incognita" changed to

"Terra Australis".

Terra Australis first appeared on a world map by Orontius in 1531 and was copied by Mercator in 1538. This map was remarkable: based on pure guesswork its outline was surprisingly like that of the real Antarctica as we know it except that it was about one-third as large with a huge bulge opposite Australia. This was the smallest "Antarctica" from the time of Ptolemy's projections until the continent was finally circumnavigated in the latter part of the eighteenth century by Captain Cook.

The first major reduction in the supposed southern landmass came with the rounding of the Cape of Good Hope by Vasco de Gama in 1497 which led many geographers to believe there was no continent at all south of Africa. In a way this was offset by Magellan in 1520. Geographers immediately assumed that Tierra del Fuego, the land south of the Straits, was a part of the great southern continent.

In 1578 Queen Elizabeth sent Sir Francis Drake to find the great southern land. His ship, the Golden Hind, was blown way south of Cape Horn, proving that the Atlantic and Pacific were one ocean there. Thus another great piece of Terra Australis was cartographically sunk.

Geographers were not deterred. The discovery of the Solomons and other Pacific Islands in the late sixteenth century and of New Zealand by the Dutch in 1642 were taken as further evidences of the South Polar continent. The myth further developed that such a continent was a veritable paradise with fertile lands and happy peoples. The economic motive to find the new land became stronger than ever.

It was, of course, inevitable that every voyage south beyond the known world should reduce the size of this hypothetical landmass. When Tasman discovered New Zealand in 1642, he thought it was part of the coast of "Terra Australis". It was left to James Cook, greatest of all Antarctic explorers and, in my opinion the greatest ship explorer of all time, to erase forever the idea of a fertile populated southern continent. During his

first voyage, from 1768 to 1771, he circumnavigated
both islands of New Zealand and thereby took
another big slice away from the unknown southern
landmass. On his second voyage, from 1772 to 1775,
Cook circumnavigated the continent of Antarctica
without actually sighting it. He deserved to discover Antarctica for he came close to it several
times and was the first explorer ever to cross the
Antarctic Circle. Upon Cook's return he observed
with prophetic clarity that if there was a southern
continent it would be so cold and inhospitable that
it could not possibly be suitable for human habita-
tion.

    After Napoleon's disastrous retreat from
Moscow, Russia emerged as a world power and the expansive mood of the Kremlin stimulated expeditions
to both the north and south polar regions. In 1818
Czar Alexander I dispatched a well-equipped expedition under the command of Captain Thaddeus von
Bellingshausen to make discoveries "as close as
possible to the South Pole". Although
Bellingshausen's course shows that he was near
enough the continent to have seen it, he does not
record such a landfall in his log. He was much
surprised to find sealers in the sub-antarctic
islands.

    On his triumphant return in 1775 Cook had re-
ported an abundance of fur seals in South Georgia
which stimulated a great increase in their exploitation by British and American sealers. At the
height of this slaughter more than 100 vessels
were operating in a single season. It would have
been strange if some of them had not inadvertently
discovered the continent.

    Most American students of the problem believe
that a youthful New England sealing captain,
Nathaniel Palmer, was the first to sight the continent in November 1820. The British are equally
sure that it was first sighted by an Englishman,
Captain Edward Bransfield, on January 30, 1820.
After an examination of the records of his voyage
the All-Soviet Geographic Congress concluded in
1949 that von Bellingshausen had discovered the
antarctic continent in the Palmer Land sector
(northward extension of what is now called the
Antarctic Peninsula).

All of these contenders have one thing in common: the assumed achievement of the discovery of Antarctica on the part of all three rests on the interpretation of imperfect records by modern investigators. It is unlikely that the matter will ever be settled to the satisfaction of all concerned. Hopefully it will forever be an item of academic interest only.

A Continent Found

The development of steam-powered ships and the gradual replacement of modern ships with iron or iron-clad vessels put greater reliance upon the magnetic compass. The Earth's magnetism became a field of great scientific importance. Sir James Clark Ross had discovered the north magnetic pole in 1831. Sparked by the work of a great German mathematician, Karl Friedrich Gauss, who predicted that there was a south magnetic pole opposite the north one and that it would be found in latitude 66° south, longitude 146° east, three expeditions were dispatched to search for it during the years 1838 to 1843.

In January 1840, a French expedition under Dumont d'Urville sighted continental land between latitudes 120° and 160° east in the region of the magnetic pole, although d'Urville did not describe his discovery as part of a continent.

An American expedition under the command of Lieutenant Charles Wilkes was dispatched by the U.S. government in 1838 to further knowledge of the prospects for a southern whale fishery as well as to carry out scientific exploration. Like d'Urville he was thwarted in his quest for the south magnetic pole since it is well inland, but he did cruise along 1,500 miles of the coastline charting many landfalls along the coast which now bears his name. On January 30, 1840, he wrote: "I make this bay in longitude 140° thirty minutes east, latitude 66° forty-five minutes south and now that all were convinced of its existence I gave the land the name of Antarctic continent". This is the first confident statement of the reality of a continent. Since Wilkes did not land, his strong statement was something of a guess but modern mapping has shown his discoveries and assumptions to be valid.

Scientific Penetration

On August 16, 1840, Sir James Clark Ross, with
the best equipped ships yet designed for navigation
in sea ice, sailed southward from Australia and was
able to penetrate through the belt of pack ice that
surrounds the continent; this had never been done
before. Although he did not reach the south magnetic pole, Ross did sail to the head of navigation
of the huge embayment that bears his name, making
some of the greatest geographic discoveries in the
history of antarctic exploration.

Following this first scientific penetration,
Antarctica was neglected for a half a century.
Then in 1893 reports of the Challenger expedition,
which had circumnavigated the globe from 1872 to
1875, were released and greatly influenced the
thinking of the International Geographical Congress
held in London in 1895. The Congress declared that
investigation of Antarctica was "the greatest piece
of geographical exploration still to be undertaken".

In 1898 Dr. John Murray, biologist on the
Challenger expedition, described the great collection of rock fragments dredged up from the sea bottom around Antarctica, which were varied kinds of
continental rocks as gneisses, granites, diorities,
sandstones, limestones and shales. Murray observed
that "there can be no doubt of their having been
transported from land situated near the South
Pole".

While Wilkes was sure he had sighted a continent in 1840, the idea continued to persist that
Antarctica might be a gigantic archipelago smother-
ed beneath the great inland ice sheet. Most geographers agreed with Murray's belief that Antarctica
was indeed a major continental landmass. Yet as
late as the beginning of the International Geophysical Year (1957-1958) some Russian scientists
supported the belief in a great archipelago.

Actually we know now that both assumptions are
valid for different parts of the continent. Seismic soundings which reveal the thickness of the inland ice show that if it were all to melt, East
Antarctica would be revealed as a true continental
shield. On the other hand West Antarctica would
become a great archipelago. But the continent is

made one by its great cover of glacial ice, for ice
is just as truly a rock as gneiss or schist or
granite.

The Heroic Age

The response to the plea from the International
Geographical Congress of 1895 has come to be known
as the "heroic age" in antarctic exploration, which
lasted from the nineteenth century well into the
second decade of the twentieth. This was the most
extensive geographic exploration of the continent
which had yet been attempted and whose results will
stand for all time among the great ones in the
history of geographic exploration.

While scientists had played important roles on
many of the early expeditions -- especially those
of Cook, Wilkes and Ross as well as some of the
sealing and whaling expeditions -- it was not until
the turn of the century that teams of scientists
were an important integral part of the voyages.
All of the expeditions of this era, except that of
Amundsen, included teams of scientists who carried
out extensive programs in their own fields of research, but it was in the realm of geography that
the major discoveries were made. It was during
this time that the real nature of Antarctica and
its environment were first understood and revealed.
Extensive mapping of the coastal areas, the first
sighting of the inland ice, significant geological
and glaciological discoveries which furnished the
basis for subsequent work and conquest of both the
geographic and magnetic poles are but a small part
of the achievements of this age.

Postwar Interest

In the twilight of the Heroic Age, after its
interruption by World War I, interest in Antarctica
was revived and a new, still continuing phase in
its exploration began, made possible by new advances in transportation and communication. For
almost four decades a series of British, Australian,
Norwegian, American, Argentine, Chilean, French and
Russian expeditions added greatly to our knowledge
of Antarctica. Among them was the first continuing
program of scientific research in Antarctica; it
was primarily oceanographic and marine biological
research, which was carried out by Scott's old ship

The Discovery which made 13 voyages from 1923-39.

The most important development in the whole field of logistics during these interim years was the introduction of aircraft.

Before the advent of the airplane no part of the interior of Antarctica except that adjacent to the sledge routes of Amundsen, Shackleton and Scott to the south pole had been uncovered. Exploration in depth beyond the coastal margin of the continent had to await aircraft.

Three men may be said to have brought the air age to Antarctica. The first flight was made by Sir Hubert Wilkins on December 20, 1928, across what is now the Antarctic Peninsula. Lincoln Ellsworth, after two failures, made a successful transantarctic flight in 1935-36 with one companion in a single engine plane -- one of the most remarkable flights in the history of aviation.

Both Wilkins and Ellsworth were concerned solely with demonstrating the practicality of the airplane for antarctic exploration. But to Commander (later Rear Admiral) Richard E. Byrd belongs credit for opening up Antarctica to the air age. Indeed, he was the dominant figure in antarctic exploration for nearly three decades. He led two expeditions of his own and played leading roles in three others.

The first Byrd Antarctic Expedition of 1928-30 was the first American expedition since that of Wilkes 90 years before and the first American party ever to winter over in Antarctica. On January 5, 1929, Byrd made his first flight. Twelve days later a flight farther east produced his first major discovery, the Rockefeller Mountains.

On November 29, 1929, Commander Byrd and two companions flew over the pole. This much publicized flight enabled the expedition to get the financial backing, which made possible important scientific programs, including extended flights over what was later to be called Marie Byrd Land and the first geological survey of the Queen Maud Mountains.

Most of the techniques of travel and communi-

cation which make the greatly extended scientific
study of Antarctica possible today were pioneered
on the first Byrd Antarctic Expedition. Today aircraft are immeasurably more flexible and efficient;
oversnow vehicles are immensely more effective, and
radios perform better.

In 1946 and again in 1947 the United States
dispatched the largest expeditions that had ever
explored Antarctica and which made extended use of
ships and ship-based aircraft.

The usual follow-up of territorial claims on
the basis of discoveries characterized most of the
expeditions of these years. Scientific cooperation
did not exist except for the Norwegian-British-
Swedish Expedition of 1949-51 which carried out a
successful exploration in Queen Maud Land. This
was the first truly international exploration in
Antarctica. In a way it was the forerunner of the
International Geophysical Year.

The IGY

There had been an International Polar year in
1882-83 and a second in 1932-33 but it seemed un-
wise to wait another 50 years for the third.

In 1950 a formal proposal was placed before
the International Council of Scientific Unions
"that the Third International Polar Year be nomin-
ated for 1957-58 and that in view of the length of
time necessary for adequate organization, an International Polar Year Commission be appointed in 1951
to supervise the planning". The resolution was approved and at the suggestion of the World Meteorological Organization the concept of a Polar Year
was extended to include the entire earth. Thus was
born the International Geophysical Year, which Hugh
Odishaw, Executive Director of the United States
National Committee, has aptly called, "the greatest
peacetime activity in man's history".

The ICSU Special Committee, which met in Rome
in 1954 to consider national programs, singled out
two areas for special attention -- outer space and
Antarctica -- observing that Antarctica was "a region of almost unparalleled interest in the fields
of geophysics and geography alike". Very little
geophysical work had ever been done in Antarctica

and on the eve of the IGY almost half the continent had not yet been seen by man.

Such significant results were achieved in both
areas that it is a matter of record that the scientific uncovering and exploration of Antarctica was
second only to the space satellite program among
the achievements of the IGY.

The first Antarctic Conference was held in
Paris from July 6-10, 1955. Gen. G. R. Laclavere
was elected president and in his opening remarks
set the tone for this conference and for the whole
program that was to follow. He emphasized the
technical character of the conference, excluding
problems of finance and politics. Tensions due to
overlapping political claims in Antarctica which
were evident at the beginning of the sessions were
laid to rest, and the following motion by General
Laclavere was unanimously adopted: "The Antarctic
Conference entirely endorses M. Laclavere's statement of purposes of the opening session and specifically his affirmation that the overall aims of the
Conference are entirely scientific". This was a
significant decision of great historic importance.
Matters of strategic and political concern were set
aside as the Antarctic IGY program was dedicated to
the sole purpose of scientific exploration. Previously, the climate caused by competitive territorial claims had discouraged the exchange of
scientific information.

Cooperation

This was the beginning of Antarctica's emer-
gence as a great natural and political science
laboratory.

From the beginning differences melted away and
the willingness to adjust national programs for
common goals prevailed. There was flexibility and
simplicity and freedom from political considerations without precedent in international scientific
cooperation. When all the problems of this initial
meeting had been ironed out, the antarctic program
emerged as the combined effort of 12 nations --
Argentina, France, Australia, Belgium, Chile,
Japan, New Zealand, Norway, South Africa, the
United States, the United Kingdom, and the Soviet
Union -- with a total of 48 new stations on the

margins and in the interior of Antarctica in add-
ition to seven stations already established by
Argentina, Chile, and the United Kingdom in the
Antarctic Peninsula.

The planet earth in its entirety is the
geophysicist's laboratory; nature performs the
experiments and man makes the observations. The
IGY consisted of those programs which were inherently global in character. For Antarctica
there were 9 programs: Aurora, cosmic rays,
geomagnetism, glaciology, gravity, ionospheric
physics, meteorology, international weather
central and seismology.

Impressive records were made in all these
fields and in the further geographic exploration
which resulted in the discovery of the last unknown major physical features on the continent.

Early in the IGY a program for the exchange
of scientists was begun whereby research workers
of one country joined in the programs of others.
This made possible the free and prolonged exchange
of scientific information which has continued with
increasing scope during the years since the IGY.

The International Antarctic Weather Central
at Little America was a further instance of effective international cooperation. Although it
was established by U.S. scientists the weather
central was truly international in character with
scientists from Argentina, Australia, France, New
Zealand, South Africa and the USSR participating
fully in its work.

Even before the IGY began it was clear that
its program of 18 months would enable scientists
to uncover but a small part of Antarctica's
secrets. Upon the recommendations of the last
Antarctic Conference before the IGY began, ICSU
approved the creation of a permanent committee to
continue the scientific cooperation of IGY. The
new committee held its organizing meeting at The
Hague in February 1958. It was designated the
Special Committee on Antarctic Research (SCAR).
Later the word "Scientific" was substituted for
"Special". The new committee consisted of delegates from each nation actively engaged in
antarctic research and representatives of various

scientific committees which would have overlapping
interests in antarctic scientific activity.

There was an important increase in scientific
programs beyond geophysics with the advent of SCAR
for not only do the various disciplines of geophysics need information for their fulfillment
which can come only from Antarctica, but
Antarctica presents environmental conditions not
duplicated elsewhere on earth. It therefore presents enormous opportunities for biological research. To IGY programs SCAR added biology, car-
tography, geology and geodesy. Antarctica had now
fully emerged as the greatest natural laboratory
on earth. In establishing continuing permanent
programs SCAR had now confirmed Antarctica as "A
Continent For Science".

Political Laboratory

Important as the scientific results of the
IGY antarctic and global programs were, in the
long run, it may be the human and social results
which will prove to have been most important.
This vast global effort was carried out in a
period of almost unprecedented worldwide turmoil
and unrest. However, in the midst of all the
political tensions, scientists of the IGY demonstrated that reasonable and rational conduct at
the scientific level was possible. And it was the
IGY cooperative efforts in Antarctica, coldest of
all the continents, that witnessed the first thawing of the cold war.

To be sure international scientific cooperation is not new. It has existed for many centuries, but the IGY did add a new and significant
dimension. It demonstrated, as never before, that
the international community of science is the most
hopeful of all examples of world cooperation and
organization.

Scientific cooperation in Antarctica led to
the creation of the first treaty ever designed to
protect a scientific program; the Antarctic Treaty
is a political document without precedent.

The treaty was signed on December 9, 1959.
The New York Times observed its tenth anniversary
on December 9, 1969 with an editorial from which

the following is an excerpt:

"There can be little doubt that this precedent helped to create the foundations of mutual
confidence on which the great diplomatic landmarks
of the past decade have been based, notably the
test ban treaty of 1963, the space compact of
1967, and the nuclear nonproliferation pact of
1968. In effect, Antarctica has become a political science laboratory, and the Antarctic Treaty a
historic, successful experiment pointing the way
for future progress toward international cooperation".

Now the task is to apply the lessons learned
from the experiment to all of the great contemporary problems where needless suspicion and rivalry
waste huge resources and endanger earth itself.

Figures 1 through 5 (see pp. 22-26) show
the historical development of man's understanding
of the continent of Antarctica. (Reprinted by
permission, *The Geographical Review*, 1957,
Antarctic Prospect, Laurence M. Gould).

22

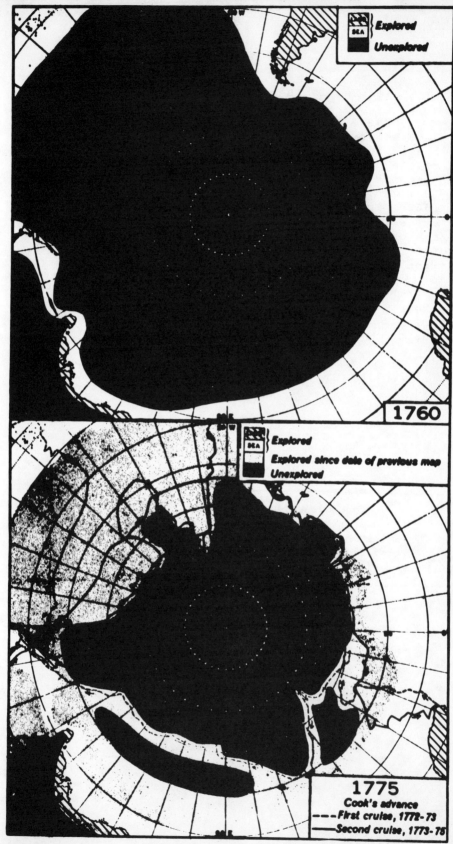

Explored
SEA
Unexplored

1760

Explored
SEA
Explored since date of previous map
Unexplored

1775
Cook's advance
---- First cruise, 1772-73
—— Second cruise, 1773-75

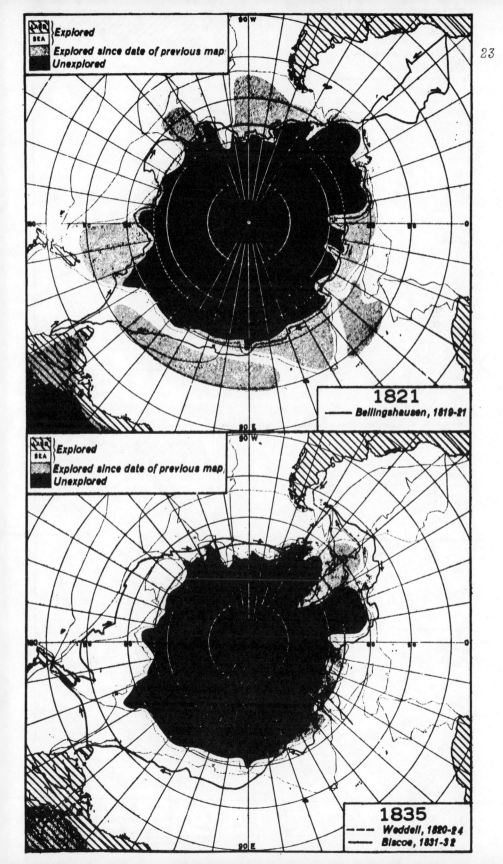

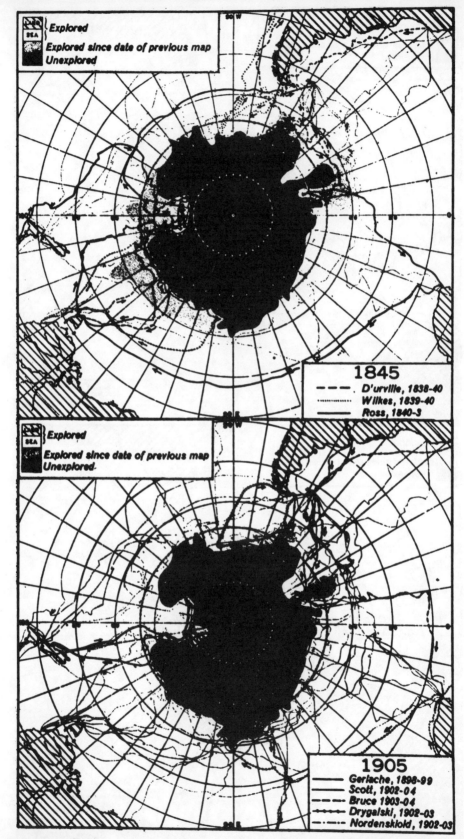

24

Explored
Explored since date of previous map
Unexplored

1845
D'urville, 1838-40
Wilkes, 1839-40
Ross, 1840-3

Explored
Explored since date of previous map
Unexplored

1905
Gerlache, 1898-99
Scott, 1902-04
Bruce 1903-04
Drygalski, 1902-03
Nordenskiold, 1902-03

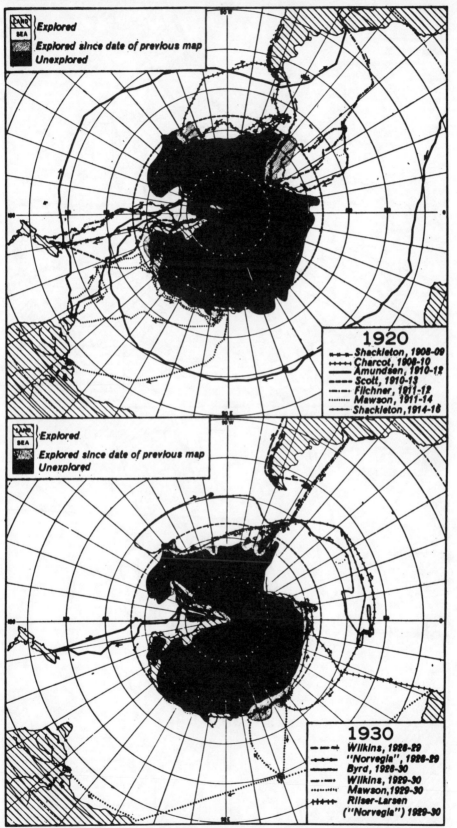

1920

⊶ Shackleton, 1908-09
⊢⊢⊢ Charcot, 1908-10
——— Amundsen, 1910-12
– – – Scott, 1910-13
–·–·– Filchner, 1911-12
·········· Mawson, 1911-14
⊶⊶ Shackleton, 1914-16

1930

– – – Wilkins, 1928-29
⊢⊢⊢ "Norvegia", 1928-29
——— Byrd, 1928-30
–·–·– Wilkins, 1929-30
·········· Mawson, 1929-30
⊢⊢⊢⊢ Riiser-Larsen
("Norvegia") 1929-30

Explored
Explored since date of previous map
Unexplored

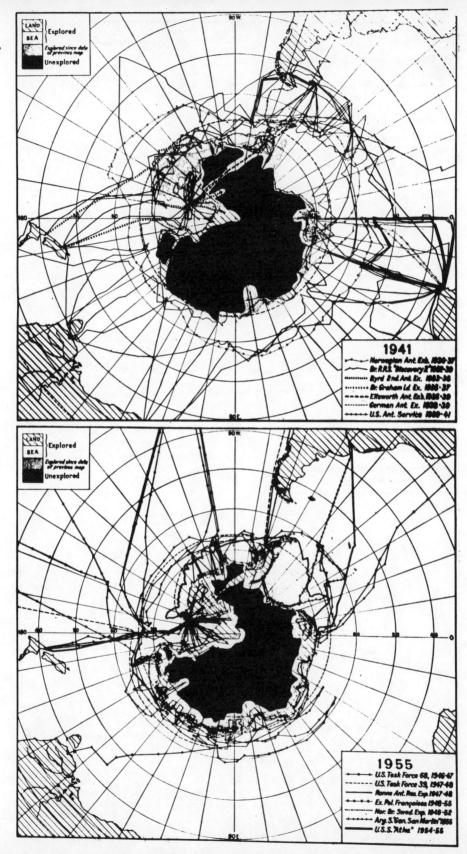

26

LAND | Explored
SEA |
| Explored since date
of previous map
| Unexplored

1941

Norwegian Ant. Exb. 1930-37
Br. R.R.S. "Discovery II" 1929-39
Byrd 2nd Ant. Ex. 1933-35
Br. Graham Ld. Ex. 1935-37
Ellsworth Ant. Exb. 1935-39
German Ant. Ex. 1938-39
U.S. Ant. Service 1939-41

LAND | Explored
SEA |
| Explored since date
of previous map
| Unexplored

1955

U.S. Task Force 68, 1946-47
U.S. Task Force 39, 1947-48
Ronne Ant. Res. Exp. 1947-48
Ex. Pol. Françaises 1948-55
Nor. Br. Swed. Exp. 1949-52
Arg. S. "Gen. San Martin" 1955
U.S.S. "Atka" 1954-55

2

Polar Research:
A Synthesis with
Special Reference to Biology

George A. Llano

"All that he [Maury] meant in his remarks was, to give fair warning that if England did not undertake these explorations, the Americans would show the way." *M. F. Maury, Captain U.S. Navy 1860*

INTRODUCTION

The arctic and antarctic regions are major fields of international scientific research. For the United States, the start was inauspicious. Growth was slow and dependent upon public awareness of the polar regions. Today, the United States is acknowledged as a leader for its contributions to polar knowledge. This result is largely due to the perseverance and dedication of a few Americans whose early work established the traditions which now identify U.S. polar science. In the beginning, because there were only a few investigators, they were readily identified by name. Now there are so many more that they are usually mentioned by discipline, if at all. While this section addresses the background, development, and present status of the life sciences, the historical pattern is not much different from other disciplines because the natural history of new regions has always held a special fascination for all men.

The Contrasting Poles

The physical differences between the two poles warrant restating because they relate to the living world and their regional flora and fauna. The most obvious difference is that the distribution of land and water is almost completely reversed in the two hemispheres. The North Pole is centered in a great ocean encircled by Eurasia, North America, and Greenland. This ocean, the North Polar Sea, is partly covered by perennial ice and receives the discharge of several great rivers which causes it to be less saline than

TABLE 1

THE CONTRASTING POLES

Arctic	Antarctic
° Ocean basin enclosed by continents.	Continent surrounded by ocean world.
° Winds, ocean currents restricted to an internal basin.	Winds, ocean currents circumpolar, uninterrupted by land masses.
° Icebergs derived from glaciers, seasonal, measured in m^3.	Icebergs derived from glaciers and shelf ice; persistent and may measure in excess of 100 km^3.
° Sea ice multiyear, circulates in polar gyre, annual thickness to 1.5m.	Sea ice annual, outward growth doubles continental extent, annual thickness to 2.5m.
° Land ice in limited areas; largest Greenland ice sheet.	90% of land ice covered in almost unbroken South Polar ice cap.
° Elevation at North Pole 1m of sea ice; bedrock 4300m below sea level.	Elevation at South Pole 2912m above sea level; bedrock 34m above sea level.
° North Pole mean annual temperature -18°C; no research station.	South Pole mean annual temperature -50°C; permanent 30 man, meteorological and geophysical research station.
° Beaches and shallow extensive continental shelf.	Beaches rare; narrow deep continental shelf backed by vertical ice cliffs.
° Frozen ground extensive, over 500m.	Frozen ground limited to ice free areas.
° Tundra well developed, extensive, marked by a tree/shrubline.	No tundra, no tree line. Subantarctic zone marked by antarctic convergence.
° 90 species of flowering plants at 82°N lat., 450 species at 66°- 70°N lat.	Crustaceous lichens at 82° lat; 2 species of flowering plants at 66°-70° S lat; vegetation primarily lichens and mosses.
° Arachnids, crustaceans, insects, and myriapods numerous and common.	Free living arthropods include insects (2), mites (150), Collembolla (6), scarce.
° Musk ox, reindeer, caribou, fox, hare, wolf, lemming, bears, etc.	No terrestrial mammals.
° Whales and porpoises (18), seals (7), amphibious mammals (1).	Whales and porpoises (14), seals (4).
° Bird species 107 (75°-80°N lat.).	Bird species 19 (70°-80° S lat.).
° Primitive man with long rich cultural record; ethnic groups circumarctic.	No record of primitive man; no native groups.
° Human population 60°N, in excess of 2 million, modern settlements, widespread expolitation and technological development.	Population 60°S sparse, scattered at scientific stations. No exploitation of terrestrial resources.
° Crossing of Arctic Circle prehistoric.	Crossing of Antarctic Circle by James Cook, January 17, 1772.

the Antarctic Ocean, providing a refuge for freshwater
fishes. The South Pole is centered in a continent almost
filling the area within the Antarctic Circle. Capped with
fresh water ice with an average thickness of 2000m, it is a
landscape without rivers but which discharges into the sea
mammoth tabular icebergs. It is a continent set in an ocean
world; and freezing of part of the ocean around the coasts
almost doubles its effective area during the austral winter.
The boundaries between subarctic and subantarctic are difficult to define and always open to question. In the Northern
Hemisphere a useful climatic boundary is the limit of the
tree line. In the Southern Hemisphere the boundary lies in
the ocean. Nevertheless, the Antarctic Convergence, at
between 55° to 60°S latitude, provides an appropriate line
of demarcation between the two life zones. The convergence
can be easily and precisely detected by a thermometer as
well as recognized visually by the change in species of birds
and animals and the changing color of the sea. (Table 1)

The distribution of plants and animals in the Arctic is
circumpolar and has historic and prehistoric ties with life
in the lands to the south. Ninety flowering plants grow at
82°N latitude in northern Greenland (Troelson, 1952) and at
latitude 66° to 70°N along the North Slope of Alaska there
are 450 species representing 53 families of flowering plants
(Spetzman, 1959). The vegetation of the tundra during the
arctic summer can be spectacular with the bloom of flowers.
The invertebrate fauna of the land and freshwaters can be
very abundant but may consist of only a few species. These
are worms, nematodes and insects in the soil and crustaceans
in freshwaters.   Species of freshwater fish include white
fish, salmon, arctic char, grayling, lake trout, black fish,
and sticklebacks. The land in summer is populous with
migratory waterfowl and shore birds which breed on the
tundra and on innumerable lakes, ponds and streams. Terrestrial and marine mammals are represented by many species of
which two, the walrus and the polar bear, are associated with
the arctic pack ice. Fay (1974) lists at least 25 species
of marine mammals in the Bering Sea. In terms of living
matter, the seas are the richest part of the arctic.

Antarctica, in contrast, is a cold desert with the most
stringent environmental conditions for life. The fifth
largest land mass on earth--it is isolated by a broad expanse
of ocean and geological eons from all other Southern Hemisphere lands. Visible vegetation is scarce, consisting
primarily of lichens, mosses and algae. North of the
Antarctic Circle on the Antarctic Peninsula where mosses and
liverworts provide some greenery to an otherwise black and

TABLE 2

A COMPARISON OF SOME BIRD GROUPS IN POLAR REGIONS

	Arctic (N of 60°)	Antarctic (S of 60°)
Passarine Birds	Many species	None
Ptarmigan	3 species	None
Shore birds	Many species	None
Waterfowl	Many species	None
Raptors	Many species	None
Cormorants	None	1 species
Skuas, Gulls, Terns	Many species	5 species
Sheathbills	None	2 species
Alciids	Many species	None
Albatross	None	Several species
Petrels	2-3 species	Several species
Storm Petrels	None	Several species
Penguins	None	4 species

white landscape, one species of grass (Deschampsia) and one
species of an herb (Colobanthus) are the only indigenous
representatives of higher plant life. Antarctica has no
true terrestrial vertebrate animals. The dominant native
invertebrate fauna are the Acarina (mites and ticks) number-
ing about 150 species, Collembola (springtails), tardigrades
and rotifers which inhabit the mosses and lichens and ice⁻
free land. These arthropods are very tolerant of low
temperatures and are widely distributed throughout the
antarctic. A flightless midge and only native insect,
Belgica antarctica, is locally restricted to the Antarctic
Peninsula; at 2.5 to 3mm in length it is the largest terrestrial organism in Antarctica. Six species of seals and
about 12 species of birds breed in or near the antarctic
coast, but these spend a much greater time at sea than on
land (Bushnell, 1967). Survival of the flightless penguins,
and the breeding success of sea birds and seals is due to the
absence of land predators. The breeding assemblages of
antarctic penguins are among the ornithological spectacles of
the world. Prévost (1976) estimates that the Spheniscidae
(penguins) in Antarctica represent 80 percent of the avian
stocks and 98 percent of the biomass for the antarctic
region; in the subantarctic penguins represent 53 percent
of stocks and 80 percent of the biomass. (Table 2)

This manifestation of birds and mammals during the brief
austral summer is due to the extreme richness of the coastal
antarctic waters and large zooplankton biomass of which
Euphausia superba, or krill, is a vital link in antarctic
food chains. It has been estimated that penguins consume
the same amount of krill as do the large whales, about 40
million metric tons, which is about half of the fish catch
landed by man.

Scientific Exploration and Research in the Arctic

The Arctic Regions, being close to European centers of
population and commerce, have a much earlier history of
exploration than the antarctic. However, even before the
Viking settlements of Greenland, the American Arctic and
Subarctic was already populated by the Eskimo, with their
remarkable uniformity of language, culture and physical type,
who were in balance with the arctic ecosystem. From the 15th
to the 18th centuries, exploratory voyages were financed by
merchants to find northern sea routes to the trading centers
of Asia. Whale and fur hunters were drawn into the arctic
regions, thereby affecting established biological systems.
Much was learned about the physical geography of the region
and contact was made with its people, but the marine and
terrestrial biogeography were barely outlined.

The Eastern Arctic

European interest in finding a northwest passage to the Orient and in arctic exploration generally during the 19th Century was carried out most vigorously by numerous large British naval expeditions. The most extraordinary event of the period was what Stefansson (1925) calls "the colossal tragedy" of the Sir John Franklin Expedition of 1847. The hunt for this lost expedition between 1849 and 1856 contributed substantially to geographical scientific knowledge of the Arctic and Alaskan Coast (Orth, 1967); while at the same time it diverted funds and public interest from antarctic exploration (Bertrand, 1971). It was also the cause for drawing U.S. public attention to the Eastern Arctic, and led the U.S. Government to search for the North Pole. However, by 1849 a fleet of 154 American whalers were already successfully taking humpback and bowhead whales in the Arctic Ocean north of the Bering Strait.

In 1850, Henry Grinnell financed the first American expedition under command of Lt. Edwin J. de Haven to assist in the search for the Franklin Expedition. The second Grinnell expedition in 1853 under E. K. Kane, sailed to northwest Greenland through the sea now called the Kane Basin. Grinnell also supported C. F. Hall who lived with Frobisher Bay Eskimos and explored eastern arctic lands from 1860-1862, and again from 1864-1869 along King William Island. In 1860, I. I. Hayes attempted to reach the North Pole on the schooner United States by sailing along the west coast of Greenland. In 1871, Hall was given command of the Polaris, the first U.S. Government sponsored expedition to the North Pole. Because the Polaris failed to return on schedule, the U.S. Navy sent the Juniata in search under Lt. Cmdr. G. W. de Long in 1873. U.S. participation in the Polar Year of 1882-1883 led to the establishment of a meteorological and magnetic station at 81° 44'N on Ellesmere Land in 1881 under the direction of Lt. A. W. Greely, U.S. Army. The expedition which suffered great hardship and the loss of all but seven of a complement of 24 men and officers was rescued in 1884. Peary's journeys in the Eastern Arctic from 1891-1909 and his success in reaching the North Pole helped to maintain U.S. public interest in the North Polar Regions until 1914. After World War I, major attention of the western world focused on Greenland. Much of the expeditionary effort consisted of small, privately financed, summer ventures which provided opportunities for exploration, scientific studies, and polar training. Work in the eastern arctic was carried out by two of Peary's colleagues, Bob Bartlett, and D. B. MacMillian of New England, and also by Louise A. Boyd of New York and E. H. Hobbs of Michigan.

Western Arctic 1867-1942

Alaska became known from the news of its rich marine mammal resources in reports of the Vitus Bering 1714 expedition and James Cook's third voyage of 1778. Over-exploitation of Alaskan fur mammals economically restricted the trade by 1820, which also coincided with the decline of the antarctic fur seal fisheries. American interest in the Western Arctic began with the North Pacific Exploring Expedition under Captain C. Ringgold and J. Rodgers, U.S. Navy, 1854-1855, which made valuable collections and observations in the area of the Aleutian Islands, north to the Bering Strait. While Alaska was still in Russian hands, the Western Union Telegraph Company Expedition of 1865-1867 carried out field activities on the Yukon and Seward Peninsula. Robert Kennicott, of the Smithsonian Institution as Chief of Exploration brought together a corps of six naturalists to assist in the scientific work. On his death in 1866, he was succeeded by his assistant, W. H. Dall. In his account in the Harriman Alaska Expedition Series (1910) Dall notes that the surveying information brought back by the "telegraph explorers" is supposed to have influenced the purchase of Alaska in 1867. According to Moore (1868), Secretary of state, W. H. Seward was also advised by Professor W. H. Brewer, Yale University, to purchase Alaska in order (1) "to keep Britain from getting it", (2) "to have a source of ice for California", (3) "to secure valuable fisheries which will be needed to feed our growing population", and (4) "to have a playground for the people of the West Coast."

Fur sealing concession to the Alaska Commercial Company by the U.S. Government was followed by indiscriminate hunting, primarily pelagic sealing which threatened the existence of the Pribilof seal herds. The situation was exposed by W. H. Elliott, one of Kennicott's naturalists and the Treasury Department assistant-agent for the Pribilof Islands through reports published in 1874, 1887 and 1896 describing conditions on the Pribilofs in 1872-74 and 1890. U.S. seizure of Canadian pelagic sealers precipitated an international crisis which was settled in 1911 with the signing of the North Pacific Sealing Convention. Thus originated Alaska's first conservation issue, as well as the policy for rational management of living resources under the Bureau of Commercial Fisheries, of Interior (now under NOAA), and the Bureau of Biological Survey of the Department of Agriculture (now Fish and Wildlife Service, Department of Interior). The whaling industry caused another dilemna through decima-

tion of caribou herds slaughtered for fresh meat for the
Arctic Ocean whaling fleet. This posed an extraordinary
hardship on coastal natives and to alleviate the situation
reindeer were introduced into Alaska from Siberia in 1872.

Scientific exploration in Arctic America was an early
interest of government agencies from which came some of the
earliest reports and collections. The Revenue Cutter Service
(now the U.S. Coast Guard) supported the Western Union
Telegraph Expedition in 1865; and since then the Coast Guard
has assisted in many scientific activities in Northern
Alaska. Its first responsibility was patrol off the Pribilof
Islands to prevent pelagic sealing. The Albatross, of the
Bureau of Commercial Fisheries initiated a number of basic
investigations on the Bering Sea fisheries. E. W. Nelson, an
employee of the U.S. Signal Service stationed at St. Michael
from 1877-1881 made extensive ethnographic collections from
the Bering Sea Eskimos for the U.S. National Museum. His
report, published by the Bureau of American Ethnology of the
Smithsonian Institution, was the first comprehensive description of an Alaskan Eskimo group, (H. B. Collins, Jr., personal communication). The U.S. Army's responsibility for
meteorological observations during the First International
Polar Year, 1882-1883, provided Sgt. John Murdoch the
opportunity for natural history and ethnological observations
at Point Barrow. Murdoch's report, published by the Bureau
of American Ethnology, is the definitive work on the Point
Barrow Eskimo. In 1894 F. Funston, U.S. Department of
Agriculture botanist made the first biological survey of the
arctic coast from the Porcupine River to Herschel Island.
The U.S. Navy detailed Lt. J. C. Cantwell and S. B. McLenegan
in 1883-1884 to explore the upper reaches of the Noatak and
Kowak rivers. From these exploratory expeditions came the
earliest observations of the inland flora and fauna. Indeed,
following the purchase of Alaska up to the turn of the
century, there were numerous and remarkable natural history
reports by adventuresome Americans. The difficulties of
travel and a short summer season restricted observations to
coastal regions. Nevertheless, from these summer field
workers-- H. M. Bannister, T. H. Bean and others--came
contributions significant to an appreciation of Alaska's
living resources. Others extended their research over the
arctic winter including M. G. Buxton, W. E. Snyder and E. A.
McIllhenny (1897-1898). At Point Barrow, R. M. Anderson
(1908)-1909) on the eastern arctic coast and Joseph Grinnell
(1898-1899) on the Kowak delta and Kotzebue Sound (Bailey,
1948). While Kennicott's naturalists and the scientific

party of the Harriman Alaska Expedition explored the Bering
Sea and Bering Strait coastal lands and islands, J. H.
Turner (1890-1893), Alaska Boundary Commission and W. H.
Osgood (1900-1903) Bureau of Biological Survey collected
plants and animals in the interior of eastern arctic and
subarctic Alaska (Orth, 1967; Reed and Ronhovde, 1971).

The single, largest privately financed expedition in the
American Arctic was the Harriman Alaska Expedition of 1899.
It included an array of about 30 leading scientists organized
with assistance from the Smithsonian Institution. The 12
volumes reporting the expedition's scientific achievements
included seven on marine and terrestrial invertebrates of
Alaska. Interest in Alaskan geography and natural history
by the National Geographic Society began in 1890 with support
of mountaineering and glacial studies. The Society also
supported the extensive botanical surveys of R. H. Griggs in
the Mount Katmai area from 1915-1919.

The 1920's marked a number of events important to
future biological field work in Alaska. One of these was the
development of aviation with early applications to aerial
photogrammetric work and for transportation to remote field
sites. Another was the establishment in 1923 of the Naval
Petroleum Reserve No. 4 on the Arctic Slope. This same year
Canada and the U.S. settled their differences on closed
fishing seasons in the Pacific by signing the Halibut Treaty.

Aside from A. M. Bailey's field work of 1921-22 on the
birds of the Arctic North Slope, the '20s and '30s were
largely dominated by startling developments in archaeology.
Archaeology in Alaska dated from 1912 when V. Stefansson
excavated at Birnirk, Point Barrow. Major archeological
research began in the late '20s with the independent discoveries by D. Jenness, A. Hrdlicka, and W. O. Geist on St.
Laurence Island and Little Diomede of what is now known as
the Old Bering Sea Culture. These finds stimulated other
studies along the Alaskan arctic and subarctic coasts. The
Point Hope site on the Chukchi seacoast was described by
Larsen (1953) as: "One of the richest archaeological localities yet discovered in the arctic." Other famous sites and
their scientific development are reported by H. B. Collins,
Jr., (1951) and H. Larsen (1953) in two excellent reviews of
arctic archaeology. The find of a Folsom-type point in 1947
drew attention to interior Alaska and at the same time, the
Aleutians and mainland coastal sites received increased
attention. Archaeology's basic contribution on man's early
culture is biologically significant for data on the ecological and environmental pre-history of Alaska. It is also an-

FIG. 1

HISTORICAL EVOLUTION OF U.S. ARCTIC BIOLOGY

PHASE I 1824-1914   PERIOD OF SCIENTIFIC EXPLORATION, NARRATIVE REPORTS, AND NATURAL HISTORY COLLECTIONS.

PHASE II 1921-1942   PERIOD OF INDIVIDUAL, INDEPENDENT STUDIES MAINLY ON SYSTEMATICS AND BIOGEOGRAPHY.

PHASE III 1947-1969   SHARP INCREASE IN SUMMER FIELD STUDIES UNDER ONR SUPPORT WITH MAJOR ACTIVITIES CENTERED AT THE NAVAL ARCTIC RESEARCH LABORATORY, BARROW, EMPHASIS ON PARTLY INTEGRATED EXPERIMENTAL RESEARCH.

PHASE IV 1970-1975   SIGNIFICANT EXPANSION OF NATIONAL AND INTERNATIONAL MULTIDISCIPLINE, INTEGRATED STUDIES ON TERRESTRIAL ECOSYSTEM UNDER THE AEGIS OF THE INTERNATIONAL BIOLOGICAL PROGRAM WITH NSF SUPPORT.

PHASE V 1976 TO DATE   DECLINING ROLE OF ONR/NARL IN ARCTIC ACTIVITIES; INCREASING SUPPORT OF NSF. EMPHASIS ON MARINE ENVIRONMENTAL ASSESSMENT STUDIES AND ON BASELINE PROJECTS IN THE SUBANTARCTIC.

other example of polar contrasts, since the absence of human cultures in Antarctica excludes the study of archeology and emphasizes again the severe isolation of the fifth largest continent.

Overall, the years 1867-1940 witnessed some remarkable events of biological importance. The exploitation of marine living resources early aroused public concern and gave rise to conservation policies and scientific management practices. During this period international treaties to the solution of biological problems on the high seas began to apply. Basic inventories of the flora and fauna expanded into systematic treatises; but generally, pre-World War II Alaskan biology was typically descriptive. The period saw the resurrection of unsuspected prehistoric cultures, revealing the antiquity of man and his long dependence on marine living resources of the region. Not withstanding 75 years of scientific progress, Alaska remained a frontier country. Biological work was limited to the short arctic summer, and generally to the most accessible regions. With the coming of winter, field work generally came to a halt as the dozen or fewer summer scientists retreated to "the lower 48." For comparison, one may consider the magnitude of effort expended by the U.S.S.R. in opening up their arctic lands during the politically complex 1930's. This includes the establishment of an Arctic Institute and numerous field stations, the forcing of the Northeast Passage, and initiation of North Pole research stations on drifting ice-floes. Unfortunately, these were times of little information exchange and no international cooperation in circumarctic scientific activities; much of the Soviet effort was not apparent to the Western World until after World War II (Figure 1).

Arctic Alaska 1944-1970

World War II brought many changes to Arctic Alaska. For one, air transportation was considerably improved and within the means of research budgets. In addition, military services in Alaska were available to qualified projects. These factors increased the number of field activities many fold; it also encouraged coordination between disciplines and fostered integration of field activities. Arctic research was also enhanced by other developments. These included the founding of the Arctic Institute of North America (AINA) in 1944 under the aegis of Canada and the United States. AINA provides a common focus for arctic science; it serves in an advisory role; and it obtains funds from government, industry and private individuals to finance research. It serves as a clearing house and its journal Arctic features contemporary

science activities. The second event in 1947 was the
establishment of the first year-round facility dedicated to
basic research under the auspices of the Office of Naval
Research (ONR). This U.S. Navy-owned, contractor-operated,
Arctic Research Laboratory at Point Barrow (later renamed the
Naval Arctic Research Laboratory, NARL) quickly became the
focus for U.S. polar science. Its origin is credited to "the
intellectual vigor and imagination characteristic of the
Office of Naval Research...." (Britton, 1964). The official
report of the Arctic Research Laboratory (Reed and Ronhoved,
1971) states; "Just who first proposed the idea of an arctic
research laboratory is not known with certainty." Actually,
the concept for an American research center in the Arctic
grew from discussions in 1944-1945 between Lt. Col. Laurence
Irving, Chief, Physiological Test Section, Proving Ground
Command, Eglin Air Force Base, Florida, and Major P. F.
Scholander, a physiologist of considerable experience and
knowledge of Greenland and Spitsbergen who looked to the end
of the war as an opportunity to resume arctic research.
Through fortunate timing, ONR entered into a contract with
Swarthmore College for the services of these two distinguished scientists. The ONR contract called for metabolic
research on warm and cold blooded animals under arctic environmental conditions, and comparisons with temperate and
tropical animals as well as the study of conservation of
heat through insulation and hibernation (Reed and Ronhovde,
1971). The 1947 Swarthmore team of seven under the direction
of civilians Irving and Scholander began comparative physiological studies with a demonstrated original experimental
approach. Both showed great tolerance for other sciences and
an immediate respect for the innate knowledge of Eskimos who
very naturally became a part of the laboratory staff. In a
very real sense, Irving and Scholander brought to Alaskan
science a new approach with emphasis on experimental studies
and team work. Irving (1972) recalls: "After travel through
Alaska during the Second World War, in 1947 I went to Barrow
with a very lively group of biologists. From their productive research developed the Arctic Research Laboratory."

This "productive research" initiated elegant experiments
and the publication of numerous, wide ranging studies. The
physiological papers have become standard sources on heat
metabolism and insulation (Scholander, P. F., et al 1953a,b).

Under George E. MacGinitie (1955), invertebrate biologist, California Institute of Technology (1949-1950), and Ira
L. Wiggins, vascular botanist, the laboratory's research
program and field activities broadened. Both men left
their professional marks, MacGinitie with the first

comprehensive study of the arctic shelf marine invertebrates;
and Wiggins with a flora of the vascular plants of the North
Slope. Britton (1964) notes the significant and influential
role of biologists in the early development of the Arctic
Research Laboratory and of the biological work which dominated "the early years and remains a source of strength."
These included studies by F. A. Pitelka on arctic avifauna
and lemming cyclic fluctuations; by J. W. Bee and E. R. Hall
on arctic mammals; by R. L. Rausch and E. L. Schiller on
parasitology in Northern Alaska; and of C. H. Arnold, H. M.
Raup, and W. C. Steere in paleobotany and phytogeography of
vascular plants and mosses, respectively, "and a galaxy of
geophysical, geological, pedological and atmospheric problems" (Wiggins, 1966). However, the percentage of biological
workers in the 1957-1966 period was the reverse of the first
10 years, and the physical scientists outnumbered biologists
until about 1970 (Reed and Ronhovde, 1971). An important
innovation in post war research was the availability of funds
from ONR for basic research. ONR's generous and relatively
unrestricted policy for supporting individual research was a
new phenomenon in U.S. science, and its application to
arctic studies was the most significant government action for
advancing science in Alaska. It assisted polar-aspiring,
young scientists and attracted senior men to the arctic. ONR
provided cost-free laboratory and field support services.
Under the leadership of NARL's first director, Laurence
Irving, ONR provided new directions, force and vitality to
Alaskan research. Expanding field operations, the complexi-
ties of growing administrative problems and rising costs have
tended in time, to institutionalize the Naval Arctic Research
Laboratory. The absence of definitive scientific objectives
and the competition between independent, multi-discipline
interests made for a common problem: "Naturally each field
researcher was most concerned about his progress" (Reed and
Ronhovde, 1971).

NARL's identification as a logistic base for mounting
research in the Arctic made it a natural choice for the 1957-
1958 IGY activities. The support and establishment of ice
island stations provided an opportunity for arctic marine
biology over a 10 year period largely by University of Southern California workers. Plans for U.S. participation in the
International Biological Year, 1967-1968 developed as the
U.S. Tundra Biome Program in 1969 under J. Brown, CRREL and
G. C. West of the University of Alaska. Barrow was favored
as the site for field work because of the wealth of information available prior to 1969 and because of NARL's excellent
facilities and access to wet, low arctic tundra. The main
thrust of the program was to more fully understand the tundra

ecosystem through predictive mechanisms. Within any one
given year, the Tundra Biome Program consisted of about 50
individual projects composed of scientists from 20 to 30
academic institutions. The research design involved highly
integrated, interdisciplinary field and laboratory studies
coupled with computerized modeling techniques. While heavily
oriented toward a summer field program and winter laboratory,
workshop and computer activities, several year-round projects
were maintained at Barrow. At the close of the 1970 and 1971
field seasons comprehensive reports were prepared; in 1972 a
major symposium was held and the published record contained
some 40 summary papers. Lead responsibility and funding in
the National Science Foundation was in the Division of Polar
Programs with contributions from the Foundation's Division
of Biological Sciences, industry and the State of Alaska
(Brown, J., and George C. West, 1973). Scientific planning,
field administration and organization at national and international meetings was coordinated among the principal investigators under the very able direction of J. Brown, Director,
Tundra Biome Center. The IBP studies were followed by a
three year study, (1975-1977) research on arctic tundra environments (RATE). RATE had 21 cooperative studies consisting
of a terrestrial project at Meade River and an aquatic project at Toolik Lake both in Alaska. RATE was designed for
information to anticipate and predict the effect of man's
activities on the terrestrial and aquatic ecosystem. Field
direction and coordination was again under J. Brown who also
served as liaison with collaborating ERDA research (Batzli,
G. O., and J. Brown, 1976; Miller, Michael C. and J. E.
Hobbie, 1976). The Division of Polar Programs also initiated
and funded The Man in the Arctic Program (MAP) - the first
comprehensive, regional social-economic study of its kind in
the U.S. North. This three year study conducted by the
University of Alaska's Institute of Social Economic and Government Resources dealt with broad environmental problems
related to the exploitation of the North Slope oil fields
(Morehouse, Thomas A. 1973). The Tundra Biome and RATE made
heavy demands on the scientific and logistic resources of the
Naval Arctic Research Laboratory. There is no question that
this excellent facility with its dependable logistics and
sophisticated equipment under the direction of the Office of
Naval Research has vitalized arctic research. In the words
of its first Director, Laurence Irving; "Considering the
novel and special interests afforded by the problems of
arctic research, the Arctic Research Laboratory can offer
splendid opportunities for pioneer work of highest quality.
I would not hesitate to recommend that its facilities be
offered to and reserved for the most important and thorough-
going research by the most competent scientists " (Reed and

Ronhovde, 1971 p. 54).

The establishment of the Arctic Aeromedical Laboratory
at Ladd Air Force Base near Fairbanks, March 1947 (Anonymous,
Polar Record 1952) served as another center for research in
physiology, psychology and arctic ecology, much of it in
collaboration with the University of Alaska and NARL scientists. The U.S. Public Health Service's, Arctic Health
Research Center established (1949) at Anchorage, later (1967)
moved to the University of Alaska's Fairbanks campus, was
organized to study problems of human adjustment to low temperature and the preservation of human health in cold
weather. From its inception, until its close in 1975, the
Center has been served by competent, highly dedicated
personnel. Their contributions cover a wide range of polar
biological problems, not the least of which were the incidence and distribution of trichinosis among carnivore marine
mammals, the cause of mortality among sea otters, the control
of biting flies, and the avifauna of Arctic Alaska (Anonymous, Polar Records 1954).

From 1949 to 1962 Laurence Irving continued the metabolic investigations begun at Barrow, as well as the migration
of arctic mammals and distribution and migration of birds at
the Physiology Branch of the Center. Among his numerous
professional papers, two may be noted: "Arctic Life of Birds
and Mammals Including Man" (1972) and "Birds of Anaktuvuk
Pass, Kobuk, and Old Crow: A Study in Arctic Adaptation"
(1960). These are illustrative of Irving's range of scientific interests, his talent for observation and obvious
pleasure for arctic research.

The University of Alaska, Fairbanks, founded in 1917
was designed to stimulate training in mining engineering.
Consequently, it was not until 1950 when the Alaska Cooperative Wildlife Research Unit was established that research
began in vertebrate zoology. The Institute of Marine
Sciences and of Arctic Biology were founded in, respectively,
1960 and 1963. Both institutes have taken active, leading
roles in biological research on many aspects of the northern
environment   (Armstrong, 1971). The Institute of Marine
Sciences has concentrated on the oceanography and ecosystems
of the Bering Sea and coastal regions of Alaska although
personnel of the Institute have participated in research on
the Beaufort and Chukchi Sea and fresh water ecosystems under
the Tundra Biome studies. The Institute of Arctic Biology
serves as a center for research in zoophysiology although its
staff has been active in Tundra Biome, RATE and taiga

FIG. 2

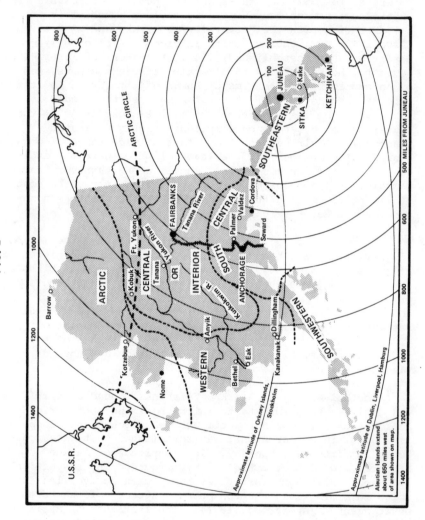

studies. In 1972 the Institute and the Alaska Cooperative
Wildlife Research Unit collaborated in the First International Reindeer and Caribou Symposium precisely 80 years
after Sheldon Jackson, missionary and educator, introduced
reindeer into Alaska from Siberia. This international symposium has served as a forum for the study of ecological
problems posed by modern technology and industry in the far
North (Luick, J. R., P. C. Lent, D. R. Klein, and R. G.
White, 1975).

Current Research 1970-1975

No other state in the United States is as dependent on
marine living resources as is Alaska. These are critical to
the subsistence and economics of a large section of its population, scattered across four time zones and along a coastline greater than the United States (Figure 2). Conservation
and management problems of living resources are topical
issues which have been brought into sharp focus by the ex-
ploitive hazards of mineral and oil extraction on the North
Slope, and the Beaufort and Bering Seas.

Alaskan research has always been influenced by the
activities of Federal Agencies. From lack of communication
or of common goals some of the Federal Activities, in retro-
spect, appear at cross-purpose. In 1968 an attempt was made
to create an open forum which evolved as the Interagency
Arctic Research Coordinating Committee (IARCC), now reconsti-
tuted as an interagency committee of the Federal Council for
Science and Technology. As the principal instrument for
coordination of scientific and technological research in the
arctic within the Federal Government, IARRC reports programs
and expenditures (Anonymous, 1975). Almost all funding is
directed toward implementing agency objectives. NSF is the
principal source of basic research support. An important
step in arctic research was the establishment of an Arctic
Research Program in the Foundation's Division of Polar
Programs in 1970. This fortuitously concided with the International Biological Program and the identification of tundra
habitats as a major world biome.

The Tundra Biome Project significantly advanced biological research in Arctic Alaska through the combined interest
of the Federal Government (NSF), the state of Alaska and
industry. It attracted skilled scientists from many disciplines and brought polar research to temperate zone colleges
and universities. In providing services for the field
research, the University of Alaska served as a logical focus
for arctic science.

FIG. 3

ESTIMATED FISCAL 1976 FEDERAL EXPENDITURES BY MAJOR DISCIPLINES AND AGENCIES IN THE ARCTIC REGION (NORTH OF 60°N)
PRELIMINARY DATA

	MARINE RESEARCH	ATMOSPHERIC SCIENCES	GEOLOGY-GEOPHYSICS	TERRESTRIAL BIOLOGY AND ECOLOGY	GLACIOLOGY	SOCIAL, ECONOMIC, AND HEALTH SCIENCES	ENGINEERING RESEARCH	HYDROLOGY	FY 1976 TOTAL BY AGENCY
EPA............	.15°	.10		.20		.92		.50	1.87
DOC............	1.62°	.19				.17			1.98
HEW............						1.58			1.58
NASA...........	.24	.10			.03				.37
FEA............	–	–	–	–	–	–	–	–	–
NSF............	2.09°	2.60	.50	.60	.57	.41	.15	–	6.92
DOI............	22.29	.01	6.93	.57		.49		1.04	31.33
DOD............	.84	.88	.63	.26	.30	.57	1.47	.12	5.07
DOT............	.03	–	.09	–	–	.01	.66	–	.79
DOA............				1.12		.04			1.16
DOS............	–	–	–	–	–	–	–	–	–
ERDA...........	.24	–	.01	1.06	–	–	.15	–	1.45
TOTAL.........	27.50	3.88	8.16	3.80	.90	4.19	2.43	1.66	52.52

° BIOLOGICAL RESEARCH SUPPORT IN WHOLE OR PART

The most recent major increase in Federal funding for Alaska, as revealed by the Fiscal 1976 table of expenditures, (Figure 3), is largely directed toward Alaskan marine environmental studies that include the Arctic Ocean. This extraordinary effort of the Outer Continental Shelf Environmental Assessment Program (OCSEAP) managed by the National Oceanic Atmospheric Administration for the Bureau of Land Management, Department of Interior (DOI), is expected to peak in the next two years. The 1975-76 research plan projects 140 investigations at a cost of about $26 million dollars.

Information in the "Current Research Profile for Alaska" for 1975 (Brommelsick and Zann, 1976) lists about 700 investigators representing some 675 projects in all areas of science and technology. Of this total, 490 are Federally funded of which 120 represent OCSEAP investigations. Approximately 200 studies are University of Alaska based projects, thus revealing the University's increasingly active role in northern research and the dramatic evolution of biology in Alaska since 1867.

The course of research in arctic Alaska is not without shortcomings. Most regrettable is the lessening influence of the Arctic Institute of North America and the declining leadership role of ONR in initiating arctic studies. One consequence is that NARL is valued more for its logistics than as a center for scientific accomplishments. In addition, there has been a reduction in the opportunities for arctic research careers which in the early years attracted young scientists and gave continuity to a wide variety of northern studies. The National Science Foundation's increasing financial support of basic research helps to compensate for ONR's cutback of support. But there is neither a philosophy nor a commitment for a center that would identify U.S. arctic interests in context with national and international circumarctic activities. A practical constraint is the high cost of arctic operations which could seal off the area to scientists. Short term contract support and mission oriented activities of other federal agencies limit the potentials for scientific continuity, afford no opportunities for graduate training, and result in a large turnover of senior scientists. Current peaking of Federal research funds is typical of past boom/bust cycles which have buffeted the state's economy since 1867. Alaskan scientists are justly apprehensive of the surge of current short range funds on their future. Finally, there is a critical need for a suitable research vessel to support biological and physical marine programs in the arctic.

FIG. 4

HISTORICAL EVOLUTION OF U.S. ANTARCTIC BIOLOGY

PHASE I	1800-1830	ACCOUNTS BY AMERICAN SEALERS AND WHALERS; AND NATURAL HISTORY REPORTS OF JAMES EIGHTS	
PHASE II	1830-1890	THE UNITED STATES EXPLORING EXPEDITION	(1838-1842)
PHASE III	1890-1957	BELGICA	F. A. COOK	(1897-1899)
		DAISY	R. C. MURPHY	(1912-1913)
		CARNEGIE	SUBANTARCTIC CRUISE	(1915-1916)
		BYRD 1ST	SIPLE	(1928-1930)
		BYRD 2ND	SIPLE/PERKINS/LINDSEY	(1933-1935)
		U. S. ANTARC. EXP.	SIPLE/PERKINS/EKLUND	(1939-1941)
		OPERATION HIGHJUMP	SIPLE/PERKINS/GILMORE	(1946-1947)
		OPERATION WINDMILL		(1947-1948)
PHASE IV	1958-TO DATE	IGY	EKLUND/LLANO/SIEBURTH/NEUSHUL	(1958-1959)
		UNITED STATES ANTARCTIC RESEARCH PROGRAM		(1960-)

Antarctica

Bertrand (1971) in his comprehensive review <u>Americans</u> <u>in Antarctica, 1775-1948</u> observes that: "American interest in the Antarctic is as old as the nation itself. While interest has waxed and waned there has been no decade when at least some Americans have not been in the Antarctic as seal hunters, whalers or explorers." Biological knowledge of the region based on observations, narratives and the study of natural history materials accumulated as a by-product of these many activities. Until the end of the 19th Century, almost all information was on marine animals and sea phenomena. Thereafter, details of the terrestrial plants and animals of coastal areas began to appear. Overall, antarctic marine resources stimulated many studies. The foremost example is the <u>Discovery</u> research on whales which also contributed most substantially to a fuller understanding of the biota of the Southern Ocean   (Mackintosh, 1964). These studies conducted during the period 1925-1939 included major studies on krill thus establishing a data base vital to contemporary fishery problems in the Southern Ocean. Following the successful pattern of international scientific cooperation established during the International Geophysical Year, biologists have expanded into every contemporary field of antarctic life sciences with particular interest on the effects of environmental degradation, and potential over-exploitation of the biological resources of the Southern Ocean   (Figure 4).

American Contributions to Antarctic Biology

The record begins with "James Eights, the first quali-fied naturalist to set foot on land south of the Antarctic Convergence" (Hedgpeth, 1971)(Figure 4). Eights accompanied the Palmer-Pendleton Expedition of 1829-1831; and the activi-ties of this expedition are described in great detail by Bertrand (1971). Hedgpeth (1971) reviewed Eights' scientific career and reproduced four of Eights' antarctic papers on the geology and life of the South Shetlands. He goes on to say: "These papers ... constitute the only solid record of the exploring expedition, and probably, had a great deal to do with gaining support for the United States Exploring Expedi-tion under the command of Charles Wilkes."

The United States Exploring Expedition of 1832-1842 also referred to as the South Sea or Wilkes Expedition is accord-ing to Bertrand (1971), one of the major South Polar expedi-tions, representing American interest in the antarctic at a time in history when England and France were competitively

engaged in extensive naval South Polar explorations. While
Wilkes has been credited with sighting Antarctica, most of
the biological collections of the expedition were made in the
subantarctic. Lieutenant Charles Wilkes' official report of
his antarctic exploration published in 1853-1854 was particularly thrilling to young American readers of this period.
Mark Twain in his Autobiography said that when he was a boy
the name of Charles Wilkes was as famous as Theodore
Roosevelt's later. Wilkes was regarded as another Columbus
who had discovered another world   (Brooks, 1947).

There was little American activity in antarctic scientific exploration in the period 1840 to 1928 except for the
biological studies of Robert Cushman Murphy in the subantarctic. Murphy visited South Georgia in 1912-1913 on the New
Bedford whaler Daisy, collecting specimens of the terrestrial
and marine fauna and flora for the American Museum of Natural
History. The results of his observations and studies
appeared in 67 scientific and popular articles. His primary
work on subantarctic birds, Oceanic Birds of South America
(1936) is still the ornithological standard on birds of the
south polar regions. Bertrand (1971) noted that Murphy's
scientific work "launched a professional career that gave
the United States, at a time when American antarctic specialists were rare, an authority of international renown on
antarctic fauna." Murphy did not see Antarctica until the
1960s and after his retirement from the American Museum of
Natural History. At this time he resumed his earlier
studies on petrels, taking keen interest in the current biological research, and speaking out on the urgency for conservation of the antarctic fauna (Murphy 1962, 1964).

In the period between 1920 and 1955, there were ten
expeditions to Antarctica from the United States (Bertrand
1971). Four of these were significant in the development of
American expertise in antarctic biological research; the
results of the scientific work included notable contributions
on the terrestrial life of the interior of Antarctica. The
Second Byrd Antarctic Expedition (1935-1937) discovered an
extensive cryptogamic flora on mountains and nunataks far
from the coast. Details of this vegetation and its ecology
were published by Paul A. Siple (1938). The southern extension of this cryptogamic flora was recorded by the find of
lichen growth at 86°07'S, 149°36'W. Siple with the assistance of three other biologists, E. B. Perkins, A. A. Lindsey
and J. W. Sterrett carried out a variety of studies including
collections of marine plankton, sampling of airborne microorganisms, and measurement, observation and branding of
Weddell seals. The latter work by Lindsey followed up on

Siple's branding work initiated during the First Byrd
Antarctic Expedition of 1929-1930 at Bay of Whales. When the
Second Byrd Antarctic Expedition returned to the U.S., they
brought with them the first collection of live emperor
penguins for exhibition.

The United States Antarctic Service Expedition, 1939-
1941, objectives included investigation and survey of the
natural resources of Antarctica. The broad scientific program included studies in botany, zoology, oceanography, and
physiological observations on expeditionary personnel. The
scientific and logistic activities were split between an East
Base on Stonington Island, Antarctic Peninsula; and a West
Base, at Bay of Whales, Ross Ice Shelf, 1600 miles apart by
air. East Base biological work by B. M. Bryant and C. R.
Eklund included observations on Adélie penguins, general
collections of lichens, marine plankton, and a series of
skeletons and embryos of the Weddell seal. Due to the
hurried and emergency evacuation of East Base, all the collections were left behind but subsequently returned to the
United States. West Base biologists under Siple included
M. Douglass and J. E. Perkins. All assisted the medical
officers, R. G. Frazier and E. E. Lockhart in carrying out
physiological tests on base personnel. Personnel of East
Base (J.D. Healy, H. Darlington, III) and of West Base (R.
G. Fitzsimmons, S. Corey, O. D. Stancliff, F. A. Wade, C. W.
Griffith) made plant collections which provided evidence of
the wide distributions and variety of the interior cryptogamic land flora. The West Base activities included a
number of wide ranging traverses, including the very successful Biological Party traverse under J. E. Perkins to the
Ford Ranges. Emperor penguins were brought to the National
Zoo in Washington, D.C. from West Base, in addition to large
botanical and zoological collections. Over 18 papers have
appeared on the flora and fauna of Marie Byrd Land (Bertrand,
1971).

The U.S. Navy projects, "Operation Highjump", 1946-1947,
and "Operation Windmill", 1947-1948, were largely sea and air
activities which provided very little opportunity for biological programs. Biologists on the former included Paul Siple,
J. E. Perkins and R. M. Gilmore. However, they made extensive observations of the biota of the antarctic pack ice, and
obtained information on whales and sea birds of the Southern
Ocean. It was at this time that the oases phenomena was
revealed to science.

The International Geophysical Year planning began with a
symposium in 1955 "to bring together scientific knowledge of

the continent", not only on the geophysical program but also
on "...other related areas of broad scientific interest"
(Crary et al, 1956). The status of antarctic zoology and
botany were addressed respectively, by C. R. Eklund (Crary
et al, 1957) and G. A. Llano (Crary et al, 1956). Both
stressed the need for biological participation on a well-
planned, continuing research basis. Eklund served as the
Wilkes Station leader for 1958-1959, Llano carried out extensive field surveys during the 1958-1959 austral summer.
Following the formation of the Committee on Polar Research
by the National Academy of Sciences in 1958, Llano was
appointed Secretary of its Panel on Biological and Medical
Sciences and instructed to initiate a biological program.
The first action of the Panel was the establishment of a
modern, permanent biological laboratory, the present Eklund
Biological Center at McMurdo Station, to encourage programs
in experimental biology. A physiological program on cold
adaptation in antarctic fish was initiated by D. Wohlschlag
of Stanford University. The Panel issued a general survey on
the opportunities for research in antarctic life sciences.
In 1960 the Academy research was absorbed by the National
Science Foundation under the United States Antarctic Research
Program.

    While the Foundation managed, coordinated and funded
antarctic biological research as a national program, the
philosophy and guidance in the formulation of life sciences
objectives from the post-IGY period to the present has come
from the Committee on Polar Research, later renamed the Polar
Research Board. These are embodied in two documents: The
Life Sciences in Antarctica (1961) and Polar Research: A
Survey (1970). Additional valuable guidance, particularly
useful in the international coordination of biology, has
come from the Scientific Committee on Antarctic Research
(1972), and the recommendations of the SCAR Working Group
on Biology reported in SCAR Bulletins. Three symposia
sponsored by SCAR since the post-IGY have invigorated the
United States program through interaction with research plans
and scientists of other Antarctic Treaty nations. The Paris
Symposium of 1962 included 15 papers by U.S. biologists on
work begun in 1958. The Cambridge, England Symposium of
1968 included 21 U.S. contributions containing new data
based largely on experimental research. The Symposium of
1974 in Washington, D.C., included 23 U.S. papers on the
structure and function of antarctic ecosystems.

    While biology was not formally included in the IGY, the
international scientific cooperation worked out in Antarctica
during the 1956-1959 years established a useful pattern.

From the beginning, U.S. biology had the interest and influential support of L. M. Gould, geologist and Chairman, U.S. National Committee for the IGY and of the scientific directors, H. Wexler, meteorologist and A. P. Crary, geophysicist. Biological plans evolved as a blend of national and international recommendations drawn from the sources previously mentioned. Broadly stated, the U.S. antarctic program goals have been directed toward:

- Obtaining fundamental knowledge about antarctic life forms and life systems

- Increasing our understanding of the environmental dynamics of the antarctic relative to the rest of the world

- Strengthening U.S. competence in polar life sciences by utilizing antarctic expeditionary research for the development of scientific careers.

In attaining these objectives, and to satisfy the demands for support of scientific work, program management has maintained a broad research approach compatible with contemporary scientific issues but aiming for a balanced research effort in the life sciences.

A synthesis of biological activities over the past 19 years is shown in Figure 5. It shows areas of priority, a gross presentation of disciplines and duration of effort in the antarctic and subantarctic. The subantarctic has had less than its due but with a high logistic investment in Antarctica it has been difficult to deflect attention from the primary target. Obviously, in so vast an ocean world, the remote and scattered subantarctic islands are key reference points to many biological questions. This figure also shows the principal facilities important in investigations of regional biology. McMurdo Station is the principal site for studies. It is a logical point for organizing field surveys into the interior. However, it is even more valuable as a site for experimental biology. This is largely due to the persistence of the sea-ice platform for conducting marine biological studies and the accessibility of a wide range of organisms suitable for physiological, biochemical, and behavioral research. From the beginning, research demands forced an upgrading of field facilities. Advanced laboratory techniques called for modern instrumentation so that biological field research early achieved a sophistication which has distinguished U.S. antarctic biology from the beginning.

FIGURE 5

ANTARCTIC BIOLOGY AND MEDICINE
A SYNTHESIS

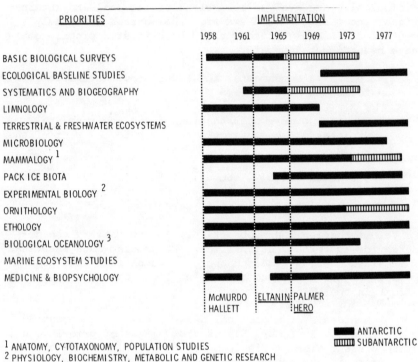

PRIORITIES

BASIC BIOLOGICAL SURVEYS
ECOLOGICAL BASELINE STUDIES
SYSTEMATICS AND BIOGEOGRAPHY
LIMNOLOGY
TERRESTRIAL & FRESHWATER ECOSYSTEMS
MICROBIOLOGY
MAMMALOGY [1]
PACK ICE BIOTA
EXPERIMENTAL BIOLOGY [2]
ORNITHOLOGY
ETHOLOGY
BIOLOGICAL OCEANOLOGY [3]
MARINE ECOSYSTEM STUDIES
MEDICINE & BIOPSYCHOLOGY

IMPLEMENTATION

1958   1961   1965   1969   1973   1977

McMURDO   ELTANIN   PALMER
HALLETT   HERO

ANTARCTIC
SUBANTARCTIC

[1] ANATOMY, CYTOTAXONOMY, POPULATION STUDIES
[2] PHYSIOLOGY, BIOCHEMISTRY, METABOLIC AND GENETIC RESEARCH
[3] INSHORE & DEEP SEA MARINE RESEARCH

FIGURE 6

ADVANTAGES OF BIOLOGICAL RESEARCH IN ANTARCTICA

o Organization and Logistic Effort Unified in Research Support
o Ring-Like Continent Gives 360^0 Scope for Research Design
o No Cultural, Technological or Industrial Presence
o Terrestrial Habitats in Summer Spectacularly Ornithological
o Large Populations of Fresh, Field Acclimated Organisms
o Tractable Seals and Birds: Low Species Interaction
o Climatic and Geographical Adaptations Found Nowhere Else
o Remoteness of Area: Highly Sensitive Gauge on Spread of
  Pollutants in Global Systems

Figure 5 fails to show these advances but one may infer from the staggered distributions of effort and the priorities that the national program in Antarctica has been one of rapid expansion and changes. The opportunity for deep sea research on <u>Eltanin</u> and <u>Hero</u> and the opening of Palmer Station on the Antarctic Peninsula were beneficial in giving U.S. biologists a total view of antarctic ecosystems and biota   (Fig. 6).

Scientific work in Antarctica is analogous to any new emerging science. In biology, the primary or descriptive stage produced much information but few breakthroughs. Mackintosh (1964) records that the biological reports from early expeditions and visits to the Antarctica "must fill much more than 100 volumes, not counting papers scattered in professional journals." In the period 1959-1969, U.S. antarctic biology matured rapidly into experimental sciences with an exponential growth of useful information and know- ledge. But this could not have happened without the data base of the earlier descriptive stage. Descriptive ecology has also been revitalized by innovative studies on the energetics of vertebrates and invertebrates, by the physio- logical and biochemical analysis of cold adaptation, by new insights into the social structure and relationship of avian colonies, and by recent effort on the population dynamics of marine birds and mammals. In the last ten years, there have been a number of intensive investigations of ecosystem dynamics. Here again we are faced with the startling asym- metry of the polar regions. Whereas the arctic is repre- sented by mature terrestrial and marine ecosystems, the antarctic terrestrial ecosystem is primitive and species poor; the fifth largest continent serves passively as a breeding and resting platform for marine birds and animals during the brief austral summer. Consequently, the antarc- tic marine ecosystem has received the lion's share of scien- tific and practical attention. A practical aspect of the Southern Ocean is that it contains the last untapped fishery resource on earth. Despite a decline of about 85-90 percent over the past 40 years in the stocks of antarctic baleen whales, whaling is still active. Fishing, a new antarctic activity and totally Russian, has since 1964 developed into a full industry based on Notothenia species. The efficiency of Soviet fishing technology may be judged from current records which show a marked drop in more recent fish catches. Attention is now being given to the commercial exploitation of the krill, which masses in swarms measuring square kilo- meters of the sea's surface. The potential catch has been estimated up to twice the present total (60.5 million tons) harvest of fish from all oceans. Experimental fishing by five nations is in progress in the Southern Ocean. By 1980,

TABLE 3

FAMILIES AND SPECIES OF POLAR MARINE FISHES

Family	Arctic	Arctic Sub-Arctic	Antarctic Family	Antarctic
Myxinidae	0	1		1
Petromyzontidae	1	2		
			Geotriidae	1
Scyliorhinidae		1		
Squalidae		4		
Rajidae		8		4
Chimaeridae		1		
Acipenseridae	1	1		
Clupeidae	1	1		
			Synaphobranchidae	1
			Halosauridae	1
Salmonidae	10	14		
Osmeridae	3	3		
Gadidae	5	21		1
			Moridae	2
			Muraenolepidae	3
Macrouridae		2		7
Gasterosteidae	1	3		
Syngnathidae		2		
Serranidae		1		
Ammodytidae	1	3		
			Nototheniidae	34
			Harpagiferidae	15
			Bathydraconidae	15
			Channichthyidae	15
			Brotulidae	1
Zoarcidae	19	26		11
Anarhichadidae		4		
Stichaeidae	1	5		
Lumpenidae	2	4		
Pholidae		2		
Gobiidae		1		
Scorpaenidae		3		
Cottidae	11	22		
Cottunculidae	2	3		
			Congiopodidae	1
Triglidae		1		
Agonidae	2	8		
Cyclopteridae	2	6		
Liparidae	7	9		5
Pleuronectidae	5	15		
Bothidae		2		2
Lophiidae		1		
TOTAL NUMBER OF SPECIES	74	180		120

Sources:
Andriyashev, A.P. 1954. Fishes of the northern seas of the U.S.S.R., Akad. Nauk S.S.S.R.
DeWitt, H.   1970   Coastal and deep-water benthic fishes of the Antarctic. Amer.
                         Geogr. Soc., Ant. Map Folio Ser. No. 15

they may well be joined by other fishing fleets   (Table 3).

Our present state of knowledge on the general quality and precision of population dynamics, and future interrelationship of food chains are inadequate for the management of modern fish harvesting technology. Exploitation of antarctic living resources with poor population assessment is bound to be disastrous. The traditional system of exploiting populations and then showing concern after catch-per-unit of effort costs rise is a treacherously poor system for highly iteroporous, slow-growing, long-lived polar species. The overall effects of exploiting new species in the antarctic ecosystem can have major and subtle effects that may be adverse, that may be irreversible, and that may be unrecognized for many years, especially in the case of a basic food component such as krill   (Wohlschlag, personal communication).

U.S. concern in these problems is deep and sincere. U.S. biologists in 1959 were instrumental in the preparation and submission of recommendations for the conservation of the flora and fauna of Antarctica. They have since supported proposals for the preservation of specially protected areas and of sites of special scientific interest. They initiated action for the conservation of antarctic seals, and supported the Convention for the Regulation of Antarctic Pelagic Sealing. U.S. biologists prepared the first environmental impact assessment on the antarctic continent. U.S. biology has made varied and useful contributions to knowledge of Antarctica. These are recorded in the Antarctic Bibliography (Thuronyi, 1974). Of 17,000 items, both U.S. and foreign, listed on all subjects, biology comprises the largest part; U.S. biologists' contributions represent approximately 12 percent (2,000 items).

Noteworthy examples of this research under the United States Antarctic Research Program include:

- The discovery of extreme cold adaptation in antarctic fish. D. Wohlschlag, University of Texas.

- The first comprehensive report on antarctic and subantarctic entomology, including the description of nearly one-third of the regions known free-living mites. J. L. Gressitt, Bishop Museum, Honolulu.

- The study of breeding behavior of antarctic terns and demonstration of bipolar migration of skuas. D. Parmelee, University of Minnesota.

- Studies of mortality among Adélie penguins showing high mortality among older breeding individuals (over 6-8 years of age), particularly females. D. Ainley, Point Reyes Bird Observatory, California.

- The first demonstration of the use of the sun as a clue to navigation in the Adélie penguins; and first demonstration that penguins use vocal recognition. R. L. Penney, Iowa.

- Circadian rhythm studies using the Adélie penguin and Weddell seals. Description of the interaction between penguins and predator/scavengers during the breeding period; and of the dimensions and function of the feeding territory of predatory skuas. D. Muller-Schwarze, State University of New York, Syracuse.

- The first recording of the underwater sound of a blue whale, representing the highest-level, sustained sound ever recorded from a natural cause. W. C. Cummings, Naval Under Sea Research and Development Center, San Diego, California.

- Discovery of large populations of southern right whales off Argentina. R. Gilmore, San Diego Museum of Natural History, California.

- Description of the physical and neurological mechanism of heat and water exchange in the respiratory passage of Adélie penguins; and neurological controls in heat exchange in feet and legs of the giant petrel. D. Murrish, Case Western Reserve University, Cleveland, Ohio.

- Demonstration of the role of blood glycopeptide in freezing avoidance in antarctic fishes, and the elucidation of the chemical structure of these antifreeze compounds. A. DeVries, University of Illinois.

- First time-depth recording of free diving in marine mammals and elucidation of diving physiology of Weddell seal and emperor penguins. J. Kooyman, University of California- San Diego.

- Elucidation of the mechanism of oxygen exchange in hemoglobin-free ice fish. E. Hemmingsen, University of California, San Diego.

- Description of metabolic pathways characteristic of cold-adapted polar invertebrates. M. A. McWhinnie, DePaul University, Chicago.

- The first comprehensive data of primary productivity in the Southern Ocean. S. Z. El-Sayed, Texas A & M, College Station.

- Demonstration of chlorinated hydrocarbons in antarctic birds. R. Risebrough, University of California, Berkeley.

- Description of chemical eutrophication in Antarctica, the biological monitoring of scientific activities; and first environmental impact assessment studies for Antarctica. B. Parker, Virginia Polytechnic Institute and State University, Blacksburg.

- First long-term study of the life history pattern and demographic characteristics of Weddell seals; characterization of leopard seal predation on crabeater seals; and description of social structure of crabeater seals during pupping and breeding. D. Siniff, University of Minnesota, St. Paul.

- First comprehensive census of antarctic seals in the pack ice. A. W. Erickson, University of Washington, Seattle.

Acknowledgments

I am grateful to colleagues with whom I exchanged ideas and whose suggestions I have incorporated in this report, principally: A. L. DeVries, J. W. Hedgpeth, D. E. Murrish, K. J. Bertrand, J. H. Lipps, J. Brown, J. E. Hobbie, D. W. Hood, B. C. Parker, and D. E. Wohlschlag. I also acknowledge and thank Horace D. Porter for editorial assistance.

References

Anonymous (1952)   The Arctic Aeromedical Laboratory at
    Fairbanks, Alaska.   Polar Record 6(43):396.

Anonymous (1954)   Arctic Health Research Center, Anchorage.
    Polar Record 7(47):70-72.

Anonymous (1975)   FY 1974 arctic research.   Arctic Bulletin
    1(6):229-300.

Armstrong, T. (1971)   Research institution of the University
    of Alaska.   Polar Record 15(97):546-548.

Bailey, A. M. (1948)   Birds of arctic Alaska.   Popular Series
    8:33-38. Denver, Colorado Mus. of Nat. His.

Batzli, G. O. and J. Brown (1976)   RATE--the influence of
    grazing on arctic tundra ecosystems.   Arctic Bulletin
    2(9):153-160.

Bertrand, K. J. (1971)   Americans in Antarctica, 1775-1948.
    New York, Amer. Geogr. Soc.   Special publication, 39.
    554p.

Britton, M. (1964)   Our arctic research laboratory.
    BioSciences 14(5):44-48.

Brown, J. and G. C. West (1973)   The Tundra Biome Program.
    Arctic Bulletin 1(2):56-60.

Brommelsick, P. H. and J. S. Zahn (1976)   Current Research
    Profile for Alaska (third edition).   Anchorage Arctic
    Environmental Information and Data, University of
    Alaska.   192p.

Brooks, V. W. (1947)   The Times of Melville and Whitman.
    New York, Dutton.

Bushnell, V. G. (editor) (1967)   Terrestrial Life of
    Antarctica: Antarctic Map Folio Series, 5.   New York
    Amer. Geogr. Soc.

Collins, H. B. Jr. (1951)   The origin and antiquity of the
    Eskimo.   In: Annual Report of the Board of Regents,
    423-468.   The Smithsonian Institution.   Washington, D.C.

Committee on Polar Research (1961) Science in Antarctica, I:
    The Life Sciences in Antarctica. Washington, D.C.,
    Nat. Acad. of Sci., Nat. Res. Council. 162p.

Committee on Polar Research (1970) Polar Research: A Survey.
    Washington, D.C., Nat. Acad. of Sci., Nat. Res. Council.
    204p.

Crary, A. P., L. M. Gould, E. O. Hurlburt, H. Odishaw, and
    W. E. Smith (1956) Antarctica in the International
    Geophysical Year. In: Geophysical Monograph, 1.
    Washington, D.C., Amer. Geophys. Union, Nat. Acad. of
    Sci., Nat. Res. Council. 133p.

Dall, W. H. (1910) The discovery and exploration of Alaska.
    In: Harriman Alaska Series 2:185-204. Washington, D.C.,
    Smithsonian Institution.

Fay, F. H. (1974) The role of ice in the ecology of marine
    mammals of the Bering Sea. In: Oceanography of the
    Bering Sea with Emphasis on Renewable Resources (Hood,
    D. W. and E. J. Kelley, editors). Fairbanks, University
    of Alaska Institute of Marine Sciences. Occasional
    paper, 2. 623p.

Hedgpeth, J. W. (1971) Perspectives of benthic ecology in
    Antarctica. In: Research in the Antarctic (Quam, L. O.,
    editor). Washington, D.C., Amer. Assoc. for the Adv. of
    Sci. Publication, 93. 3-45.

Irving, Laurence (1960) Birds of Anaktuvak Pass, Kobuk, and
    Old Crow: a study in arctic adaptation. U.S. Nat. Mus.
    Bulletin, 217. 409p.

Irving, Laurence (1972) Arctic Life of Birds and Mammals
    Including Man. Heidelberg, Berlin, Springer-Verlag.
    192p.

Laresen, H. (1953) Archaeological investigations in Alaska
    since 1939. Polar Record 6(45):593-607.

Luick, J. R., P. C. Lent, D. R. Klein, and R. G. White (1975)
    Proceedings of the First International Reindeer and
    Caribou Symposium, 8-11 August, 1972. In: Biological
    Papers of the University of Alaska, Special Report, 1.
    Fairbanks, University of Alaska. 551p.

MacGinitie, C. E. (1955) Distribution and ecology of the
    marine invertebrates of Point Barrow, Alaksa. In:
    Smithsonian Miscellaneous Collections 128(9):1-201.

Mackintosh, N. A. (1964) A survey of antarctic biology up
    to 1945. In: Biologie Antarctique. 651p. Paris, Hermann.

Maury, M. F. (1861) On the physical geography of the sea, in
    connection with the antarctic regions. Proceedings of
    the Royal Geographical Society 5:22.

Miller, M. C. and J. E. Hobbie (1976) RATE--the Toolik Lake
    Program. Arctic Bulletin 2(9):161-164.

Moore, T. (1968) Alaska's first American century: the view
    ahead. Polar Record 14(88):3-13.

Morehouse, T. A. (1973) Social and economic research in the
    U.S. arctic: the Man in the Arctic Program. Arctic
    Bulletin 1(2):43-46.

Murphy, R. C. (1936) Oceanic Birds of South America. New
    York, MacMillian. 2 volumes. 1,245p.

Murphy, R. C. (1962) Antarctic conservation. Science 93:
    303-309.

Murphy, R. C. (1964) Conservation of the antarctic fauna.
    In: Biologie Antarctique. Paris, Hermann. 651p.

Orth, D. J. (1967) Dictionary of Alaska place names. In:
    U.S. Geological Survey Professional Paper, 567. Wash-
    ington, D.C., U.S. Government Printing Office. 1,052p.

Prevost, J. (1976) Population Biomass and Energy
    Requirements of Antarctic Birds. 17p. (9 tables).
    Unpublished.

Reed, J. C. and A. C. Ronhovde (1971) A History (1947-1966)
    of the Naval Arctic Research Laboratory at Point Barrow,
    Alaska. Washington, D.C., Arctic Institute of North
    America. 748p.

Scientific Committee on Antarctic Research (1972) SCAR
    Manual (second edition). Scott Polar Research Institute.
    Cambridge, England.

Scholander, P. F., W. Flagg, R. J. Hock, and L. Irving (1953)
Studies on the physiology of frozen plants and animals
in the Arctic. Journal of Cellular and Comparative
Physiology 42:1-56 .

Scholander, P. F., W. Flagg, U. Walters, and L. Irving (1953)
Climatic adaptations in arctic and tropical poikilotherms. Physiol. Zoology 26:67-92.

Science and Technology Division, Library of Congress
(Thuronyi, Gezat, editor) (1974) Antarctic Bibliography,
7. 465p. Washington, D.C., U.S. Government Printing
Office.

Siple, P. A. (1938) The Second Byrd Antarctic Expedition,
Botany 1. Ecology and geographical distribution. In:
Annals of the Missouri Botanical Gardens 25(2):467-514.
St. Louis, Missouri Botanical Gardens.

Stefansson, V. (1925) The Adventure of Wrangel Island.
New York, MacMillan. 424p.

Spetzman, L. A. (1959) Vegetation of the arctic slope of
Alaska. In: U.S. Geological Survey Professional Paper,
302-B, 58p. Washington, D.C., Department of the
Interior, U.S. Geological Survey.

Troelson, J. C. (1952) Danish Pearyland Expedition, 1947-50.
Polar Record 6(44):417-473.

Wiggins, I. C. (1966) The Arctic--its discovery and past
development. In: Arctic Biology (Hansen, H. P., editor)
Corvallis, Oregon State University: 261.

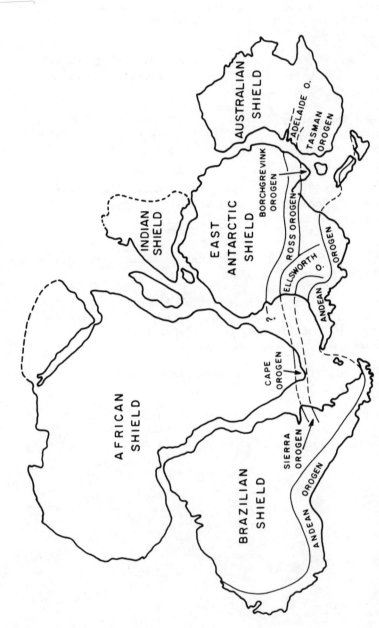

Figure 1. Schematic tectonic map of Gondwanaland in the early Mesozoic before fragmentation, with the addition of the younger late Mesozoic-early Cenozoic Andean orogen. The shapes and structures of the Gondwanaland fragments as they exist today have been used in this reconstruction. Areas in the western Pacific which today lie north of Australia-New Zealand and which may have been part of Gondwanaland are not included.

3

Antarctica and Gondwanaland

Campbell Craddock

Although the idea of drifting continents had
appeared earlier, it was not until late in the
nineteenth century that geologists first suggested
the existence of a large ancestral continent in
the southern hemisphere in the geologic past.
This hypothetical protocontinent - now termed
Gondwanaland - included present-day South America,
Africa, Arabia, Madagascar, Ceylon, peninsular
India, Antarctica, Australia, and New Zealand
(Fig. 1). Because of its position in the reassembly, Antarctica clearly must play an important role in determining the reality and history of
Gondwanaland. Despite its great importance to the
concept, however, the geology of Antarctica was almost unknown when Gondwanaland was first postulated. Only in the past few years has knowledge of
Antarctica, the last fragment of the supposed
supercontinent to be explored, advanced to a point
where meaningful geologic tests of the Gondwanaland hypothesis are possible.

Antarctica was probably first sighted about
1820 from ships sailing near the tip of the
Antarctic Peninsula; this discovery confirmed the
long-suspected existence of a southern polar continent. Later expeditions collected continental
rocks such as granite and sandstone from icebergs,
but the first geologic specimens obtained on the
continent were collected in the 1890's at Cape
Adare, south of New Zealand. The next twenty years
saw vigorous exploration by expeditions from several nations, and the broad pattern of antarctic
geology began to emerge. Other private and
national expeditions before and after World War II
added more geologic information, but large areas

of the continent still remained unexplored and unknown as late as 1955.   Most of these early geologic observations were confined to the coastal
fringe of Antarctica; except for the South Pole
parties of Ernest Shackleton, Roald Amundsen and
Robert F. Scott, and the Laurence M. Gould party
in support of Byrd's polar flight.   The vast interior of the continent remained geologically unknown.

    In 1937 the great South African geologist
Alexander Du Toit published a book (Our Wandering
Continents) which must be rated among the most important ever written in the field of geology.   In
this brilliant synthesis he set forth in detail
the geologic evidence then available for continental drift and for the existence of Gondwanaland.
Regarding Antarctica, he stated:

        "The role of the Antarctic is a vital
        one.   As will be observed...the shield
        of East Antarctica constitutes the
        'key-piece' - shaped surprisingly like
        Australia, only larger - around which,
        with wonderful correspondences in out-
        line, the remaining 'puzzle-pieces' of
        Gondwanaland can with remarkable pre-
        cision be fitted".

    Because so little was then known about the
geology of Antarctica, Du Toit's Gondwanaland reassembly in effect predicted the geologic patterns
to be expected in the antarctic interior.   It is a
tribute to his genius and foresight that subsequent geological studies in Antarctica have
largely confirmed these predictions.   When
Du Toit's book was published, the Gondwanaland hypothesis had few advocates, particularly among
northern hemisphere scientists.   Unfortunately,
Du Toit did not live to see the wide respect and
acceptance accorded his work today.

    Since the International Geophysical Year in
1957-58, ski-equipped aircraft and oversnow tracked vehicles have opened the entire continent to
geological study.   Only a few significant rock exposures remain unvisited by geologists today.   Our
knowledge of the geology of this remote continent
has more than doubled during the past twenty
years.

Geology of Antarctica

Early in this century, after geologic data became available from the Antarctic Peninsula, the
Ross Sea region, and other coastal localities, it
was recognized that Antarctica could be divided into two major geologic provinces. The first comprises the larger part of the continent that faces
mainly upon the Atlantic and Indian Oceans; since
most of this province lies in the area of east
longitudes, it is commonly known as East
Antarctica (see Fig. 1). The second province consists of the smaller part of the continent that
faces mainly upon the Pacific Ocean; it is commonly known as West Antarctica. East Antarctica is
a typical continental shield or stable platform,
consisting of a foundation of igneous and metamorphic rocks overlain by a sequence of younger,
flat-lying stratified sedimentary and volcanic
rocks. By contrast, West Antarctica is composed
of generally younger rocks that are widely deformed and metamorphosed; the age and nature of the
basement rocks are poorly known. Intrusive and
extrusive igneous rocks are abundant, and some
volcanic activity continues there today. The
geology of Antarctica is portrayed on a
1:5,000,000 geologic map of the continent
(Craddock, 1972a).

Rock exposures comprise less than five percent
of the area of the continent, and those in East
Antarctica occur in an oval belt that includes the
coastal region and the Transantarctic Mountains.
The nunataks (rocky peaks protruding through the
ice) and mountain ranges within this belt reveal a
basement complex composed mainly of high-grade
metamorphic rocks and intrusive igneous rocks.
Gneisses of the granulite facies are the most
abundant rocks, but lower grade metamorphic rocks
of the amphibolite and greenschist facies occur in
some localities. A wide range of igneous rocks
has been reported, but felsic varieties such as
granite are most common. These crystalline basement rocks record a complex geologic history in-
volving several cycles of deformation, regional
metamorphism, and emplacement of igneous intrusives.

In contrast to the other continents, Antarctica

Table 1.   Classification of Phanerozoic time,
           after Van Eysinga (1975).

Era	Period	Epoch	Millions of years before present that it began
Cenozoic			
	Quaternary		2
	Tertiary		
		Pliocene	5
		Miocene	22
		Oligocene	38
		Eocene	55
		Paleocene	66
Mesozoic			
	Cretaceous		141
	Jurassic		195
	Triassic		231
Paleozoic			
	Permian		280
	Carboniferous		345
	Devonian		395
	Silurian		435
	Ordovician		500
	Cambrian		600

has so far revealed few rocks with apparent ages
greater than 1.8 billion years. This fact may imply that, 1) the oldest rocks in the basement of
East Antarctica are truly younger than those of
other continental shields, 2) insufficient sampling has yet taken place to discover the oldest
rocks present, or 3) later metamorphic events, especially in the early Paleozoic era, have reset
the mineral clocks, causing apparent radiometric
ages younger than the true ages of the rocks
(Table 1). The youngest known rocks in the East
Antarctic basement complex are fossiliferous Upper
Precambrian and Cambrian strata, generally folded
and metamorphosed, that occur in the Transantarctic Mountains and at a few coastal localities.

Overlying the East Antarctic basement complex
is a succession of mainly flat-lying sedimentary
and volcanic rocks. These beds have been named
the Beacon Supergroup (sedimentary) and the Ferrar
Group (igneous), and they represent the Gondwana
sequence, as described from peninsular India and
the other southern continents, in Antarctica. The
Beacon Supergroup contains rocks as old as Devonian, and the Ferrar Group rocks as young as
Jurassic. Beacon and Ferrar strata are widely exposed in the Transantarctic Mountains, but they
have been found in place at only a few localities
along the coast of East Antarctica.

The geologic history of West Antarctica is complex and not well established. All rocks whose
ages are known appear to have formed during the
last 600 million years; no definitely Precambrian
rocks have yet been discovered. In much of West
Antarctica the oldest rocks are igneous intrusive
and metamorphic varieties that form a basement
complex believed to be Paleozoic in age. Sedimentary and volcanic sequences of probably Paleozoic and Mesozoic age are widely distributed, and
most of these rocks are strongly folded and somewhat metamorphosed. Intrusive igneous rocks were
emplaced throughout much of West Antarctica during
the Mesozoic, and perhaps the early Cenozoic. Upper Cenozoic volcanic and sedimentary layers on
the Antarctic Peninsula and to the west are flat-
lying and undisturbed. Volcanism which began in
the middle Tertiary has continued into recent
times in much of coastal West Antarctica.

The geologic composition and history of a continent can be effectively studied from a tectonic
map, which shows the age and distribution of the
major structural units that define the architecture of the continent (Craddock, 1970, 1972b). In
particular, such maps portray shields (stable areas
with a basement complex of ancient igneous and
metamorphic rocks overlain by younger flat-lying
strata) and orogens (belts of folded and metamorphosed strata, commonly intruded by large bodies
of granite, the modern or ancient sites of mountain
chains). The major tectonic units of Antarctica
are the East Antarctic shield, four orogens in the
Transantarctic Mountains and West Antarctica, and
a Cenozoic volcanic province. The delineation of
these tectonic provinces allows a major test of
the Gondwanaland hypothesis, the geologic compati-
bility of the opposing coasts.

Evidence for Gondwanaland

In fitting Antarctica into his Gondwanaland reassembly, Du Toit (1937) had to depend largely on
the shape of the continent because so little was
then known about its geology. Since that time,
progress in antarctic geology has yielded a number
of discoveries that bear on the Gondwanaland
problem. Some lines of evidence that seem especially significant are summarized below:

1. The basement rocks of coastal East Antarctica
are similar, both in a general way and in some details, to those along the matching coasts of the
other Gondwanaland fragments in Du Toit's reassembly. Work by geologists of several nations has
shown that the structural grain in these ancient
antarctic rocks is compatible with that in like
rocks of the suggested matching coast. The basement rocks of all these areas are compositionally
similar, consisting of high-grade metamorphic
rocks such as granulite gneisses, along with
igneous intrusives such as granite. In particular,
an unusual hypersthene-bearing granitic rock,
termed charnockite, is widespread in eastern
Africa, Ceylon, eastern India, and coastal East
Antarctica.

2. The rocks of the Beacon Supergroup in
Antarctica are generally similar to the Paleozoic
and Mesozoic Gondwana sedimentary sequences on the

other southern continents and continental islands.
The lower Beacon consists of detrital sedimentary
rocks as old as Devonian in some localities. Beds
of ancient tillite were first discovered in the
Transantarctic Mountains in 1958, and many other
Paleozoic tillite localities are now known in
Antarctica. These tillites occur in the Beacon
sequence and are considered Carboniferous or
Permian in age. Overlying these glacial beds are
younger Permian strata which commonly include coal
beds and bear the Glossopteris flora. This
succession of distinctive rock types can be match-
ed, at least in part, in Australia, India,
Madagascar, Africa, the Falkland Islands and South
America.

3. With the discovery of the tillites in
Antarctica, evidence for late Paleozoic glaciation
is now known from all the major Gondwanaland fragments. Similar deposits had been previously found
in South America, Africa, India, and Australia,
and their existence in Antarctica had been predicted. The character and distribution of these
ancient glacial beds imply the presence of Paleozoic ice sheets of continental dimensions. However, along some coasts directional indicators
show that the ice flowed onto the present-day continent from the adjacent ocean basin. If we ac-
cept modern geography as that of the Permian, both
the anomalous flow directions and the wide latitudinal range of continental glaciation are awk-
ward to explain. Recent studies have shown, however, that the Gondwanaland reconstruction presents an attractive alternative in understanding
this early glacial period (Crowell, 1977).

4. The Paleozoic and Mesozoic fossil record in
Antarctica, only now emerging in detail, bears a
strong resemblance to that found in the other
southern continents. Marine fauna are as old as
Cambrian and include archaeocyathids, trilobites,
gastropods, bryozoans, fish, echinoderms, brachio-
pods, and pelecypods. These animals flourished in
shallow waters close to land under conditions
similar to those on modern continental shelves.
Although these fossil fauna are similar to those
of Australia, South America, and South Africa, it
is unlikely that such animals migrated across deep
ocean basins. Land animals are less abundant but
also show close affinities to the fauna of the

Figure 2. Glossopteris leaf from the Polarstar Formation, Ellsworth Mountains, Antarctica.

other southern continents. Recent discoveries of
Triassic reptiles and amphibians in the Transantarctic Mountains are of great importance because these animals, such as Lystrosaurus, must
have moved over land routes. Antarctic fossil
flora, especially the Permian-Carboniferous
Glossopteris flora (Fig. 2), bear a strong similarity to other southern flora. The pronounced
overlap between the Glossopteris flora of
Antarctica and India, for instance, poses two
questions if we suppose that Permian and modern
geography are identical. Can a reasonable dispersal mechanism, such as wind or water currents, be
found to connect these distant lands? And is it
possible that these two widely separated lands,
one polar and the other tropical, could support
nearly identical flora when their climates would
have been so different?

Thus, the fossil animal and plant record in
Antarctica strongly suggests that the present geographic isolation of the continent did not exist
during Paleozoic time and at least early Mesozoic
time.

5. The deformed and metamorphosed rocks underlying the Beacon strata in the Transantarctic
Mountains can be compared to rocks in southeastern
Australia. Strata in both areas were folded and
intruded by granitic rocks during Paleozoic time.
Each continent reveals an early Paleozoic orogen
paralleled by a middle Paleozoic orogen lying to
the east, or away from the Precambrian shield
(Fig. 1). Structural trends in both areas are
anomalous in being nearly perpendicular to the
present shoreline, but they roughly parallel the
coast in the Gondwanaland reassembly.

6. The Ellsworth Mountains orogen (Fig. 3)
formed in early Mesozoic time, and it probably
represents the continuation of the Cape orogen of
South Africa and a part of Du Toit's (1937)
Samfrau geosyncline. Between the Transantarctic
Mountains of East Antarctica and the coastal belt
of West Antarctica lies a large region that has
been explored only during the last twenty years.
Bedrock exposures in this area are found in the
Ellsworth Mountains and in nunatak groups and
small ranges to the south and west. On the basis
of lithologic similarity and structural continuity,

Figure 3.   Folded Paleozoic quartzites in the southern
Ellsworth Mountains, Antarctica.

most of these outcrops have been assigned to a new
tectonic province, the Ellsworth Mountains orogen.
The thick sedimentary sequence is mainly Paleozoic
in age (some Precambrian strata may be present)
and has undergone strong post-Permian folding.
Some of these formations resemble the Beacon strata
in the Transantarctic Mountains, but differ in being both considerably thicker and strongly folded.
In part of the province these deformed Paleozoic
strata are invaded by granitic bodies that were
emplaced during late Triassic to early Jurassic
time. In its present setting the Ellsworth Mountains fold belt is a discordant tectonic fragment
resting between East Antarctica and coastal West
Antarctica. Both in stratigraphy and in structural style, however, it bears strong resemblance to
the Cape fold belt of southern Africa and the fold
mountains of eastern Argentina. In the Gondwanaland reassembly it represents the natural continuation of a fold belt that begins in Argentina and
continues across southern Africa into Antarctica.

    7. Jurassic igneous rocks, mainly basaltic in
composition, are widespread in Antarctica. These
rocks occur both as volcanic deposits and as shallow intrusive bodies such as sills and dikes.
They are common throughout the length of the Transantarctic Mountains, where they have been termed
the Ferrar Group. These Jurassic mafic igneous
rocks may be compared to rocks of similar age and
composition that occur over large areas of Brazil,
southern Africa, and Tasmania. In the Gondwanaland reassembly it is reasonable to interpret the
rocks of all these areas as belonging to a single
igneous province, one perhaps related to the
initial fragmentation of the protocontinent.
Jurassic volcanic rocks of more varied composition
are abundant in the Antarctic Peninsula and common
along the coast of West Antarctica. These latter
rocks, along with counterparts in Argentina and
Australia, may be the products of tectonism along
an active margin of Gondwanaland.

    8. Late Cretaceous to early Tertiary igneous
bodies, mainly granitic in composition, are widespread in the Antarctica Peninsula and westward
along the coastal sector of West Antarctica.
Similar intrusive rocks are typical of the western
margin of the Americas from Alaska to Tierra del
Fuego. The presence of such plutons, along with

geologically young deformation and abundant
Cenozoic volcanism, suggest that coastal West
Antarctica may be considered part of the circum-
Pacific mobile belt. One anomaly, however, is the
presently aseismic character of Antarctica; elsewhere the circum-Pacific belt is typified by
numerous modern earthquakes.

9. Magnetic anomaly belts parallel to and sym-
metrical about the mid-ocean ridges strongly suggest that sea-floor spreading and continental displacement have occurred. Within the last twenty
years oceanographic surveys have revealed this un-
expected pattern of parallel belts of high and low
magnetic intensity, a pattern which initially de-
fied explanation. Concurrent studies of paleomagnetism from both lava flow and marine sediment
sequences, however, produced evidence that the
earth's magnetic field appears to undergo periodic
reversals of its polarity. If the alternating
high- and low-intensity belts are ascribed to
these polarity reversals, then the slowly spreading sea-floor can be thought of as a magnetic tape
which freezes in the effects of the existent magnetic field as new crust is formed at the mid-
ocean ridges by the cooling of silicate melts from
the earth's interior. If this interpretation is
correct, we can eventually learn both the rates of
sea-floor spreading and the times when the various
fragments of Gondwanaland began to separate.

10. The antarctic ice sheet appears to have
formed at least 7 million years ago, suggesting
that Antarctica was a separate polar continent by
that time. The late Cenozoic history of the continent is obscure because few deposits of this age
are known in areas of rock outcrop. A limited
number of paleomagnetic measurements suggest that
Antarctica was in its present latitude even at the
beginning of the Cenozoic, some 66 million years
ago. Tertiary flora from the Antarctic Peninsula
area indicate that moderate temperatures prevailed
there during part of the era, but fossil penguins
have been recovered from beds considered Miocene
in age. Early Tertiary microflora have been identified in glacial erratics in the Ross Sea area,
but these rocks have not been found in place.
Volcanic rocks at least 7 million years old over-
lie a glaciated surface in the Jones Mountains of
coastal West Antarctica, and late Cenozoic

volcanos to the west in the same province contain
deposits that suggest eruption of the lava through
the ice sheet. An interesting record of glacial
and volcanic events of the last few million years
is preserved in some of the deglaciated valleys of
the Transantarctic Mountains. Thus, although there
remains much to be learned about the Cenozoic history of Antarctica, it seems clear that by 7 million years ago the continent was isolated from the
other Gondwanaland fragments and was in a geographic position favorable to the growth of an ice
sheet.   Indeed, recent oceanographic work discussed later suggests that both the isolation and
glaciation of Antarctica date from middle Tertiary
time.

   11. Better knowledge of the bathymetry of the
southern ocean allows more critical testing of the
morphological fit of the Gondwanaland fragments.
The earliest speculations about continental drift
were fostered by the similarity in shape of opposing coasts, especially the Atlantic coasts of
South America and Africa. The coastline, however,
may undergo significant modification with only a
small change in sea level, and a more realistic
comparison may be obtained by using a submarine
contour near the edge of the continental shelf or
part way down the continental slope. Although
subject to some modification by erosional and de-
positional processes, such a contour is a natural
border for the continent and may be little changed
in shape since the time of separation from its ad-
joining landmass. Recent oceanographic surveys
have yielded greatly improved bathymetric maps of
the antarctic continental shelf and slope.
Studies using these new maps have shown that good
morphological matches can be obtained between
Africa and Antarctica, and between Australia and
Antarctica, as required by the Gondwanaland hypothesis.

   Du Toit's reassembly of Gondwanaland, if correct, predicts that certain geologic features
should exist in Antarctica. The basement rocks of
coastal East Antarctica must resemble in composition and structure those of the matching coasts
of the other Gondwanaland fragments. The Beacon
strata should be present throughout the length of
the Transantarctic Mountains and should resemble
the Gondwana sequences of the other southern con-

tinents. Upper Paleozoic glacial beds should
occur in Antarctica. The Paleozoic and Mesozoic
fossil record should consist of forms resembling
those elsewhere in Gondwanaland rather than unique
forms developed in an isolated continent. The
eastward extension of the Samfrau geosyncline and
the Cape fold belt from southern Africa should be
found in Antarctica. The southward-trending
Paleozoic orogens of southeastern Australia should
continue in the northern Transantarctic Mountains.
Jurassic mafic igneous rocks can be expected in
the Transantarctic Mountains along with the strata
of the Beacon Supergroup.

The rapidly accumulating geologic data from
Antarctica strongly suggest that each of these
predictions will be proven correct. The accuracy
of Du Toit's predictions, the striking geologic
similarities between Antarctica and the other
southern lands, and the new evidence from the
oceans for sea-floor spreading combine to provide
a very strong case for the reality of Gondwanaland.

Recent delineation of the tectonic provinces of
Antarctica allows comparison with those of the
other landmasses and permits a more accurate reconstruction (Fig. 1). Tectonic ties between
Antarctica and Australia are provided by the early
Paleozoic Ross and Adelaide orogens, and by the
middle Paleozoic Borchgrevink and Tasman orogens.
The early Mesozoic Ellsworth orogen in Antarctica
is the continuation of the Cape orogen in southern
Africa. That the present map of Gondwanaland,
based on the swift advances in antarctic geology
in recent years, differs so little from that drawn
by Du Toit in 1937 is ample testimony to the skill
and vision of that great geologist.

Origin of Gondwanaland

Although Gondwanaland seems to have existed by
late Precambrian time, its early history remains
obscure. Uncertainty surrounds the mode and place
of formation of the individual Precambrian shields;
nevertheless a fairly satisfactory mid-Phanerozoic
reconstruction of Gondwanaland is possible (Fig.1).
Embleton and McElhinny (1975) present paleomagnetic evidence for positioning Madagascar off
Kenya and Tanzania, as shown by Du Toit (1937).

Harrington and others (1973) have shown the likelihood of two phases of large lateral displacement
in the Australia-New Zealand-East Antarctica sect-
or. However, McElhinny (1973) warns that separate
blocks within a present continent may have moved
independently, and Embleton and others (1974) postulate a large rotation of southeast Australia
since the Silurian. The existence and extent of
the Precambrian shield in West Antarctica and in
southernmost South America remain problematic.

The development of the Gondwanide shields is
part of the general problem of the early Precambrian history of the lithosphere. Hargraves
(1976) proposes a model in which shields are
created from an early lithospheric segregation by
convection during the early Precambrian and by
plate tectonic processes during the late Precambrian; some Precambrian orogens are considered
as probably intracratonic, but others formed along
the edges of the cratonic nuclei. All the main
shields within Gondwanaland contain early Precambrian rocks, and some of the oldest rocks yet
discovered occur in southern Africa. However, the
study of all these Precambrian terranes, and especially the key central fragments of Africa and
East Antarctica, is complicated by a widespread
late Precambrian-early Paleozoic thermal event
which clouds the meaning of radiometric ages and
paleomagnetic determinations. Thus while these
shields clearly began to form during the early
Precambrian, their relative positions at various
times during the Precambrian are poorly known.

The identification of tectonic and/or metamorphic belts within one shield, and their probable
continuations in other shields, is an important
tool for, (a) refining the Gondwanaland reconstruction, and (b) establishing at what times now-
separated shields were in continuity. Such belts,
however, are presently poorly defined in the Precambrian rocks of the Gondwanide shields. Rutland
(1976) recognizes three main basement provinces in
Australia, with the oldest in the west and the
youngest in the east. Ravich and Kamenev (1972)
identify three kinds of tectonic elements in the
East Antarctic shield, but Elliot (1975) concludes
that insufficient data exist yet to define clearly
the tectonic-chronologic provinces. Orogenic and
metamorphic zones in the Precambrian of Africa are

reviewed by Clifford (1974), who emphasizes the
complications created by widespread retrograde metamorphism during the 600 m.y.B.P. Pan-African event.
A few attempts have been made to correlate Precambrian belts between Gondwanide shields. Katz,
M.B. (1972, 1974) postulates ties between granulite
belts in India, Madagascar, and Africa, and
Crawford (1974) matches granulite belts in India
and Ceylon with those in Enderby Land, Antarctica.
Possible continuations of African Precambrian
structures in South America are shown on a map by
Hurley and Rand (1973).

Paleomagnetic polar wander curves from different
crustal blocks provide some information about the
early history of Gondwanaland, though much remains
to be learned. Briden (1973) and Piper and others
(1973) argue that Africa was intact and joined to
South America after about 2300 m.y.B.P. Facer
(1974), however, emphasizes differences between the
Australian Precambrian curve and those of other
shields, and suggests the likelihood of relative
movements during the Precambrian. Curves from 2400
m.y.B.P. for Africa, India, and Australia are given
by Giddings and others (1973); convergence of these
curves about 800 m.y.B.P. may indicate the time of
origin of Gondwanaland. Veevers and McElhinny
(1976) concluded that the Australian platform was
intact between 1800 m.y.B.P. and 450 m.y.B.P., and
McElhinny and others (1974) indicate that Gondwanaland had formed by 750 m.y.B.P. or earlier.
Hailwood (1974) infers from the curves that Gondwanaland was intact by the early Paleozoic, but
some separations may have existed during the
Cambro-Ordovician (Embleton, 1972; Klootwijk,
1973). In his comprehensive review McElhinny
(1973) concluded that Gondwanaland had certainly
formed by the Ordovician and that it remained
essentially intact into the Mesozoic, although some
minor disruptions may have occurred during late
Paleozoic or Triassic time.

Comparison of fossil fauna (Runnegar, 1977) and
flora can provide tests for the continuity of
Gondwanaland at different times during the Phanerozoic. Lower Paleozoic fossils, however, are rare
through much of Gondwanaland. Firm conclusions are
not possible at present about Cambrian paleogeo-
graphy; additional comparative studies are needed,
especially for the Cambrian fauna of South America,

Antarctica, and Australia. Palmer (1973) points
out that the dissimilarity of Cambrian trilobite
fauna from Argentina and Antarctica may be due to,
(1) simple latitudinal differences, or (2) separation of one or both areas from the rest of
Gondwanaland at that time. Studies of Devonian
fossils, however, indicate the unity of Gondwanaland by that time. Devonian marine fauna of
Antarctica are typical of a province that includes
southern Africa, the Falkland Islands, and southern
South America; ties between Antarctica and New
Zealand are also probable (Boucot and others, 1967).
Devonian fish fossils in southeastern Australia are
similar to those in the Transantarctic Mountains.
The Permian flora and the Triassic and younger
vertebrate fauna (Colbert, 1977) indicate that
Gondwanaland remained essentially intact well into
the Mesozoic.

Tectonic Evolution of Gondwanaland

Although the early history of Gondwanaland remains obscure, some facets of its tectonic evolution from the late Precambrian until its break-up
in the Mesozoic can be described. The Pacific
border of Gondwanaland, along the edges of the
Brazilian, African, East Antarctic, and Australian
shields, was an active continental margin during
this time interval (Craddock, 1975). Three main
orogenic episodes are defined by deformation,
igneous activity, and regional metamorphism, and
these orogens can be traced intermittently along
this restored continental margin. The importance
of these belts in refining the Gondwanaland reconstruction is shown in the accompanying map (Fig. 1).

Thick sedimentary and volcanic sequences of late
Precambrian-early Paleozoic age, which underwent
Cambro-Ordovician orogeny, occur along much of the
Pacific border. In South Australia the rocks of
the Adelaide geosyncline were deformed during the
Delamerian orogeny, and in addition, the late
Precambrian Penguin orogeny has also been recognized in Tasmania (Rutland, 1976). Harrington and
others (1973) postulate large strike-slip displace-
ments along latitudinal faults in this region, and
thus the Tasmanian segment of this belt may be well
east of its original position. The Ross orogen can
be traced almost across Antarctica, where it roughly parallels the Transantarctic Mountains, but its

continuation in Africa is in doubt. It may be represented by the Cambrian Cape granites, or it may
be related to the ENE-trending Damaran belt farther
north. The tectonic history of southern South
America is poorly known, but the early Paleozoic
orogen may have reached this part of Gondwanaland
as well (Borrello, 1969).

Evidence for a second orogenic peak during the
Devonian can be found along the Gondwanaland border
from Australia to South America. The main deformation in the western Tasman orogen was during the
Devonian Tabberabberan orogeny (Rutland, 1976), and
Devonian plutonism and regional metamorphism has
been identified in western New Zealand (Suggate and
Grindley, 1972). Evidence for this orogeny in
Antarctica occurs in the Borchgrevink orogen of
northern Victoria Land and at scattered localities
along the coastal belt of West Antarctica (Craddock,
1972a, 1972b). Some deformations near the southern
tip of Africa appear to be pre-Karroo (Haughton,
1969), and these structures may also record
Devonian orogeny. The Paleozoic history of southern South America is poorly known, but Harrington
(1967) reports deformation in the Andean geosyncline of late Devonian-Carboniferous age.

A third orogenic cycle of Permo-Triassic age,
the Gondwanide orogeny of Du Toit (1937), affected
rocks along the Pacific border of Gondwanaland
from Australia to South America. The principal
phase of deformation in the eastern Tasman orogen
was the Permian Hunter-Bowen orogeny (Rutland,
1976), and some granite intrusives of Permo-
Triassic age occur in New Zealand (Suggate and
Grindley, 1972). The Ellsworth orogen in
Antarctica was described by Craddock (1964), and
its significance was discussed by Craddock (1972a)
and Ford (1972). The Cape orogen in southernmost
Africa developed in strata of the Cape and Karroo
Systems, probably during the Permian and early-
middle Triassic (Bishop and Van Eeden, 1971;
De Beer and Van Zijl, 1974). The westward con-
tinuation of this belt in the Sierra orogen by
Argentina was identified by Du Toit (1937), and
evidence for probably related deformation in the
Andean belt is given by Borrello (1969) and
Gansser (1973a). Dalziel (1972) emphasized the
role of early Mesozoic orogeny in southern South
America, the Scotia Arc, and the Antarctic

Peninsula.

Thus the Pacific border of Gondwanaland was an active margin which underwent successive cycles of deposition, orogeny, and cratonization. In Australia these orogenic belts are progressively younger from the shield toward the Pacific Ocean, but this pattern is not so clear elsewhere. The three orogens discussed here have indistinct boundaries in time and space; they represent deformation peaks during a long interval of tectonic activity. In most cases the ensimatic or ensialic character of the orogen has not been established, and some may have formed in marginal basins with continental crust on the seaward side. Thus, this active margin of Gondwanaland was the site of extensive folding, regional metamorphism, igneous activity, faulting, and probably horizontal displacement of some crustal blocks. Nevertheless, Gondwanaland appears to have remained mainly intact from the late Precambrian well into the Mesozoic, although the first indications of the eventual break-up may have appeared in the late Paleozoic (McElhinny, 1973; Klootwijk, 1975; and Valencio, 1975b).

Fragmentation of Gondwanaland

Recent geological and geophysical studies on land and at sea have clarified the history of the break-up of Gondwanaland. It remains difficult, however, to establish exactly the time of separation of one continental block from another. In some cases, early manifestations of crustal extension, such as faulting, volcanic activity, subsidence, and marine transgression, preceded by millions of years the ultimate parting and formation of new sea floor. Hence, for any given case separation dates based on land geology may differ considerably from dates based, for example, on marine magnetic anomalies. Twelve events in the Gondwanaland fragmentation are discussed briefly below, roughly in chromologic order:

1. Possibly the first separation to occur was that of West Gondwanaland (South America-Africa) from East Gondwanaland (Antarctica-India-Australia). On the basis of paleomagnetic polar wander curves, Valencio (1975a) suggested that this separation may have begun as early as the Permian. Ravich (1973) favors a Triassic age, and several writers argue

that the widespread Jurassic volcanics mark the start of separation. Marine magnetic anomalies in this area are too poorly defined at present to resolve this uncertainty.

2.   Northwestern Australia was the site of rifting and faulting in the early Jurassic, and sea floor spreading began there in the late Jurassic (Larson, 1975; Exon and Willcox, 1976). It is not clear, however, whether a continental fragment was detached from this coast.

3.   At least twelve papers since 1970 have offered estimates of the time of separation of Africa and South America, based on paleomagnetic curves, sea floor magnetic anomalies, or geologic evidence. Larson and LaFountain (1970) inferred from paleomagnetic data that separation began during the Triassic, but most subsequent studies have yielded a late Jurassic or early Cretaceous estimated age for this event.

4.   The time of separation of India from Antarctica is poorly defined, but it was probably late Jurassic or early Cretaceous. Laughton and others (1973) summarize the history of the Indian Ocean and date this separation as older than 75 m.y.B.P. Veevers and McElhinny (1976) place the time at 130 m.y.B.P., and Casshyap (1976) reports evidence for a possible seaway off the modern east coast of India during the early Cretaceous. Crustal extension normal to the east coast of India may have caused subsidence, block-faulting, and marine transgression in the late Jurassic (Aditya and Sinha, 1976; Sastri and others, 1976).

5.   Broken Ridge separated from the Kerguelen Plateau by the early Tertiary, and it is possible that these features may in part represent continental fragments detached from Gondwanaland. Quilty (1973) reports Cenomanian foraminifera from sediments northeast of the Kerguelen Plateau and concluded that the initial separation of Broken Ridge had occurred by 92 m.y.B.P. Watkins and others (1974) studied Kerguelen Island and found that it is not older than late Oligocene in outcrop; no evidence for a continental origin of the island was discovered. Luyendyk (1976) postulates that both Broken Ridge and the Kerguelen Plateau began to form more than 100 m.y. ago through the activity of

the Kerguelen Islands hot spot.

6.   The history of the spreading ridge in the
southern Pacific and Indian Oceans, an important
factor in the break-up of Gondwanaland, was discussed by Bowin (1974).   In his model a spreading
ridge had formed in the southeastern Pacific by the
late Cretaceous, and it migrated westward into the
Indian Ocean by the early Tertiary and northwest-
ward to the Gulf of Aden by the late Tertiary.
This ridge system played an important role in the
movements of New Zealand, Australia, and India
away from Antarctica.

7.   On morphological grounds it is probable
that the New Zealand Plateau formerly lay adjacent
to West Antarctica.   Some geologic similarities
exist, but the geology of coastal West Antarctica
is too poorly known to permit a detailed comparison.   Magnetic anomalies south of the New Zealand
Plateau suggest separation from Antarctica during
the late Cretaceous, and the date has been estimated at 81-85 m.y.B.P.   (Falconer, 1973; Molnar
and others, 1975; Wellman, 1976).

8.   New Zealand is a microcontinent that was
probably attached to Australia before the opening
of the Tasman Sea.   This separation appears to have
begun in the late Cretaceous and to have ended in
the early Tertiary.   The period of separation is
placed at 81-60 m.y.B.P. by Molnar and others
(1975) and at 85-55 m.y.B.P. by Griffiths (1976).

9.   The low region of largely unknown geology
between the Transantarctic Mountains and coastal
West Antarctica, along with the unusual trend of
the Ellsworth Mountains, make horizontal displacement of West Antarctica relative to East Antarctica
highly probable.   If such movement occurred, it was
probably during the late Cretaceous and early
Tertiary (Craddock, 1975; Molnar and others, 1975).

10.   The separation of Australia from East
Antarctica may have begun as long as the Jurassic
(Harrington and others, 1973), but the final break
with the formation of new sea floor took place
53-55 m.y.B.P. (Sclater and Fisher, 1974; Molnar
and others, 1975; Veevers and McElhinny, 1976).

There have been about 500 km of dextral bending of
the New Zealand geosyncline and another 500 km of
dextral strike-slip displacement on the Alpine
fault, probably all since the Eocene (Carter and
Norris, 1976) although earlier movements have been
argued (Jones and Roots, 1974; Grindley, 1976).
The bending may have begun only about 40 m.y.B.P.
(Molnar and others, 1975), and movement on the
Alpine fault may have commenced about 20 m.y.B.P.
(Griffiths, 1976; Wellman, 1976).

   11. The northward-moving Indian shield eventually collided with the mainland of Asia, but it is
difficult to establish the exact time of this
event. Although Ravich (1973) advocates connection
in latest Cretaceous time, most writers argue for
collision during the late Eocene or early Oligocene
(Raiverman, 1972; Athavale, 1973; Colchen, 1975;
Molnar and Tapponier, 1975; Blow and Hamilton,
1975; Sclater and others, 1976). If the Siwalik
beds were derived from the rising Himalayas, then
collision was underway by the Miocene (Gansser,
1973b; Verma, 1973; Dutta and Grigorescu, 1975).

   12. The separation of South America from
Antarctica may have been the last major event in
the break-up of Gondwanaland. Many writers have
stressed similarities between the geology of
southern South America and the Antarctic Peninsula, but Katz, H.R. (1972, 1973) have argued for
contrasting histories since the late Jurassic.
Dalziel and Elliot (1973), however, postulate a
narrow land connection between South America and
West Antarctica at the beginning of the Tertiary.
Dalziel (1974) infers crustal extension from the
widespread middle and upper Jurassic volcanics
around the Scotia Sea, perhaps related to the
separation of South America (and Antarctica?) from
Africa. Barker and Griffiths (1972) postulate detachment of South America from the Antarctic
Peninsula in the early Tertiary, and sea floor
magnetic anomalies suggest opening of the Drake
Passage during the late Oligocene (Barker and
Burrell, 1976). Thus differing interpretations
have been offered for the Mesozoic-Cenozoic
history of this complex region. Some results of
recent deep sea drilling in this region are
summarized in the following section.

Deep Sea Drilling in the Southeast Pacific Basin

Leg 35 of the Deep Sea Drilling Project was conducted in the Southeast Pacific Basin during 1974
(Craddock and Hollister, 1976). Some of the objectives of this cruise were to determine, 1) the
age and character of the oceanic basement, 2) the
age and nature of the marine sediments, 3) the
history of deep and surface paleocirculation patterns, and 4) the history of continental glaciation
of West Antarctica. In particular, in order to
clarify the tectonic evolution of the region, it
was important to discover whether any pre-Cretaceous sea floor exists in the Southeast Pacific
Basin.

Four holes were drilled south of 60° south latitude in the area northwest of the Antarctic Peninsula. Two of these holes were on the antarctic
continental rise; one failed at shallow depth in
Pliocene sand, but the other reached lower Miocene
or Oligocene sediments. The other two holes were
drilled into the Bellingshausen abyssal plain, and
both bottomed in basaltic rock. Both abyssal plain
holes have probable unconformities caused by deep-
sea scour during the Oligocene or early Miocene
(Fig. 4).

The information from these four holes, integrated with the results of marine geophysical
surveys, clarifies considerably the geologic
history of this interesting region. The Southeast
Pacific Basin seems to have been a deep oceanic
region since the late Paleozoic or earlier, a part
of the vast sea that formerly bordered Gondwanaland. No oceanic crust older than late Cretaceous
has been found, however, and it is unlikely that
any pre-Cretaceous oceanic crust exists here.

The tectonic history of the region during the
last 100 m.y. has been dominated by three spread-
ing-ridge axes (Fig. 5). The Pacific-Antarctic
Ridge existed by the Cretaceous, and its westward
propagation helped to fragment Gondwanaland, de-
taching New Zealand during the late Cretaceous and
Australia during the early Tertiary. To the south
a newly discovered ridge, parallel to the margin
of West Antarctica and the Antarctic Peninsula,
may have formed during the Cretaceous and seems to
have propagated northeastward. The southwestern

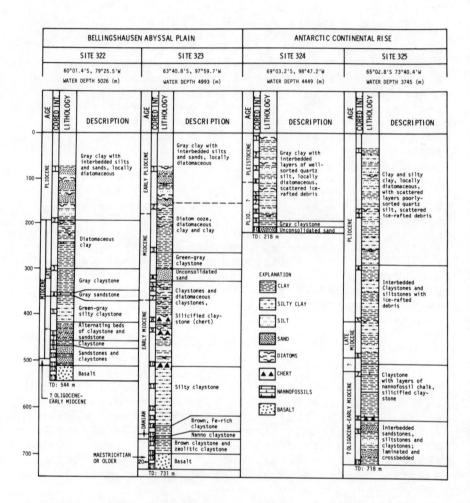

Figure 4.   Stratigraphic columns of the four holes drilled during Leg 35 of the Deep Sea Drilling Project.

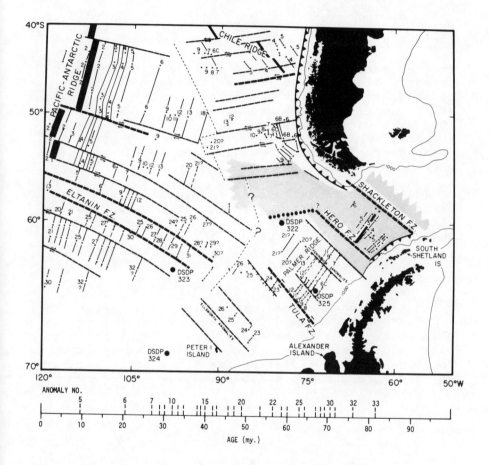

Figure 5. DSDP Leg 35 drillsites, magnetic anomalies, and principal tectonic features in the Southeast Pacific Basin (after Herron and Tucholke, 1976).

segment of this ridge was subducted beneath West
Antarctica during the Eocene, but the segment to
the northeast was active during the Eocene and was
subducted beneath the Antarctic Peninsula in the
early Miocene. The southern Chile Ridge may also
have formed in the Eocene or Oligocene and have
been subducted beneath southern South America in
the early Miocene.

Deep-sea sediment erosion during the Oligocene
or early Miocene, inferred at the abyssal plain
Sites 322 and 323, is attributed to the initiation
of the Antarctic Circumpolar Current. The age of
this event is in agreement with the Scotia Sea
magnetic anomalies in suggesting that the final
opening of the Drake Passage occurred during the
middle Tertiary.

Ice-rafted debris occurs in sediments as old as
early Miocene (about 16-17 m.y.B.P.) at Site 325
off the Antarctic Peninsula. Interpretation of
the cored sediments suggests that Antarctica
glaciation was weak in the early Miocene but
reached full development sometime during the late
Miocene.

Hence, although Antarctica has probably been in
a polar position since Cretaceous time, the present
glaciation seems to have developed during the last
25 million years, after the continent achieved its
total geographic isolation and the modern patterns
of oceanic circulation had been established.

References

Aditya, S. and R.N. Sinha (1976) Evolution of the
    coastal sedimentary basins, south of Latitude
    18°N., India, in Proceedings of Workshop on
    Coastal Sedimentaries of India-South of 18°N.
    Latitude, Oil and Natural Gas Commission,
    Madras, 23.

Athavale, R.N. (1973) Inferences from recent Indian
    paleomagnetic results from the northern margin
    of the Indian plate and the tectonic evolution
    of India, in Implications of Continental Drift
    to the Earth Sciences, Eds. D.H. Tarling and
    S.K. Runcorn, Acad. Press, London, 1:117-130.

Barker, P.J. and J. Burrell (1976) The opening of
    the Drake Passage, Abstracts, 25th Inter-
    national Geological Congress, Sydney, 881.

Barker, P.J. and D.H. Griffiths (1972) The evolu-
    tion of the Scotia Ridge and Scotia Sea, Phil.
    Trans. Royal Soc. London, Series A, 271:151-183.

Bishop, D.W. and O.R. Van Eeden (1971) Explanatory
    text for the tectonic map of Africa: areas co-
    ordinated by the Southern Group, in Tectonics
    of Africa, UNESCO, Paris, 561-585.

Blow, R.A. and N. Hamilton (1975) Paleomagnetic
    evidence from DSDP cores of northward drift of
    India. Nature, 257:570-572.

Borrello, A. (1969) Los Geosinclines de la
    Argentina, Direc. Nacional de Geol. Miner.
    Annales 14, 188 p.

Boucot, A.J., G.A. Doumani, J.G. Johnson, and
    G.F. Webers (1967) Devonian of Antarctica, in
    International Symposium on the Devonian System,
    Ed. D.H. Oswald, Alberta Soc. Petroleum
    Geologists, Calgary, 1:303-307.

Bowin, C. (1974) Migration of a pattern of plate
    motion. Earth and Planetary Science Letters,
    21 (4):400-404.

Briden, J.C. (1973) Applicability of plate tec-
    tonics to pre-Mesozoic time. Nature, 244:
    (5416) 400-405.

Carter, R.M. and R.J. Norris (1976) Cenozoic
   history of southern New Zealand: an accord between geological observations and plate-
   tectonic predictions. Earth and Planetary
   Science Letters, 31:85-94.

Casshyap, S.M. (1976) Paleocurrents and continental assembly: a comparison from Paleozoic coal-
   fields of India, Antarctica, South Africa and
   Australia, Abstracts, 25th International Geological Congress, Sydney, 238-239.

Clifford, T.N. (1974) Review of African granulites
   and related rocks. Geol. Soc. Amer. Sp.
   Paper 156, 49 p.

Colbert, E.H. (1977) Gondwana vertebrates. Proceedings IV International Gondwana Symposium,
   Calcutta, Section III, 18 p.

Colchen, M. (1975) Paleogeographic and structural
   evolution of the Tibetan area of the Nepal
   Himalaya (Annapurna region). Himalayan
   Geology, 5:83-103.

Craddock, C. (1964) The structural relation of
   East and West Antarctica, in Rock deformation
   and tectonics, Ed. R.K. Sundaram. 22nd International Geological Congress, Part IV, New
   Delhi, 278-292.

Craddock, C. (1970) Tectonic map of Gondwanaland,
   in Geologic Maps of Antarctica, Eds. V.C.
   Bushnell and C. Craddock, Antarctic Map Folio
   Series, American Geographical Society, New
   York, Plate XXIII.

Craddock, C. (1972a) Geologic Map of Antarctica,
   1:5,000,000 American Geographical Society,
   New York.

Craddock, C. (1972b) Antarctic tectonics, in
   Antarctic Geology and Geophysics, Ed. R.J.
   Adie, Universitets-forlaget, Oslo, 449-455.

Craddock, C. (1975) Tectonic evolution of the
   Pacific margin of Gondwanaland, in Gondwana
   Geology, Ed. K.S.W. Campbell, ANU Press,
   Canberra, 609-618.

Craddock, C. and C.D. Hollister (1976) Geologic evolution of the Southeast Pacific Basin, in Initial Reports of the Deep Sea Drilling Project, C.D. Hollister, C. Craddock and others, U.S. Government Printing Office, Washington, D.C., 35:723-743.

Crawford, A.R. (1974) Indo-Antarctica, Gondwanaland, and the distortion of a granulite belt. Tectonophysics, 22:141-157.

Crowell, J.C. (1977) Problems concerning the late Paleozoic Glaciation of Gondwanaland, Abstracts, Fourth International Gondwana Symposium, Calcutta, India, Section IV, 10 p.

Dalziel, I.W.D. (1972) Large scale folding in the Scotia Arc, in Antarctic Geology and Geophysics, Ed. R.J. Adie, Universitetsforlaget, Oslo, 47-55.

Dalziel, I.W.D. (1974) Evolution of the margin of the Scotia Sea, in The Geology of Continental Margins, Eds. C.A. Burk and C.L. Drake, Springer-Verlag, New York, 567-580.

Dalziel, I.W.D. and D.H. Elliot (1973) The Scotia Arc and Antarctic margin, in The Ocean Basins and Margins, Eds. A.E.M. Nairn and F.G. Stehli, The South Atlantic, 1:171-246.

DeBeer, J.H. and J.S.V. VanZijl (1974) Plate tectonic origin for the Cape fold belt. Nature, 252 (5485):675-676.

Du Toit, Alex L. (1937) Our Wandering Continents. Oliver and Boyd, Edinburgh, 366 p.

Dutta, A.K. and D.A. Grigorescu (1975) Towards a correlation of the Mammalian fauna of the Siwaliks with their equivalents in southeastern Europe, including Crimea and Caucasus, in Recent Researches in Geology, Ed. V.K. Verma. Delhi, 2:265-274.

Elliot, D.H. (1975) Tectonics of Antarctica: a review. Amer. Jour. Sci., 275-A:45-106.

Embleton, B.J.J. (1972) On the unity of Gondwanaland during the lower Palaeozoic. Search, 3 (9):338-339.

Embleton, B.J.J., M.W. McElhinny, A.R. Crawford, and G.R. Luck (1974) Paleomagnetism and the tectonic evolution of the Tasman orogenic zone. Geol. Soc. Australia Jour., 21 (2):187-193.

Embleton, B.J.J. and M.W. McElhinny (1975) The Palaeoposition of Madagascar: paleomagnetic evidence from the Isalo Group. Earth and Planetary Science Letters, 27:329-341.

Exon, N.F. and J.B. Willcox (1976) Structure and tectonic evolution of the Exmouth Plateau area off western Australia, Abstracts, 25th International Geological Congress, Sydney, 345-346.

Facer, R.A. (1974) Apparent polar wander relative to Australia during the Precambrian. Earth and Planetary Science Letters, 22:44-50.

Falconer, R.K.H. (1973) Numerical studies of Cretaceous magnetic anomalies in the southwest Pacific Ocean, in Oceanography of the South Pacific, N.Z. Comm. UNESCO, Wellington, 257-262.

Ford, A.B. (1972) Weddell Orogeny-Latest Permian to Early Mesozoic deformation at the Weddell Sea margin of the Transantarctic Mountains, in Antarctic Geology and Geophysics, Ed. R.J.Adie. Universitetsforlaget, Oslo, 419-425.

Gansser, A. (1973a) Facts and theories on the Andes. Jour. Geol. Soc. London, 129:93-131.

Gansser, A. (1973b) Ideas and problems on Himalayan geology, Seminar on Geodynamics of the Himalayan region, Nat. Geophy. Res. Inst., Hyderabad, 97-103.

Giddings, J., A. Crawford, J.J. Embleton, and M.W. McElhinny (1973) Precambrian paleomagnetism in Australia: evidence for the date of formation of Gondwanaland. Geol. Soc. Amer. Abstracts with Programs, 5 (7):635.

Griffiths, J.R. (1976) A plate tectonic model for the southwest Pacific, Abstracts, 25th International Geological Congress, Sydney, 84.

Grindley, G.W. (1976) Palaeomagnetic evidence for
    New Zealand's Cretaceous-Cenozoic drift and
    rotation, Abstracts, 25th International Geo-
    logical Congress, Sydney, 84-85.

Hailwood, E.A. (1974) Paleomagnetism of the Msissi
    Norite (Morocco) and the Paleozoic reconstruct-
    ion of Gondwanaland. Earth and Planetary
    Science Letters, 23 (4):376-386.

Hargraves, R.B. (1976) Precambrian geologic his-
    tory. Science, 193 (4251):313-371.

Harrington, H.J., K.L. Burns, and B.R. Thompson
    (1973) Gambier-Beaconsfield and Gambier-Sorrell
    fracture zones and the movement of plates in
    the Australia-Antarctica-New Zealand region.
    Nature Physical Science, 245 (146):109-112.

Harrington, Horacio J. (1967) Devonian of South
    America, in International Symposium on the
    Devonian System, Ed. D.H. Oswald. Alberta.
    Soc. Petroleum Geologists, Calgary, 1:651-671.

Haughton, S.H. (1969) Geological History of South-
    ern Africa. Geological Society of South Africa,
    Cape Town.

Herron, E. and B.E. Tucholke (1976) Sea-floor
    magnetic patterns and basement structure in the
    southeastern Pacific, in Initial Reports of the
    Deep Sea Drilling Project, Eds. C.D. Hollister,
    C. Craddock, et al., Government Printing Office,
    Washington, D.C., 35:263-278.

Hurley, P.M. and J.R. Rand (1973) Outline of Pre-
    cambrian chronology in lands bordering the
    South Atlantic, exclusive of Brazil, in The
    Ocean Basins and Margins, Eds. A.E.M. Nairn and
    F.G. Stehli. The South Atlantic, Plenum Press,
    New York, 1:391-410.

Jones, J.G. and W.D. Roots (1974) Evolution of the
    Tasman Sea. Nature, 252 (5484):613-614.

Katz, H.R. (1972) Plate tectonics and orogenic
    belts in the Southeast Pacific. Nature, 237
    (5354):331-332.

Katz, H.R. (1973) Tectonic setting and evolution
of continental margins in the Southeast Pacific,
in Oceanography of the South Pacific, N.Z. Comm.
UNESCO, Wellington, 340.

Katz, M.B. (1972) Paired metamorphic belts of the
Gondwanaland Precambrian and plate tectonics.
Nature, 239 (5370):271-273.

Katz, M.B. (1974) Paired metamorphic belts in Precambrian granulite rocks in Gondwanaland.
Geology, 2 (5):237-241.

Klootwijk, C.T. (1973) Paleomagnetism of upper
Bhander sandstones from central India and implications for a tentative Cambrian Gondwanaland reconstruction. Tectonophysics, 18 (1-2):
123-145.

Klootwijk, C.T. (1975) Paleomagnetism of upper
Permian red beds in the Wardha valley, central
India. Tectonophysics, 25 (1-2):115-137.

Larson, E.E. and L. LaFountain (1970) Timing of
the breakup of the continents around the
Atlantic as determined by paleomagnetism.
Earth and Planetary Science Letters, 8 (5):341-
351.

Larson, R.L. (1975) Late Jurassic sea-floor
spreading in the eastern Indian Ocean. Geology,
3 (2):69-71.

Laughton, A.S., J.G. Sclater, and D.P. McKenzie
(1973) The structure and evolution of the
Indian Ocean, in Implications of Continental
Drift to the Earth Sciences, Eds. D.H. Tarling
and S.K. Runcorn. 1:203-212.

Luyendyk, B.P. (1976) Deep Sea Drilling on the
Ninety East Ridge: synthesis and a tectonic
model, Abstracts, 25th International Geological Congress, Sydney, 895-896.

McElhinny, M.W. (1973) Palaeomagnetism and Plate
Tectonics. Cambridge University Press, 357 p.

McElhinny, M.W., J.W. Giddings, and B.J.J.
Embleton (1974) Palaeomagnetic results and late
Precambrian glaciations. Nature, 248 (5449):
559-561.

Molnar, P., T. Atwater, J. Mammerickx, and S.W.
    Smith (1975) Magnetic anomalies, bathymetry, and
    the tectonic evolution of the South Pacific
    since the late Cretaceous. Geoph. Jour., 40
    (3):383-420.

Molnar, P. and P. Tapponnier (1975) Cenozoic tec-
    tonics of Asia: effects of a continental colli-
    sion. Science, 189 (4201):419-426.

Palmer, A.R. (1973) Cambrian trilobites, in Atlas
    of Palaeobiogeography, Ed. A. Hallam, Elsevier,
    Amsterdam, 3-11.

Piper, J.D.A., J.C. Briden, and K. Lomas (1973)
    Precambrian Africa and South America as a single
    continent. Nature, 245 (5423):244-248.

Quilty, P.C. (1973) Cenomanian-Turonian and Neogene
    sediments from northeast of Kerguelen Ridge,
    Indian Ocean. Geol. Soc. Australia Jour., 20
    (3):261-271.

Raiverman, V. (1972) Time series and stratigraphic
    correlation of Cenozoic sediments in foothills
    of Himachal Pradesh. Himalayan Geology, 2:
    82-101.

Ravich, M.G. (1973) Superkontinent iuzhnogo
    polushariia, Chelovek i stikhuua, nastol'nyi
    gidrometeorologicheskii kalendar;, 201-202.

Ravich, M.G. and E.N. Kamenev (1972)
    Kristallicheskii Fundament Antarkiticheskoi
    Platformy, Leningrad, 658 p.

Runnegar, B. (1977) Marine fossil invertebrates of
    Gondwanaland: palaeogeographic implications.
    Proceedings Fourth International Gondwana
    Symposium, Calcutta, Section III, 25 p.

Rutland, R.W.R. (1976) Orogenic evolution of
    Australia. Earth Science Reviews, 12 (2/3):
    161-196.

Sastri, V.V., A.T.R. Raju, R.N. Sinha, B.S.
    Venkatachala, and R.K. Banerji (1976) Strati-
    graphy and evolution of Cauvery basin, India, in
    Proceedings of Workshop on Coastal Sedimentaries
    of India - South of 18°N. Latitude, Oil and
    Natural Gas Commission, Madras, 34-35.

Sclater, J.G. and R.L. Fisher (1974) Evolution of the east central Indian Ocean with emphasis on the tectonic setting of the Ninety east Ridge. Bull. Geol. Soc. Amer., 85 (5):683-702.

Sclater, J.G., B.P. Luyendyk, and L. Meinke (1976) Magnetic lineations in the southern part of the Central Indian Basin. Bull. Geol. Soc. Amer., 87 (3):371-378.

Suggate, R.P. and G.W. Grindley (1972) Geological Map of New Zealand, 1:1,000,000, N.Z. DSIR, Wellington.

Valencio, D.A. (1975a) The paleomagnetism of South American rocks and its significance for the fragmentation of Gondwanaland, in Gondwana Geology, Ed. K.S.W. Campbell. ANU Press, Canberra, 3-8.

Valencio, D.A. (1975b) The South American paleo-magnetic data and the main episodes of the fragmentation of Gondwanaland. Physics of the Earth and Planetary Interiors, 9 (3):221-225.

Van Eysinga, F.W.B. (compiler) (1975) Geological Time Table, 3rd edition, Elsevier, Amsterdam.

Veevers, J.J. and M.W. McElhinny (1976) The separation of Australia from other continents. Earth Science Reviews, 12 (2/3):139-159.

Verma, R.K. (1973) Paleomagnetism of Indian rocks and the birth of the Himalaya, in Seminar on Geodynamics of the Himalayan Region, Nat. Geoph. Res. Inst., Hyderabad, 49-58.

Watkins, N.D., B.M. Gunn, J. Nougier, and A.K. Baksi (1974) Kerguelen: continental fragment or oceanic island? Bull. Geol. Soc. Amer., 85: 201-202.

Wellman, H.W. (1976) Sea floor reconstruction for the last 85 million years and the bending and faulting of the New Zealand region, Abstracts, 25th International Geological Congress, Sydney, 106-107.

4

The Role of the Polar Regions in Global Climate Change

Joseph O. Fletcher and John J. Kelley

INTRODUCTION

The ocean and atmosphere constitute what may be conceived as a single thermodynamic engine. Each fluid in this climate machine is driving the other by mechanical stress or by thermal forcing. Annual fluctuations in the intensity and character of the circulation constitute climate change and such fluctuations are associated with changing patterns of thermal forcing. In the tropical heat source region large variations in the intensity and distribution of heating are related to variations in cloudiness and rainfall. Variations in the polar heat sink regions are related primarily to the extent of ice on the ocean. How these variable factors interact with each other is important, but still obscure.

The north and south polar regions are dominated by rigorous cold and months of continuous cold alternating with equal periods of darkness. In almost every respect the Arctic and Antarctic are strikingly different.

The north pole lies near the center of a deep ocean basin surrounded by land. Except for oceanic openings through the Bering Strait and off east Greenland arctic waters are isolated from other northern oceans. The south polar region is dominated by a high land mass surrounded by the Atlantic, Pacific and Indian Oceans.

Antarctica is the fifth largest continent, with an area of 5.5 million square miles--larger than the United States and Mexico combined. This area doubles in the winter as the sea freezes around the periphery of the continent. Antarctica reflects the continental character of one region and the oceanic nature of the Arctic. Polar atmospheric circulations strongly influence weather and

9

climate at the lower latitudes. Variations in the sea ice
cover would almost certainly have a profound effect on the
global heat balance and on the world's weather and climate.

Meteorology and climatology constitute a broad field
of study of practical interest to polar research. Meteorological and climatological processes are closely associated
with other geophysical phenomena. Understanding of the
interactions of air, sea, land, and ice is critical to a
knowledge of the dynamic systems that govern both the arctic
and antarctic and the entire world.

Observational techniques and adequate areal coverage
have in the past limited studies. Recent advances in technology have opened up new frontiers for investigation
particularly in synoptic meteorology and tropospheric
processes, stratospheric and mesospheric circulations,
climatology, heat balance, and atmospheric chemistry. Year
by year, especially since the advent of the International
Geophysical Year, we have witnessed the utilization of these
new technologies-- for example: satellites, sounding rockets,
balloons, remotely operated stations, instrumented aircraft,
as well as new breakthroughs in numerical treatment of data
through advanced computer technology. New advances in
numerical modeling have enhanced the traditional role between
theory and observation in polar meteorology.

The importance of the polar regions is of critical
importance to the continued improvement of our knowledge of
climatic processes and the possibilities of influencing them.
It may be that human activity may already be inadvertently
and irreversibly doing so (Fletcher, 1969). If this is true,
it can further be expected that human activity will increase
manifold in only a few decades, thus affecting world food
production and social conditions. Man already has the technological capability to carry-out many climate-influencing
schemes such as the modification of large inland seas, the
deflection of ocean currents, the seeding of extensive cloud
or surface areas, and perhaps even the removal of sea ice.

The nature of the problem is in understanding the
physical basis of climate and understanding how and why
changes occur in the boundary conditions which influence the
global pattern of thermal forcing of the atmosphere. The
climate machine is closely coupled with the ocean/atmosphere/
cryosphere systems in which the atmosphere drives the ocean,
mainly by momentum exchange and the ocean drives the
atmosphere primarily by heat exchange. The "short-memoried"

atmosphere dominates the short range future but the ocean
dominates the longer range future. The difference in response times for the two media may be illustrated by the
following physical characteristics:

	OCEAN		ATMOSPHERE
Heat Capacity	1600	:	1
Mass	400	:	1
Momentum	4	:	1
Kinetic Energy	.04	:	1

and by comparison of typical circulation and residence times
(in years).

	ICE CAPS	DEEP OCEAN	SURFACE OCEAN	ATMOS
Circulation Time	10,000	1,000	10	1/10
Residence Time of Water	100,000	5,000	100	1/50

About 10 percent of the ocean area in the Northern
Hemisphere is covered by floating ice in winter; in the
Southern Hemisphere the figure is about 13 percent. The
extent of this pack ice varies greatly during the year and
from year to year. It has long been observed that these
variations show a close correlation with many indices of
climatic change (Fletcher, 1972). As the arctic ice pack
recedes, storm tracks tend to go further north, and the midlatitude rainfall patterns tend to shift eastward. Therefore, the variable extent of the ice on the sea is a very
sensitive lever that can amplify the effects of small changes
in global heating (Figure 1).

It is necessary to look closely at the behavior of all
the heat-budget components (Figure 2) in order to understand
fully why the presence or absence of ice cover has such a
large effect on the heat budget of the atmosphere. The presence of an ice cover effectively prevents heat exchange
between the ocean and atmosphere, both in winter and summer.
For example, in January the mean air temperature at the
earth's surface in the Central Arctic is about -30°C, while
2 or 3 m below the surface, the temperature of the ocean
water is near -2°C. However, the ice and its snow cover
provide good enough insulation that one $kcal/cm^2/month$
reaches the surface from below. The ice surface radiates
heat to space, and heat loss cools the ice surface until it
is cold enough to drain from the atmosphere the heat needed
to balance the loss. The thermal participation of the ocean
is greatly suppressed when ice is present. Without the ice

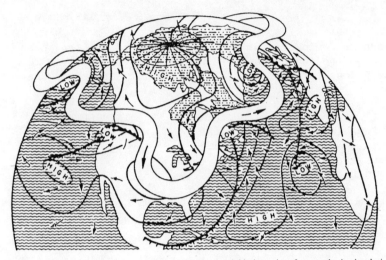

Figure 1. Variable extent of arctic pack ice as related to variable intensity of atmospheric circulation. The general circulation of the atmosphere is forced by gradients arising from the net heat loss to space in polar regions and net heat gain at low latitudes. The intensity of polar cooling is influenced by the extent of ice on the ocean.

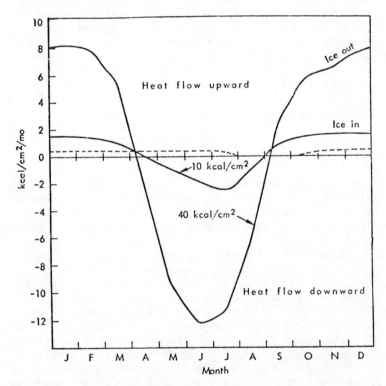

Figure 2. Heat flow to the surface from below under present ("ice-in") conditions and as estimated for an ice-free Arctic Ocean. (After Fletcher, 1965).

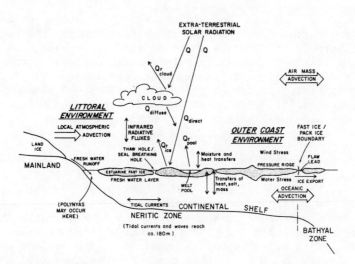

Figure 3. Schematic diagram of the water-fast ice-atmosphere inter-relationships in summer (Q=incoming short-wave radiation; Qr=reflected short-wave radiation) (after Jacobs, 1975)

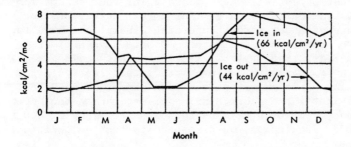

Figure 4. Atmospheric cooling in the central arctic under "ice-in" and hypothetical "ice-out" conditions (after Fletcher, 1965)

cover most of the atmospheric heat would be obtained from
the relatively warm ocean.

In summer, an open ocean would absorb about 90 percent
of the solar radiation reaching the surface, while the pack
ice reflects 60 or 70 percent of the incident sunlight.
Thus, the presence of the ice suppresses heat loss by the
ocean in winter and heat gain by the ocean in summer. For
the atmosphere, a reciprocal relation applies. A more
complicated relationship is shown in Figure 3 when effects
of air-sea-ice-and-land are to be considered (Jacobs, et al,
1975).

The effects of heat flow from an ice-covered and ice-
free Arctic Ocean have been estimated (Fletcher, 1965),
Figure 4. The "ice-in" curve shows the amount of heat
reaching the surface from below during each month of the
year. The heat gained in summer is about 10 kcal/cm^2. This
is enough to warm the ice mass and about a third of its
thickness. A similar amount is supplied to the surface
during winter, and most of this comes from cooling the ice
mass and some freezing. The actual upward flux of sensible
heat from the liquid ocean is shown by the dotted curve.

The "ice-out" curve shows heat flow to the surface from
below as estimated for an ice-free arctic Ocean. According
to these estimates, the ocean would gain about 40 kcal/cm^3
in summer and would lose a similar amount in winter, for a
net balance of about zero. Important assumptions have to
be made to obtain such estimates. Others have estimated
(Donn and Shaw, 1966; Budyko, 1962) somewhat smaller heat
loss during winter with the prediction that ice would not
soon return. This important question cannot be answered
definitely until the uncertainties of estimation have been
reduced and until we have a better basis for judging how the
atmospheric circulation would respond to such a condition.

An estimate of the annual variations of atmospheric heat
loss is enormous over the arctic basin under present conditions. The atmosphere over the pack ice loses 6 to 8 kcal/
cm^2/month during winter, but in summer it loses less than a
third of this amount. Once an ice-free arctic, the annual
pattern would be almost the inverse, with strongest atmospheric cooling during summer and with winter values much
smaller. Because the arctic basin is centrally located with
respect to the main planetary westerly circulation, it would
be expected that more intense atmospheric heat loss over the
arctic would mean stronger northward temperature gradients

and stronger westerly winds around the periphery of the
arctic basin. Again, a realistic model of the entire planetary circulation under the assumption of an ice-free Arctic
Ocean is not yet available and it is not possible to draw
firm conclusions suggesting whether or not an ice-free
Arctic Ocean would remain free.

VARIATIONS IN THE EXTENT OF THE PACK ICE

There are sound physical reasons why the extent of ice
on the sea should influence atmosphere circulation, in addition to the traditional arguments about cyclones tending to
follow the pack ice boundary. Some of the most important
factors causing year-to-year variations are shown in Figure
5. The upper curve shows the monthly values of solar radiation at the Earth's surface after taking into account reflection and depletion by the atmosphere above. The total
annual value of solar radiation at the surface is about
73 kcal/cm^2, but the highly reflecting surface absorbs only
about 18. Moreover, maximum absorption does not occur in
June, when radiation intensity is greatest, but in July when
radiation is rapidly decreasing. The reason for this is
that the disappearance of the snow cover and meltwater on
the ice causes a greater fraction of available radiation to
be absorbed which occurs after the radiation intensity has
already passed its maximum. If the event occurred three or
four weeks earlier, it would make a large difference in the
heat budget, and the dotted line is sketched to indicate
the larger amount of heat that might be absorbed in such a
case. The square, representing quantity of heat, is drawn
to show how much heat it would take to melt 2 m of ice,
about two-thirds of the total pack ice thickness. There is
more than enough solar heat available at the surface to melt
the whole ice pack if the absorptivity of the surface were
sufficiently high.

The total amount of melting in summer is extremely sensitive to factors that influence the date of first melting. A
greater than usual number of cyclones advecting warm air
during May and June is probably the most important factor
for the melting of the pack ice (Fletcher, 1972). A small
positive air-temperature anomaly and higher wind speeds
would greatly increase turbulent heat flow from the air to
the ice surface. The resulting advance in melting date
greatly increases absorption of solar heat.

Data from the arctic drifting stations over the last 15
years show year-to-year variations to be on the order of 8

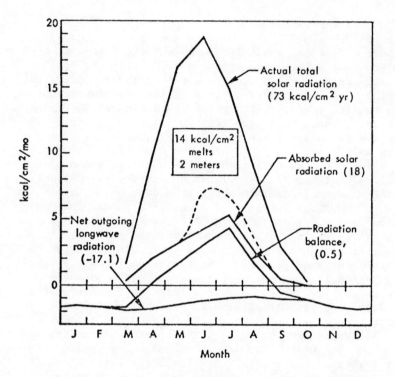

Figure 5. Radiation components at the surface in the central arctic (long-term mean values).

$kcal/cm^2$, half the area of the square shown in Figure 5.   It may be surmised that any general increase in the strength of global circulation during May and June, whatever the planetary cause, would tend to cause melting of the arctic pack ice. Anomalies of winter air temperature appear to be much less effective in influencing ice thickness.

There are other factors which affect the extent and variability of sea ice. The surface heat balance is also determined by the amount of heat advected in by ocean currents and the amount of ice exported. The magnitude of the ocean heat transport into the arctic basin is relatively small, about 5×10^{17} kcal/yr (Aagaard, et al, 1973). However, the oceanic input of heat is important also to the size of the arctic pack. Most of the heat is transported into the Arctic Ocean between Greenland and Svalbard. The inbound Greenland current is relatively warm. The outbound West Spitzbergen current is relatively cold. A final contribution to heat input is the export of ice between Greenland and Scandinavia.

Man can inadvertently produce climate changes by diverting rivers. It has been pointed out (Aagaard and Coachman, 1975) that a relatively small accumulation of fresh water in the southern Eurasian basin for example, is an important feature, because the shallow and weak salinity gradient forms a lid on the warmest and most saline water in the Arctic Ocean. It is postulated that if the thin veneer of fresh water were to be substantially removed then the high sensible heat content of the Atlantic water would become readily available for surface exchange. The likely and climatically important results would be: prolonged ice-free conditions because of deep reaching convection in the Arctic Ocean, the release of large amounts of heat from the warm deep water during the cold months, and the elevation of more saline water into close proximity with the sea surface leading to deep water formation. Other mass-induced peculiarities to the sea-ice environment, such as large oil spills combined with the dynamics of the ice pack, may alter the albedo and the arctic heat balance.

ANTARCTIC REGIONS

Since climate changes are global in nature, the antarctic regions must be addressed in order to understand climate changes. The far south can be divided into three regions, in each of which the heat exchanges are reasonably uniform. The three regions are the antarctic continent, the

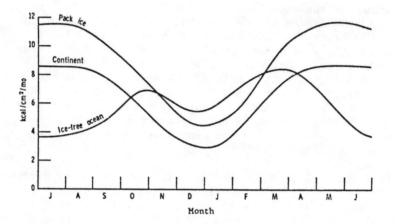

Figure 6. Annual pattern of heat loss by atmosphere
over the antarctic continent, over the pack ice, and
over the ice-free regions of the surrounding ocean.

ice-covered sea around the continent, and the ice-free sea around the continent.

An apparent pattern of heat loss (Figure 6) by the atmosphere over the antarctic continent, over the pack ice, and over the ice-free regions of the surrounding ocean is shown. The time scale has been displaced by half a year to make it easier to relate cooling patterns to their counterparts in the Northern Hemisphere. It can be seen that the annual pattern of heat loss by the atmosphere over the antarctic continent, which is roughly the area of the arctic basin, is very similar to that over the antarctic pack ice which at its maximum extent is about 1.5 times greater in area than the continent. This annual pattern is caused by: strong solar heating during summer, which partly compensates for heat loss to space, so that atmospheric heat loss is reduced; maximum atmospheric heat loss in winter, when there is no sun; and rapid heat loss in the fall, as solar energy decreases and loss to space is high because of the warmer temperatures. Over the continent, the atmospheric heat loss is considerably lower than over the pack ice. With so little heat reaching the surface from below over the high snow-covered antarctic continent, the radiative loss from the surface lowers the temperatures of the surface until it attains approximate radiative equilibrium with the warmer atmosphere above. Very low surface temperatures, -30°C in the warmest month and -70°C in the coldest month are typical. The heat loss to space is reduced by the generally lower temperatures of both the surface and atmosphere.

Over the ice-free ocean the pattern of atmospheric heat loss is very much different. In winter, most of the heat loss to space is supplied by the ocean, and atmospheric heat loss is small. During summer this heat flux from the ocean is suppressed by the change in the air/surface temperature gradient, so that the atmospheric heat loss increases. However, the considerable absorption of solar heat by the atmosphere causes a second minimum in summer. The result is two maxima of atmospheric heat loss near the equinoxes. The general pattern, seen also in the estimate for an ice-free Arctic Ocean, is even more pronounced in the North Pacific and North Atlantic. The causal factors are high latitude, cold winter advection over an ice-free ocean, and large solar absorption by a moist cloudy atmosphere subjected to long hours of sunlight. The net heat loss of the atmosphere over an ice-free Antarctic Ocean in the winter is very much smaller than the heat loss over the continental regions or over an ice-covered ocean. In the summer, the net atmospheric heat loss over an ice-free ocean is somewhat greater than over continental or ice-covered oceanic regions. These differences in patterns of atmospheric heat loss have corresponding effects on the thermal forcing of atmospheric circulation. In the antarctic, as in the arctic, patterns of atmospheric heat loss are closely related to atmospheric circulation. The mean winds at the periphery of the continent closely follow the pattern of cooling over the interior.

VARIATIONS IN THE EXTENT OF ANTARCTIC PACK ICE

The extent of ice on the sea is a sensitive "climatic lever" that regulates heat exchange between the ocean and atmosphere in both the arctic and antarctic. In the arctic, the annual maximum extent in area covered by pack ice is about 5 percent of the hemisphere and the annual variation is about a quarter of this. In the antarctic (Figures 7 and 8), the maximum area of pack ice is about 3 percent of the hemisphere and the annual variations of the area of pack ice in the antarctic is 85 percent of the maximum pack-ice area (Treshnikov, 1967) from 18.8×10^6 km^2 in September to 2.6×10^6 km^2 in March. Thus, the annual variation of the area covered is some six times greater in the antarctic than in the arctic. The relative magnitude of year-to-year and long-term variations may be correspondingly large. However, there is very little data on these variations.

The influence of seasonal anomalies of ice extent on the oceanic heat budget is enormous, especially when the ice boundary shrinks earlier than usual. Variations in ice extent on the southern ocean can amplify the long-term changes in radiation intensity. In winter, the ice cover affects the oceanic heat budget by suppressing heat loss by the ocean, i.e., the more ice cover, the less the heat loss. Quantitative estimates for winter are more uncertain because the location of open leads and polynyas can alter the picture.

Observational evidence of climatic variations is meager for the area of the southern heat sink. Evidence from surface air temperatures at Archangel (Prik, 1968) in the Northern Hemisphere and at Orcadas (Rubinstein and Polozova, 1966) in the Southern Hemisphere indicates that warming and cooling occurs in an opposite sense to warming and cooling trends for the Northern Hemisphere and most of the Southern Hemisphere. Variations of ice extent on the Southern Ocean correspond to significant variations in the

intensity of the southern heat sink and occur in a sense
which reinforces the concurrent variations in global atmospheric circulation.

The hypothesis that emerges is one in which changes
in solar radiation intensity in Antarctica are amplified
by variations in the extent of sea ice, causing variations
in the Southern Hemisphere circulation. The weaker
Northern Hemisphere circulation follows the trends of the
Southern Hemisphere, especially during the northern summer.
The extent of the sea ice in the north is also an influential lever on local atmospheric behavior, but its waxing
and waning (Ahlmann, 1945; Lamb, 1966) is most sensitive
to warm air advection in summer and is basically a response
to the vigor of global circulation during May, June and
July, the Southern Hemisphere's winter. The waxing and
waning of the sea ice in the Northern and Southern Hemispheres occurs asynchronously. In both polar regions, more
extensive sea ice tends to intensify atmospheric cooling
and increase circulation. In the Southern Hemisphere,
these factors seem to act in the same direction, but in the
Northern Hemisphere the ice extent is to a greater extent
influenced by, rather than influencing, the global system.

Man's inadvertent influences on global climate up to
now appear to be small, but in future decades may become
dominant. The influencing pollutants most frequently
suggested are carbon dioxide, heat and stratospheric dust,
and moisture. Other anthropogenic gases also contribute
to the thermal modification to an uncertain degree. These
gases include chlorofluoromethane, nitrous oxide, methane,
carbon tetrachloride, and others.

Carbon dioxide is generally believed to be a most
important influence. It is one of the three important
radiation absorbing gases in the atmosphere along with
water vapor and ozone. Fluctuations in atmospheric carbon
dioxide are evident. There is a seasonal variation, decreasing during the summer growing season of the Northern
Hemisphere. This seasonal variation appears at all clean
air monitoring sites. The amplitude over Scandinavia
(Bolin and Bischof, 1970) and northern Alaska (Kelley,
1968) is more than twice that found at Mauna Loa (Keeling,
et al, 1976a) which, in turn, is larger than that at the
South Pole (Keeling, 1976b). A long-term upward trend is
also noted and presumed to be a consequence of the combus-
tion of fossil fuels. The growth rate of carbon dioxide
has been essentially constant at about 4.3 percent per year

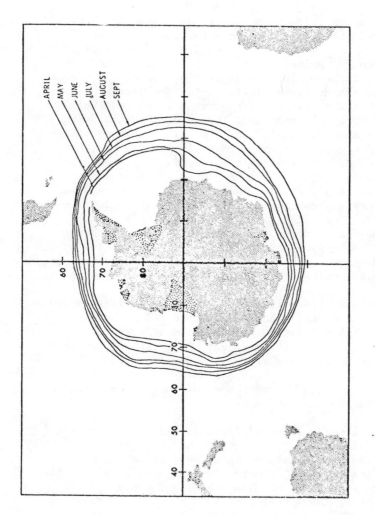

APRIL
MAY
JUNE
JULY
AUGUST
SEPT

Figure 7. Monthly variations in the boundary of the
pack ice in the antarctic winter. (Adapted from "Atlas
of Antarctica," in Soviet Geography, Moscow, 1966).

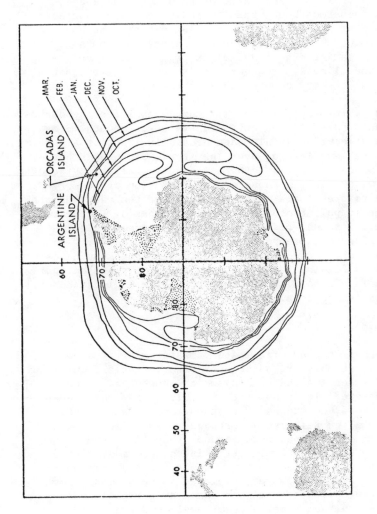

Figure 8. Monthly variations in the boundary of the pack ice in the antarctic summer. (Adapted from "Atlas of Antarctica," in Soviet Geography, Moscow, 1966)

from the late 1940's to the early 1970's. Current estimates
of future trends, based on the assumption that the rate of
burning of fossil fuels will continue to increase at 2 to 4
percent per year, and that half of this CO_2 produced will
remain in the atmosphere, seem to indicate a mean surface
temperature of 1°C by the end of this century. Such a
strong warming would be further reinforced by substantial
changes in sea-ice extent and might trigger other variations in the climate. However, it is a possibility that
other influences may counter these trends.

Shaw (1976) reports that minimum aerosol loading occurs
at the South Pole Station at a mean value of about 2.3 mg
m^{-2}. The same value is also approached in interior Alaska.
However, the mass loading over the Arctic Ocean near Barrow
has always been observed to be larger than this by a factor
of 2 to 10, possibly because of the formation of ice crystals due to open leads in the pack ice or the carry-over of
anthropogenic pollutants into the arctic basin. Ultimately,
to derive the actual climatic impact of the aerosols, one
must incorporate the aerosol parameters into a climate
model that takes account of the various feedback mechanisms
and infrared feeding terms. It can be roughly stated that
the aerosols act to slightly heat the polar regions and cool
the equatorial regions.

FUTURE CLIMATIC TRENDS

The basic causes of climate variations are too poorly
understood but they are associated with variations in global
patterns of heating and cooling which cause the motion of
the atmosphere. It is not yet possible to forecast future
climatic trends on the basis of cause-and-effect relationships. Even the relative importance of such factors as
atmospheric dust, cloudiness, ozone production, and carbon
dioxide has not been firmly established, and many of the
complicated interactions between the ocean and atmosphere
are still obscure. However, progress is being made; for
example, there is a spatial and temporal correspondence in
Pacific sea surface temperature (Newell and Weare, 1977)
and changes in atmospheric CO_2.

More comprehensive observations of the behavior of the
global system over a period of time will eventually clarify
many of these questions, and more sophisticated mathematical
models of ocean-atmosphere circulation will make it possible
to simulate variations in global circulation caused by
specific changes in basic causal factors. Forecasts of

future climatic trends, for the present, will continue to be based on projection in time of empirical relationships between climatic changes and other physical factors.

REQUIREMENTS FOR FUTURE RESEARCH

It has long been a goal of meteorology to study the global thermodynamic system as a whole. Past technology has not allowed this. However, these technological barriers are being steadily removed. Modern computers are making it possible to approach solutions of complex mathematical models. Satellites have become indispensible through observation of cloud patterns and ice extent. The development of quantitative sensors to monitor important heat-exchange patterns and other physical parameters is increasing. To provide input to dynamical climate models it is necessary to obtain reliable data over the whole planet of heat gain and loss by the stratosphere and ocean.

Ice cores provide an opportunity to reconstruct climatic conditions over a long time span and to enhance an understanding of the behavior of the global system. The antarctic ice offers a unique opportunity to explore global climatic history. A series of cores from the South Pole to the Antarctic Peninsula, together with South American records from tree rings and other sources, offers hope toward a better understanding of the past climate and possible future projection. A better understanding of the ocean circulation and its driving forces, especially the antarctic circumpolar flow and the large oceanic gyres east and west of the Antarctic Peninsula, is essential.

A question of major interest in the arctic regions is the exchange of heat, mass, and salt between the Arctic Ocean and Atlantic most of which takes place through a narrow gap between northeast Greenland and Spitzbergen.

Observations of climatically important chemical constituents continue to play a role in understanding climate change. Long records provide a basis for comparison with other climatic variables. Other important factors for observation in the polar regions are the seasonal patterns of heat exchange over the land and oceanic regions and the extent and location of pack ice, open leads and polynyas especially during winter, and the variation and mean area albedo during summer. Continuing monitoring programs should be carried out that will give us permanent and reliable data about year-to-year variations. Realization of the magnitude of these potential changes and their possible impacts on our society makes it imperative that we reach a much better understanding of the dynamics of our global climate machine just as soon as we can.

References

Aagaard, K.; C. Darnall and P. Coachman (1973). Year-long current measurements in the Greenland-Spitzbergen passage. Deep Sea Research. $\underline{20}$:743-746.

Aagaard, K. and L. K. Coachman (1975). Toward an ice-free Arctic Ocean. Trans. of the Amer. Geophys. Union. $\underline{56}$:484-486.

Ahlmann, H. W. (1945). The organization of Soviet Arctic research in Polarbroken, Stockholm, Sweden. 32.

Bolin, B. and W. Bischof (1970). Variations of the carbon dioxide content of the atmosphere in the northern hemisphere. Tellus. $\underline{22}$:431-442.

Budyko, M. I. (1962). Polar ice and climate. 12v. Akad. Nauk. SSSR., Ser. Geogr. $\underline{6}$

Donn, W.L. and D. M. Shaw (1966). The stability of an ice free Arctic Ocean. J. Geophys. Res. $\underline{71}$:1086-1095.

Fletcher, J. L. (1965). The heat budget of the Arctic basin and its relation to climate. RAND Corp. Rept. R-444-PR, Santa Monica, California.

Fletcher, J. O. (1969). Controlling the planet's climate in impact of science on society, UNESCO, $\underline{XIX:2}$:151-168.

Fletcher, J. O. (1972). Ice on the ocean and world climate, in Beneficial Modifications of the Marine Environment, National Academy of Sciences, Washington, D.C. 4-49.

Jacobs, J. D., R. G. Barry and R. Weaver (1975). Fast ice characteristics with special reference to the eastern Canadian Arctic. Polar Record. $\underline{17:110}$:521-536.

Keeling, C. D., R. B. Bacastow, A. E. Bainbridge, C.A. Ekdahl, P. R. Guenther, L. S. Waterman and J. S. Chin (1976a). Atmospheric carbon dioxide variations at Mauna Loa observatory, Hawii. Tellus. $\underline{28}$:538-551.

Keeling, C. D., J. A. Adams, C. A. Ekdahl and P. R. Guenther (1976b). Atmospheric carbon dioxide variations at the South Pole. Tellus. 28:552-564.

Kelley, J. J. (1968). Carbon dioxide and ozone studies in the arctic atmosphere in Arctic Drifting Stations. Arctic Institute of North America. 155-156.

Lamb, H. H. (1966). The changing climate. Methuen, London.

Newell, R. E. and B. C. Weare (1977). A relationship between atmospheric carbon dioxide and Pacific sea surface temperature. Geophys. Res. Letters. 4:1-2.

Prik, Z. M. (1968). On the fluctuations of the climate of the Arctic and the reasons for them. Tr. Arkt. Antarkt. Inst. 274.

Rubenstein, E. S. and L. G. Polozova (1966). Souremennoe Izmeneniye Klimata, Hydrometerological Publishing House, Leningrad.

Shaw, G. E. (1976). Properties of the background global aerosol and their effects on climate. Science. 192:1334-1336.

Treshnikov, A. F. (1967). The ice of the southern ocean. Proc. Symposium on Pacific Antarctic Sciences. Eleventh Pacific Science Conference, Tokyo.

5

Polar Oceans:
Similarities and Differences
in Their Physical Oceanography

Theodore D. Foster

Abstract. The physical oceanography of the polar oceans is compared, and it is found that the Arctic Ocean proper is quite different from the Southern Ocean. The primary causes of this difference are the relative isolation of the Arctic Ocean, which results in nearly permanent ice cover, and the large amount of fresh water runoff from the northern rivers, which causes the upper waters of the Arctic to be very stable. The Greenland Sea bears a closer resemblance to the Southern Ocean and, in particular, to the Weddell Sea in that both have cyclonic circulation, a three-layer structure, and are major source areas for bottom water formation.

Oceanographers have challenged the polar oceans to reveal their secrets for many years, and they have been surprisingly successful when one considers the low temperatures, high winds and seas and, perhaps most importantly, the ice cover. In recent years several comprehensive reviews of the physical oceanography of the polar oceans have appeared, notably Deacon's (1963) paper on the Southern Ocean and Treshnikov and Baranov's (1972) and Coachman and Aagaard's (1974) papers on the Arctic Ocean. We will not, therefore, attempt to present another review of polar physical oceanography. Rather we will endeavor to compare and contrast the oceans in the south and north.

On first consideration one thinks of the polar oceans as merely cold and icy and probably very

Fig. 1a Arctic bathymetry (after American Geographical Society, 1975). Depth contours
every 1000 m. Light shading indicates
depths less than 3000 m.

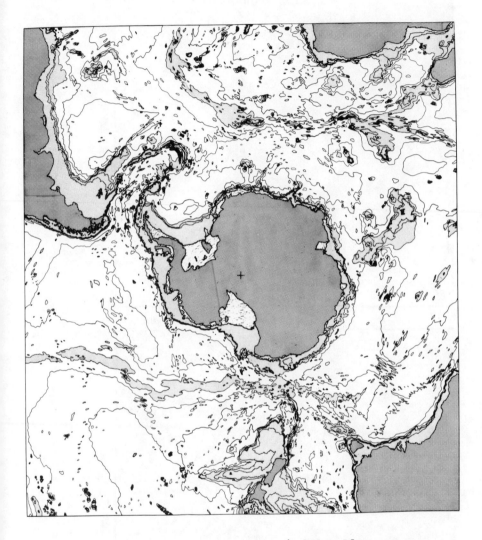

Fig. 1b Antarctic bathymetry (after Glavnoe
Upravlenie Geodezii i Kartolrafii, 1974).
Depth contours every 1000 m. Light shad-
ing indicates depths less than 3000 m.

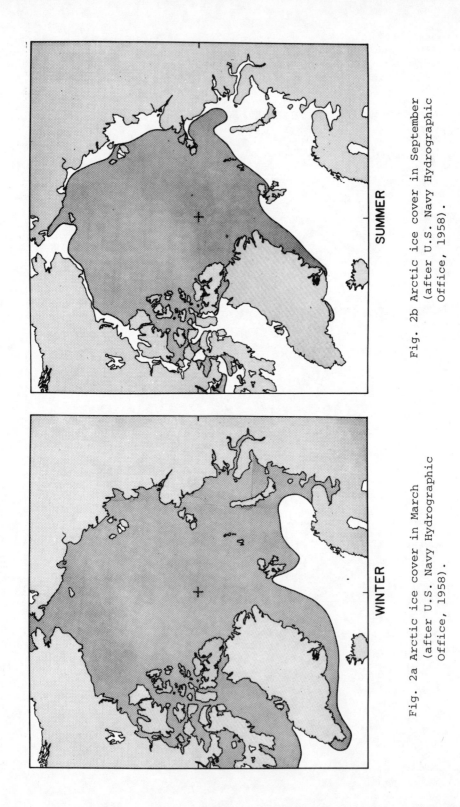

WINTER

Fig. 2a Arctic ice cover in March
(after U.S. Navy Hydrographic
Office, 1958).

SUMMER

Fig. 2b Arctic ice cover in September
(after U.S. Navy Hydrographic
Office, 1958).

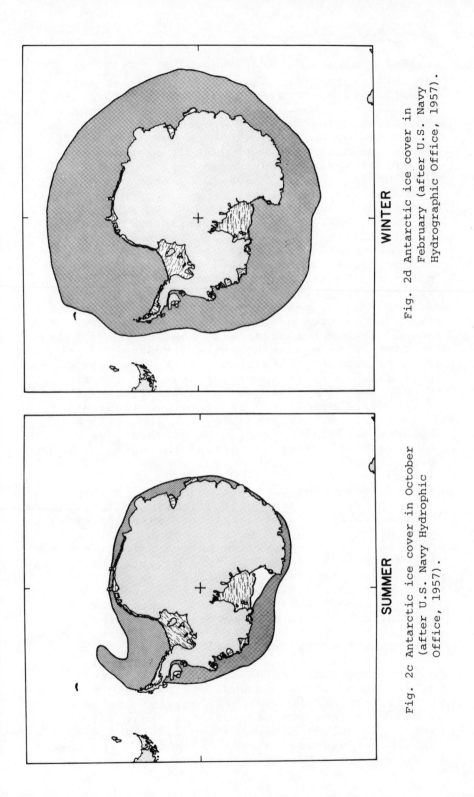

SUMMER

Fig. 2c Antarctic ice cover in October (after U.S. Navy Hydrophic Office, 1957).

WINTER

Fig. 2d Antarctic ice cover in February (after U.S. Navy Hydrographic Office, 1957).

similar. However, if one looks at a chart (Fig. 1)
one quickly realizes that the north polar region
is quite different from the south. In the north
one finds an ocean, the Arctic Ocean, surrounded
by land, and in the south, a continent, Antarctica,
surrounded by an ocean, the Southern Ocean. The
Arctic Ocean is nearly closed off from the remainder of the World Ocean except for the passage between Greenland and Spitsbergen, which allows in-
terchange with the Atlantic Ocean. Additional exchange of water occurs through the Barents Sea,
the Canadian Archipelago and the Bering Strait,
but these passages are shallow and thus limit the
exchange considerably. The Southern Ocean on the
contrary freely communicates with the Atlantic,
Indian and Pacific Oceans at all depths. In fact,
most cartographers show these oceans extending all
the way up to the antarctic continent and do not
give the Southern Ocean the status of a separate
ocean. Polar oceanographers, however, have found
it convenient to designate the circumpolar ring of
ocean surrounding Antarctica as the Southern Ocean.
The relative isolation of the Arctic Ocean makes
it much less important to the overall circulation
of the World Ocean than the freely communicating
Southern Ocean, excepting for the subarctic seas,
the Greenland and Norwegian Seas, which, as we
will see later, have a profound influence upon the
North Atlantic Ocean.

The geographical situation of the polar
oceans results in some similarities due to their
location at high latitudes. The low atmospheric
temperatures cause the oceans in both north and
south to acquire a covering of sea ice. There are
also large seasonal variations in solar heating in
both oceans; however, the seasonal variation of
sea ice in the Arctic Ocean is very much less than
in the Southern Ocean (Fig. 2). There seems to be
two causes for this difference. First, the Arctic
Ocean is nearly entirely at latitudes greater than
$70^{\circ}N$ while the Southern Ocean is mostly at latitudes less than $70^{\circ}S$. Thus the average solar
heating in the Arctic Ocean is less than that in
the Southern Ocean. Second, and probably more important, the Arctic Ocean is largely confined by
land and the sea ice recirculates about the Arctic
Basin with only a small portion flowing out
through the passage between Spitsbergen and Greenland. On the other hand, the Southern Ocean is

unconfined at its northern boundary and the ice
cover formed in winter can easily spread northward
away from the antarctic continent to melt at higher latitudes. Thus the ice cover of the Arctic
Ocean is relatively permanent and the sea ice
grows for several years to form multiyear ice 2 to
4 meters thick. In the Southern Ocean the greater
portion of the sea ice melts each year so that
most of the ice is first-year ice 1 to 2 meters
thick. Since the sea ice, especially when it is
covered with a layer of snow, acts to prevent
solar radiation from penetrating the upper layers
of the ocean, the biological productivity of the
Arctic Ocean is low except for the coastal regions
that are ice-free in summer. In the Southern
Ocean large areas of the deep ocean are ice-free
in summer and the productivity is correspondingly
high there.

The average atmospheric pressure at sea level
in the polar regions shows a similar pattern in
north and south with higher pressure at the poles
than at subpolar latitudes (Fig. 3). This pattern
is much more clearly developed in the south polar
region than in the north. Thus the winds in the
south are more consistent with the simple picture
of polar easterlies and midlatitude westerlies.
Probably this is due to the preponderance of ocean
in the south and the largely zonal distribution of
land and sea there. The southern polar easterlies
are further intensified by the katabatic winds
blowing off Antarctica. Thus the surface circulation in the Southern Ocean is characterized by the
Antarctic Circumpolar Current, or West Wind Drift,
flowing to the east in subpolar latitudes north of
about $60°S$ and the Antarctic Coastal Current, or
East Wind Drift, flowing to the west close to the
continent (Fig. 4a). The region between these two
nearly zonal currents is made up of a series of
mainly cyclonic eddies that are poorly defined
with the possible exception of the Weddell Sea.
Here there is a fairly well-defined cyclonic gyre,
confined by the Antarctic Peninsula in the west
and extending eastward possibly beyond $30°E$. In
the Arctic Ocean the surface circulation has been
determined mainly from the ice drift (Fig. 4b).
In the Canadian Basin there is a large anticyclon-
ic gyre while in the Eurasian Basin the flow is
mainly almost straight across the basin from the
Bering Strait to the passage between Spitsbergen

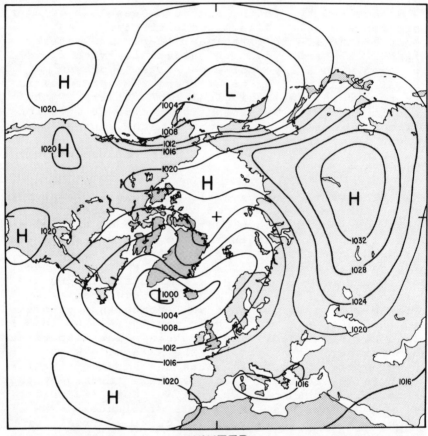

WINTER

Fig. 3a Arctic surface atmospheric pressure in winter (after Namias, 1975).

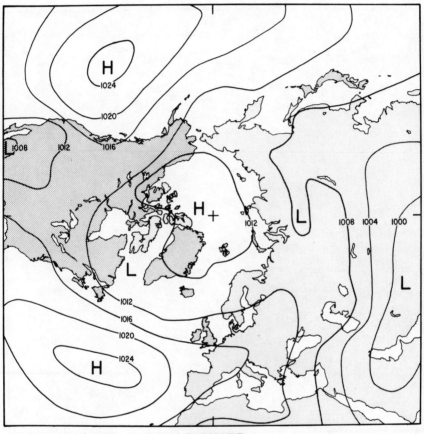

SUMMER

Fig. 3b Arctic surface atmospheric pressure in
summer (after Namias, 1975).

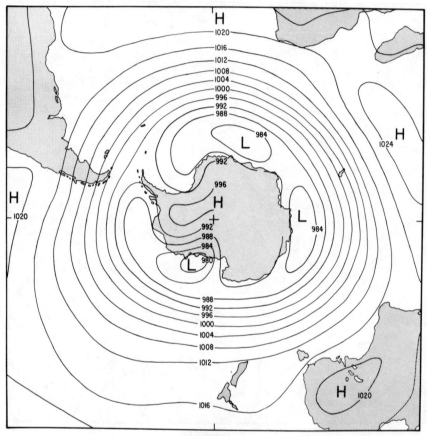

Fig. 3c Antarctic surface atmospheric pressure in
August (after Taljaard et al, 1969).

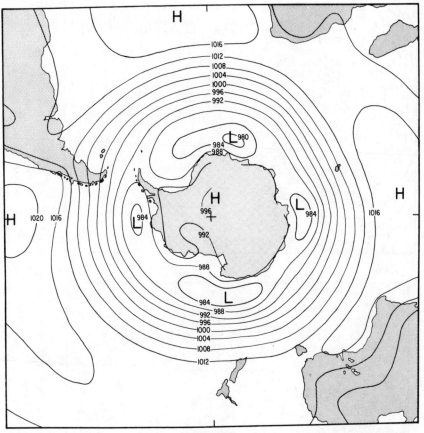

SUMMER

Fig. 3d Antarctic surface atmospheric pressure in
February (after Taljaard <u>et</u> <u>al</u>, 1969).

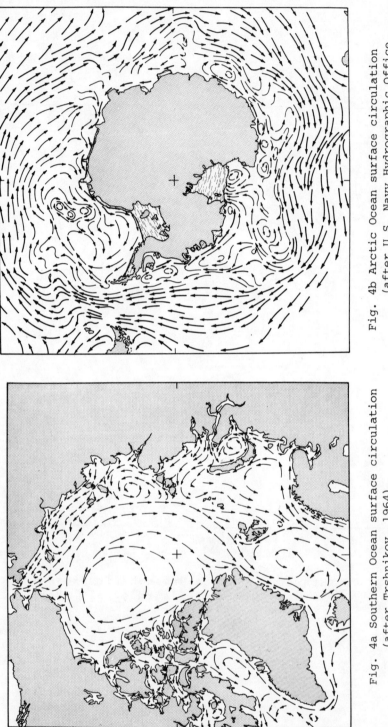

Fig. 4b Arctic Ocean surface circulation (after U.S. Navy Hydrographic Office, 1958).

Fig. 4a Southern Ocean surface circulation (after Trshnikov, 1964).

and Greenland. At lower latitudes around the
periphery of the Arctic Ocean proper several poor-
ly-defined cyclonic eddies are found. In the
Greenland Sea there is a fairly well-defined cyclonic gyre with the West Spitsbergen Current on
the eastern side, the East Greenland Current on
the west and the Jan-Mayen Ridge and Mohns Rise
forming a southern boundary.

The temperature and salinity structure of the
Arctic Ocean show qualitative resemblances to that
of the Southern Ocean in that deep areas of both
oceans typically have a surface layer of cold,
relatively fresh water overlying an intermediate
layer of warmer, saltier water and a colder bottom
layer. In the arctic the bottom water is at very
nearly the same salinity as the intermediate water,
but in the antarctic the bottom water usually has
a salinity less than the intermediate water. The
temperature and salinity profiles (Fig. 5) show
that the resemblances are superficial as the
arctic surface water usually has a lower salinity
than the antarctic surface water. The strong
halocline in the Arctic Ocean causes the stability
of the upper ocean to be very great even in winter
when sea ice formation increases the salinity of
the surface layer. In the Eurasian Basin the surface salinity is somewhat higher, but it is only
in the Greenland Sea that the stability approaches
the very low stability found in the Weddell Sea.
The low salinity of the arctic surface water is
primarily due to the large amount of fresh water
runoff from rivers into the Arctic Ocean. In the
Southern Ocean the runoff takes the form of tabular icebergs which break off from the ice shelves
surrounding Antarctica. Some melting of these
icebergs and subsequent mixing of fresh water into
the surface layers takes place, but large numbers
of the icebergs are advected north away from
Antarctica before they melt in the circumpolar
current or further north. The Arctic Ocean also
has an influx of low salinity water through the
Bering Strait (Coachman, Aagaard and Tripp, 1975),
which further strengthens the halocline in the
Canadian Basin.

The relatively strong halocline in the Arctic
Ocean causes several effects. First, convection
is suppressed and is generally confined to a depth
of 25 to 30 meters. Thus the heat transported by

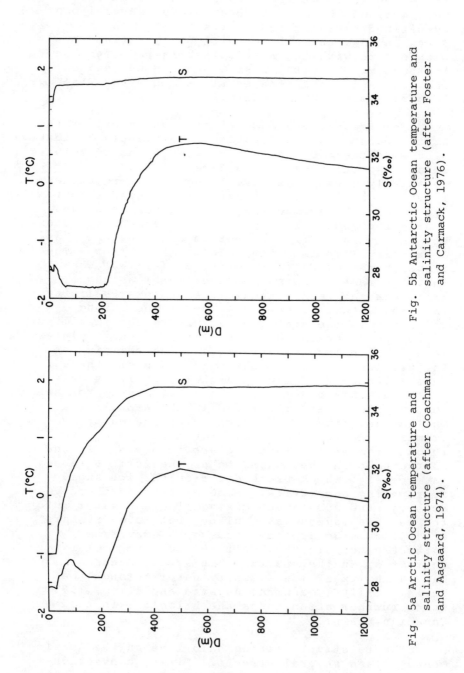

Fig. 5a Arctic Ocean temperature and salinity structure (after Coachman and Aagaard, 1974).

Fig. 5b Antarctic Ocean temperature and salinity structure (after Foster and Carmack, 1976).

the warm intermediate water, the Atlantic water,
into the Arctic Basin is only very slowly transmitted to the overlying surface water and sea ice.
This has the important consequence that the ice
cover is stable in the arctic. Aagaard and
Coachman (1975) have recently speculated that if
the Siberian rivers were diverted from entering the
Arctic, the halocline would be weakened in the
Eurasian Basin. Thus Deep convection could take
place and heat transferred from the Atlantic Water
at a much higher rate, which might result in a substantially ice-free Arctic Ocean. Furthermore,
deep water formation, which does not take place in
the Arctic Ocean proper now, might occur there.
Second, the halocline in the Arctic Ocean effectively decouples the flow of the arctic surface
water from the flow of the Atlantic water, with the
former mainly flowing in a clockwise manner around
the Canadian Basin while the latter flows nearly
contrarily in an anti-clockwise manner. In the
Southern Ocean the weaker halocline results in low
stability of the whole water column, which in turn
causes the currents to generally extend from top to
bottom. In the Weddell Sea, in particular, the
surface, intermediate and bottom waters all flow in
a clockwise manner around the sea.

     One last difference in the water masses is
that the Atlantic Water forms the intermediate
water mass in the Arctic Ocean by sinking of
Atlantic surface water as it passes into the
Eurasian Basin from the Greenland Sea. On the
other hand, the Warm Deep Water forms the intermediate water in the Southern Ocean largely by the
rising of North Atlantic Deep Water as it reaches
the region of the circumpolar current.

     A north-south hydrographic section through the
Atlantic Ocean (Fig. 6) shows a layer of cold water
at the bottom. The slope of the isotherms seems to
indicate that this cold bottom water originates in
both the northern as well as southern extremes of
the Atlantic. It also appears that North Atlantic
Deep Water (which originates in the north) over-
rides the Antarctic Bottom Water (which originates
in the south) at midlatitudes in the North Atlantic,
and that the Antarctic Bottom Water has a relatively low salinity. Intermediate water masses also
apparently originate at subpolar latitudes in both
the North and South Atlantic Ocean. Though inter-

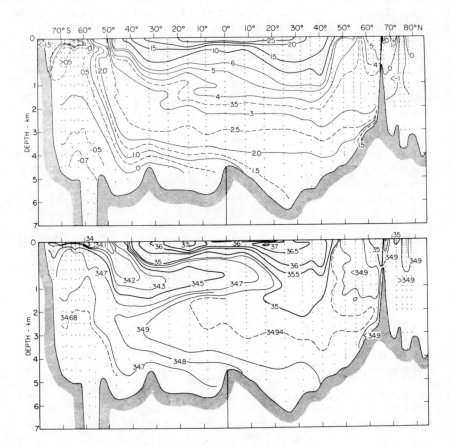

Fig. 6   North-south hydrographic sections through Atlantic Ocean (Reid and Lynn, 1971).

mediate water masses also originate in the Pacific
and Indian Oceans, there does not appear to be any
large sources of bottom water there.

Cold, dense Norwegian Sea Water flows intermittently over the ridges between Greenland and
Scotland into the North Atlantic Ocean proper, and
in recent years the measurement of this flow has
been the subject of the several international
"Overflow" Expeditions. Worthington (1970) has
estimated that 6×10^6 m^3/sec of Norwegian Sea
Water flow over the ridge and entrain Atlantic
Water to form about 10×10^6 m^3/sec of North
Atlantic Deep Water. Dietrich (1967) and Meincke
(1972) among others have shown that the overflow is
highly variable. The Norwegian Sea Water actually
forms in the Greenland Sea (sometimes called the
northern part of the Norwegian Sea) where the highly saline Atlantic Water in the West Spitsbergen
Current is cooled and sinks. The classical explanation of this process, due mainly to Nansen (1906),
is that the deep water of the Greenland Sea forms
from the cooling of the surface water in winter until the entire water column overturns. This is
similar to the deep convection observed by the
Medoc Group (1970) in the western Mediterranean.
More recently Carmack and Aagaard (1973) have presented evidence that the Greenland Sea Deep Water
forms by subsurface modification of Atlantic Water
through the double-diffusive process. More detailed winter observations in the Greenland Sea will be
necessary to decide between these possible mechanisms for the formation process. In the Arctic
Ocean proper the low salinity of the surface layer
prevents deep convection, and thus the Arctic Ocean
bottom water apparently also forms in the Greenland
Sea and flows in beneath the Atlantic Water.

An examination of the distribution of properties in the bottom water of the Southern Ocean, in
particular the potential temperature (Fig. 7), has
led to the belief that the major source of Antarctic
Bottom Water is in the Weddell Sea (Deacon, 1937;
Carmack, in press). Bottom water formation in the
Weddell Sea evidently is mainly due to the increase
in salinity, induced by sea ice formation
(Brennecke, 1921) and thus is quite different from
that in the Greenland Sea where the primary process
is cooling of sea water that already has relatively
high salinity. The freezing process has its greatest effect over the continental shelf regions of

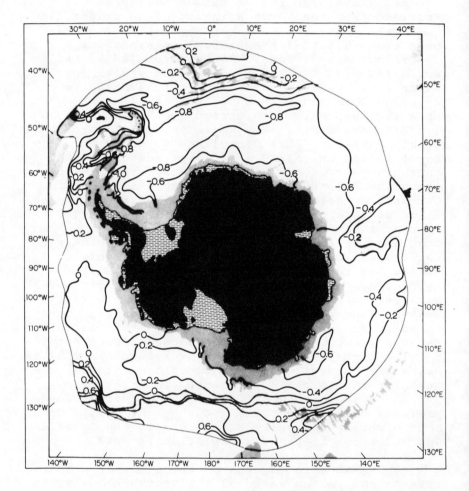

Fig. 7   Near-bottom values of potential temperature for depths greater than 2000 m in the
Southern Ocean (Carmack, in press).

the southern and western Weddell Sea where haline convection can mix the entire water column to form cold, highly saline Shelf Water. This Shelf Water subsequently mixes with the intermediate water, the Warm Deep Water, and flows down the continental slope (Mosby, 1934). Gill (1973) and Foster and Carmack (1976) have shown that an intermediate process whereby the Warm Deep Water mixes with cold, low salinity Winter Water, which it underlies, occurs before it mixes with the Shelf Water (Fig. 8). The traditional Antarctic Bottom Water then forms as this newly-formed bottom water mixes with the overlying Warm Deep Water as it flows out of the Weddell Sea. Although the rate of sea ice formation is greater in winter, bottom water formation can proceed all year around since there is a supply of high salinity shelf water on the southern and western Weddell Sea continental shelf even in summer (Elder and Seabrooke, 1970). Hydrographic sections in the western Weddell Sea in summer (Fig. 9) show a continuous layer of cold water extending from the abyssal plain right up onto the shelf and support the conjecture of year-round bottom water formation (Foster, 1976). It is estimated that from 2 to 5 x 10^6 m^3/sec of bottom water are formed in the Weddell Sea (Carmack and Foster, 1975). Long-term current measurements (Foldvik and Kvinge, 1974) at the shelf break show that bottom currents are somewhat stronger in winter than in summer, but similar year-long current measurements on the abyssal plain (Foster and Middleton, 1976) do not show a clear-cut seasonal variation. Thus it is probable the bottom water flow out of the Weddell Sea is much less intermittent than that of North Atlantic Deep Water since there is no ridge acting as a barrier as there is south of the Norwegian Sea.

We have seen that though the Greenland and Weddell Seas are quite similar in several respects the bottom water processes probably proceed quite differently. The Arctic Ocean proper is quite different in all respects from the Southern Ocean in that the Arctic Ocean is nearly always ice covered and highly stratified and consequently plays only a small role in the general circulation of the World Ocean while the Southern Ocean plays an important part in providing communication between the three major oceans and in renewing the bottom waters.

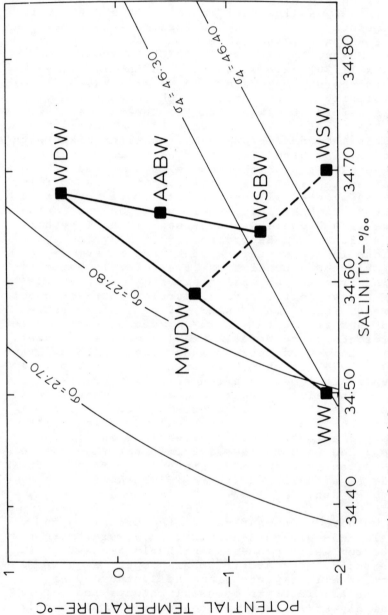

Fig. 8 Potential temperature-salinity diagram showing mixing
processes involved in the formation of Antarctic
Bottom Water (Foster and Carmack, 1976).

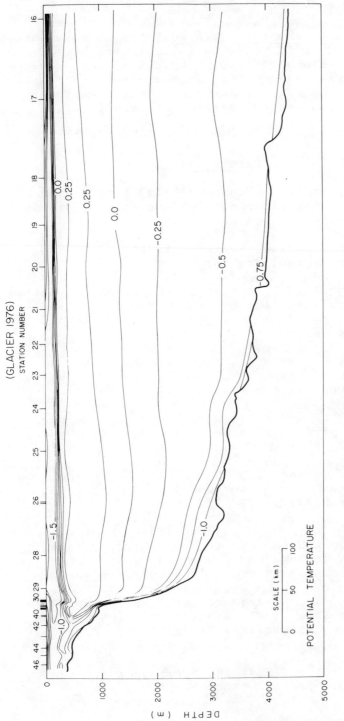

Fig. 9   Potential temperature section in the western Weddell Sea
(Foster, 1976).

Acknowledgements. This work has been supported for a number of years by the Division of Polar
Programs, National Science Foundation, most recently
by Grant DPP75-14936. The author wishes to thank
K. Aagaard and L. K. Coachman for their advice and
comments on an earlier version of this paper.

References

Aagaard, K. and L. K. Coachman (1975) Toward an
    ice-free Arctic Ocean. Transactions, American
    Geophysical Union 56:484-486.

American Geographical Society (1975) Map of the
    Arctic Region, New York.

Brennecke, W. (1921) Die ozeanographischen Arbeiten
    der deutschen antarktischen Expedition 1911-
    1912. Aus dem Arkiv der Deutschen Seewarte
    39:214 pp.

Carmack, E. C., Water characteristics of the South-
    ern Ocean south of the Polar Front. Deep-Sea
    Research. (in press)

Carmack, E. C. and K. Aagaard (1973) On the Deep
    Water of the Greenland Sea. Deep-Sea Research
    20:687-715.

Carmack, E. C. and T. D. Foster (1975) On the flow
    of water out of the Weddell Sea. Deep-Sea
    Research 22:711-724.

Coachman, L. K. and K. Aagaard (1974) Physical
    Oceanography of arctic and subarctic seas.
    Marine Geology and Oceanography of the Arctic
    Seas. Ed. Y. Herman. Springer, 1-72.

Coachman, L. K., K. Aagaard and R. B. Tripp (1975)
    Bering Strait, The Regional Physical Ocean-
    ography. University of Washington Press,
    172 pp.

Deacon, G. E. R. (1937) The hydrography of the
    Southern Ocean. 'Discovery' Reports 15:
    124 pp.

Deacon, G. E. R. (1963) The Southern Ocean. The
Sea, Vol. II. Ed. M. N. Hill. Interscience,
281-295.

Dietrich, G. (1967) The international "Overflow"
Expedition (ICES) of the Iceland-Faroe Ridge,
May-June 1960. Rapports et Procès-Verbaux des
Réunions. Ed. J. B. Tait. 157, Ch. 10.

Elder, R. B. and J. M. Seabrooke (1970) Oceanography of the Weddell Sea. U.S. Coast Guard
Oceanography Report No. 30, 98 pp.

Foldvik, A. and T. Kvinge (1974) Bottom currents
in the Weddell Sea. Report No. 37, Geophysical Institute, Div. A, University of Bergen,
43 pp.

Foster, T. D. (1976) International Weddell Sea
Oceanographic Expedition, 1976. Antarctic
Jour. U.S. 11:73-76.

Foster, T. D. and E. C. Carmack (1976) Frontal
zone mixing and Antarctic Bottom Water formation in the southern Weddell Sea. Deep-Sea
Res. 23:301-317.

Foster, T. D. and J. H. Middleton (1976) Long-term
current measurements in the bottom water of
the central Weddell Sea. Transactions, Amer.
Geophys. Union 57:940-941.

Gill, A. E. (1973) Circulation and bottom water
formation in the Weddell Sea. Deep-Sea Res.
20:111-140.

Glavnoe Upravlenie Geodezii i Kartolrafii (1974)
Bathymetricheskaya Karta Antarktiki, Moscow.

Medoc Group (1970) Observation of formation of
deep water in the Mediterranean Sea, 1969.
Nature 227:1037-1040.

Meincke, J. (1972) The hydrographic section along
the Iceland-Faroe Ridge carried out by R. V.
"Anton Dohrn" in 1959-1971. Berichte der
Deutschen Wissenschaftlichen Kommission fur
Meeresforschung 22:372-384.

Mosby, H. (1934) The waters of the Atlantic
    Antarctic Ocean. Scientific Results of the
    Norwegian Antarctic Expeditions 1927-1928,
    1(11):131 pp.

Namias, J. (1975) Northern hemisphere seasonal sea
    level pressure and anomaly charts, 1947-1974.
    California Cooperative Oceanic Fisheries In-
    vestigations, Atlas No. 22, 243 pp.

Nansen, F. (1906) Northern waters: Captain Roald
    Amundsen's oceanographic observations in the
    Arctic Seas in 1901. Vid. Selskabets Skrifter,
    I. Math.-Naturv. Klasse, No. 3. Christiania,
    145 pp.

Reid, J. L. and R. J. Lynn (1971) On the influence
    of the Norwegian-Greenland and Weddell Seas
    upon the bottom waters of the Indian and
    Pacific Oceans. Deep-Sea Res. 18:1063-1088.

Taljaard, J. J., H. van Loon, H. L. Crutcher and
    R. L. Jenne (1969) Climate of the Upper Air:
    Southern Hemisphere, Vol. 1, Temperature,
    Dewpoints, and Heights at Selected Pressure
    Levels. U.S. Department of Commerce, ESSA.

Treshnikov, A. F. (1964) Surface water circulation
    in the Antarctic Ocean. Soviet Antarctic Ex-
    pedition 2(45):81-83 (English translation).

Treshnikov, A. F. and G. I. Baranov (1972) Water
    Circulation in the Arctic Basin. Leningrad,
    Gidrometeoizdat, 145 pp. English translation.
    National Technical Information Service,
    TT72-50088.

U.S. Navy Hydrographic Office (1957) Oceanographic
    Atlas of the Polar Seas; Part I, Antarctic.
    Washington, 70 pp.

U.S. Navy Hydrographic Office (1958) Oceanographic
    Atlas of the Polar Seas; Part II, Arctic.
    Washington, 149 pp.

Worthington, L. V. (1970) The Norwegian Sea as a
    mediterranean basin. Deep-Sea Res. 17:77-84.

6

Primary Productivity and Estimates of Potential Yields of the Southern Ocean

Sayed Z. El-Sayed

I. INTRODUCTION

Interest in the biological productivity of the Southern Ocean dates back to Captain James Cook's second voyage of discovery (1772-75). In his account he drew attention to the productivity of these southern waters. The richness of the Antarctic seas in plant and animal life has been recognized during the EREBUS and TERROR expedition (1839-43), under James Clark Ross. During this expedition J. D. Hooker, the famed botanist-surgeon, collected plankton samples and sent them to Ehrenberg, who in 1844 published the first paper on Antarctic diatoms. Durmont D'Urville in his "Voyage au Pole Sud et dans l'Oceanie" published in 1845, also wrote an interesting account of the richness of the Antarctic waters.

In the following one hundred years the data from the numerous Antarctic expeditions served to perpetuate the belief in the extreme richness of the Antarctic seas. The enormous catches of baleen whales taken from these waters, together with the teeming of the coastal waters with seals, winged birds and penguins, lend support to this belief. The initiation of the DISCOVERY investigations (1925-39) laid the foundation of our knowledge of the general oceanography of the Southern Ocean. These investigations contributed substantially to our understanding of the distribution and abundance of phytoplankton, zooplankton (with special emphasis on krill, Euphausia superba) fish and whales. However, it was not until the early 1960's (with the use of the radioactive

141

carbon-14 method in primary productivity measure-
ments) that the first direct estimates of primary
productivity of the Antarctic seas were obtained
(Klyashtorin, 1961; Ichimura and Fukushima, 1963;
El-Sayed, Mandelli and Sugimura, 1964; Saijo and
Kawashima, 1964; Volkovinsky, 1966).

Thanks to the extensive cruises of the USNS
ELTANIN, the U.S.S.R. OB and other research
vessels in the 60's and early 70's, sufficient
data on primary production have now accumulated to
allow estimates of the productivity of the
Southern Ocean (Mandelli and Burkholder, 1966;
El-Sayed, 1967, 1968a,b; El-Sayed and Jitts, 1973;
El-Sayed and Turner, in press; Holm-Hansen,
El-Sayed, Franceschini and Cuhel, in press). These
estimates, which are largely based on station data
taken by oceanographic ships at different times
and often in different years, vary widely. The
estimates clearly reflect the great variability
in the productivity values obtained in the circum-
Antarctic waters. They also pointed to the
marked differences between the more productive
coastal regions and the poorer oceanic waters
(El-Sayed, 1970).

The growing interest by several countries in
recent years in the exploitation of the living
resources of the Southern Ocean (e.g. whales,
seals, krill, squid, fish, etc.) is reflected in
the recent expeditions to the Antarctic by
research vessels, commercial factory trawlers and
ice-breakers of the Federal Republic of Germany,
Poland, U.S.S.R., Japan, France, Argentina, U.S.A.
and Taiwan. Scientists and several international
organizations (e.g. the Scientific Committee on
Antarctic Research (SCAR), the Scientific
Committee on Oceanic Research (SCOR), and the Food
and Agriculture Organization of the UN (FAO), have
expressed concern over the need for the proper
management and conservation of these resources
(El-Sayed, 1976). The SCAR/SCOR newly formed
Group of Specialists on Living Resources of the
Southern Ocean has recently stressed the necessity of adopting an ecosystem approach to the
understanding of the Southern Ocean and its
exploitable resources (see SCAR Bulletin No. 55,
January, 1977, and SCOR Proceedings Vol. 12,
December, 1976). In order to obtain the information upon which management decisions must be

based, there is a need for a greater understanding
of the complex ecosystem of which these resources
are integral components. There is also the need
for a better understanding of the efficiency of
transfer of organic carbon from the primary producers level to the secondary, tertiary and other
high consumer levels.

In this paper we will review the subject of
primary productivity of the Southern Ocean in
light of the more recent data collected during
ELTANIN Cruises 38, 46 and 51 (Fig. 1). With the
impending commercial exploitation of the Antarctic
living resources, an accurate assessment of the
primary productivity of the Southern Ocean is of
considerable importance for the proper management
of these resources. For instance, one wishes to
know how such a system is capable of supporting as
it once did, huge catches of baleen whales and fur
seals, and whether the system is capable of sustaining a krill catch of 100-200 million tons per
year, as some fishery experts have predicted. In
order to provide answers to these questions,
estimates of the faction of annual primary production required to support the krill, fish, bird
and mammalian populations were made. However,
before discussing these estimates, it would be
instructive to review the distribution and abundance of the primary producers and of the factors
which govern their productivity. For detailed
information regarding these subjects, reference
should be made to the papers by El-Sayed (1970);
El-Sayed and Turner (in press); Holm-Hansen et al
(in press) and Fogg (in press).

II. PHYTOPLANKTON STANDING CROP AND PRIMARY
     PRODUCTION

1. Standing Crop

Diatoms are the dominant components in
antarctic phytoplankton; next are the dinoflagellates and silicoflagellates. Nearly 100 species
of diatoms have been found in antarctic waters,
with more than 60 species of dinoflagellates and
only one species of silicoflagellates.

Our knowledge of the distribution and abundance of Antarctic phytoplankton has substantially
increased thanks to the extensive investigations

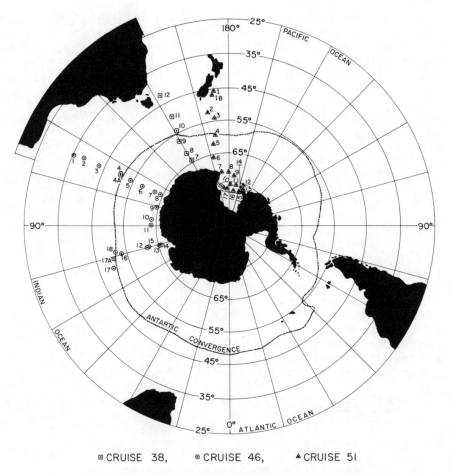

□ CRUISE 38,   ⊙ CRUISE 46,   ▲ CRUISE 51

Figure 1. Positions of Stations Occupied During
USNS ELTANIN Cruises 38, 46 and 51.

carried out by the late J. T. Hart of the
DISCOVERY and, more recently, by Soviet and U.S.
scientists. As a result of these investigations,
we know that there are conspicuous geographic and
seasonal variations in the distribution of the
standing crop (biomass per unit area or volume).
Large biomasses are found in the Scotia Sea, west
of the Antarctic Peninsula, in the Ross Sea, and
in the southwestern Weddell Sea (El-Sayed, 1970).
Coastal waters off the Antarctic continent and the
sub-Antarctic Islands are, in general, characterized by much higher standing crop than in the
oceanic (i.e. offshore) regions.

The vertical distribution of chlorophyll a
shows that maximum values are found at subsurface
depths. Following these maxima, there is a
gradual decrease in the chlorophyll values to the
depth of 200 m, below which chlorophyll concentration is greatly reduced (El-Sayed, 1970; El-Sayed
and Turner, in press). At several stations
occupied by the ELTANIN in the Pacific and Indian
sectors of the Antarctic and in the Ross Sea, substantial amounts of phytoplankton were found below
the euphotic zone (Fig. 2). The data collected
during ELTANIN Cruise 51 in the Ross Sea showed
that the magnitude of the photosynthetic activity
of the phytoplankton below the euphotic zone cannot be overlooked (El-Sayed and Turner, in press;
Holm-Hansen et al., in press).

2. Primary Production

Primary productivity data of the Southern
Ocean, in general, showed good correlation with
the distribution of the phytoplankton standing
crop. For instance, low values were reported in
the Drake Passage, the Bellingshausen Sea, the
Antarctic Convergence, and in the oceanic waters
in general (El-Sayed and Mandelli, 1965; Walsh,
1971). High values were found in coastal regions
and in the vicinity of Antarctic and sub-Antarctic
islands. For example, El-Sayed (1967) recorded
3.2 gC/m^2/day in February 1965 in the Gerlache
Strait; Mandelli and Burkholder (1966) reported
3.62 gC/m^2/day also in February 1965 near
Deception Island. Horne, Fogg and Eagle (1969)
found a peak of productivity of 2.8 gC/m^2/day in
early February 1967 in the inshore waters of Signy
Islands, South Orkney Islands. These values which

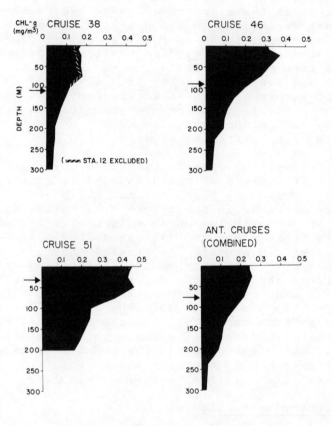

Figure 2.   Vertical Distributions of Average
           Chlorophyll a Values of ELTANIN Cruises
           38, 46, 51 and for the Three Combined
           Cruises. Arrows indicate depth of the
           Euphotic Zone.

are comparable to any of the highly productive
areas off Peru, southeast Arabia, Somalia, southwest Africa, etc., no doubt have perpetuated the
belief of the proverbial richness of the Antarctic
waters. They may also have contributed to the
premature high primary productivity estimates
published in the mid-sixties.

As to the vertical distribution of primary
production, maximum photosynthetic activity
occurred at depths corresponding to between 50%
and 25% of surface light intensity (Fig. 3).
During ELTANIN Cruise 51, we observed that the
photosynthetic activity of the phytoplankton at
the bottom of the euphotic zone was higher than
the average productivity at any depth of the other
two cruises (38 and 46). The depths of the
euphotic zone at the stations occupied during
ELTANIN Cruises 38, 46 and 51, ranged between 30 m
and 135 m, with an average of 78 m.

Based on in situ primary productivity experiments conducted by the author during ELTANIN
Cruises 38, 46 and 51, a mean primary productivity
value of 0.134 $gC/m^2/day$ was calculated. The
discrepancy between this figure and those given
earlier by the author (El-Sayed, 1967), as well as
those by other investigators, stems from the fact
that these early estimates were based on data
collected from the more productive coastal regions
of the Scotia Sea, Bransfield Strait, Gerlache'
Strait, and the waters west of the Antarctic
Peninsula, whereas the ELTANIN data (Cruises 38,
46 and 51) were generally taken in the less productive oceanic waters. Since the Southern Ocean
is essentially a deep ocean with a narrow shelf
region (areal extent of the shelf is about
2.1×10^6 km^2 compared to 36×10^6 km^2 for the
Southern Ocean), we believe that the in situ data
of the ELTANIN cruises are more representative of
the Southern Ocean as a whole than the former
estimates made largely in coastal regions.

III. FACTORS AFFECTING PRIMARY PRODUCTION IN THE
      SOUTHERN OCEAN

In seeking an explanation for the great variability of the productivity values reported from
the Southern Ocean, several attempts were made to
explain this variability in terms of the physical,

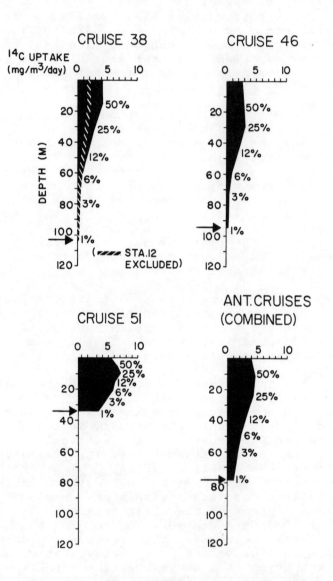

Figure 3.   Vertical Distributions of Average ^{14}C
            Uptake Values of ELTANIN Cruises 38, 46,
            51, and for the Three Combined Cruises.
            Arrows indicate depth of the Euphotic Zone.

chemical and biological factors which govern
phytoplankton production in that ocean. El-Sayed
and Mandelli (1965) discussed five factors which
they thought are likely to control production in
these waters. They listed: (1) temperature, (2)
inorganic nutrient salts, (3) light, (4) turbu-
lence and (5) grazing. Unfortunately, however,
little has been added in recent years to improve
our understanding of the role played by these
factors in affecting primary production. However,
based on the ELTANIN data collected during Cruises
38, 46 and 51, Holm-Hansen et al.,(in press)
attempted to update the information included in
El-Sayed and Mandelli's paper. A summary of the
recent findings regarding the factors governing
phytoplankton production in the Southern Ocean is
given below. A fuller description will appear in
Holm-Hansen __et al__. (in press).

(1)   Temperature

     In El-Sayed and Mandelli's paper mentioned
above, they discussed some of the conflicting
views in regard to the effect of temperature on
the metabolic activities of phytoplankton in
Antarctic waters. They cited Gran's (1932) work
in the Weddell Sea, and Hart's (1934) observations
in the vicinity of the South Georgia Islands.   .
Both Gran and Hart reported high standing crop of
phytoplankton coincident with low temperatures.
However, one should remember that the abundance of
phytoplankton in water near freezing point, while
indeed striking (witness the extensive bloom of
phytoplankton observed in the southwestern Weddell
Sea where surface temperature of $-1.69^{\circ}C$ was
recorded, El-Sayed, 1971), does not necessarily
imply high primary production. On the basis of
respiratory and photosynthetic data, antarctic
phytoplankton show a sharp metabolic drop-off at
temperatures above $10^{\circ}C$, (Jitts and Carpenter,
unpublished). Thus, it would seem that these
algal cells are obligate psychrophiles in that
they are adapted to low temperatures and will not
grow at higher temperatures. Moreover, the
highest specific growth rate (μ) found in
Antarctic waters was 0.33 doublings per day, which
suggests that low temperatures of Antarctic waters
do limit algal growth rates (Holm-Hansen __et al__.,
in press).

(2) Radiant Energy

Variations in incoming solar radiation between summer and winter in the Antarctic are
extreme. The effects these variations have on
marine plant life in the circum-Antarctic waters
were discussed by El-Sayed (1971). Furthermore,
light penetration in Antarctic waters is determined not only by the intensity and angle of
incidence of light, surface reflectance, and the
absorption of suspended particles, but also by
the presence of thick fast ice and pack ice which
appreciably reduce the amount of submarine illumination. Despite this reduced illumination,
Bunt (1964) presented evidence of the presence of
prolific growth of microalgae in the lower layers
of the sea ice. He also found that this assem-
blage of microalgae and plankton under extensive
ice cover in McMurdo Sound exhibited a high degree
of shade adaptation which enabled them to make net
gains at very low light intensities.

At the stations occupied during ELTANIN
Cruises 46 and 51, a high correlation between the
intensity of the incident solar radiation and
photosynthetic rates in the euphotic zone was
found (Holm-Hansen et al., in press). These
authors found, for instance, that on days when
light intensity was high, photosynthetic rates
were low in the surface waters, and these rates
increased with depth. On the other hand, when
incident light was low during the in situ
incubation period, photosynthetic rates either
remained fairly constant in the upper waters of
the euphotic zone or they were highest in surface
waters. These results are most probably caused
by photo-inhibition whereby high light intensity
causes a decrease in the photosynthetic rates.
Holm-Hansen et al.,(in press) found that on bright
days (100 to 160 cal/cm^2/half-light day) the maximum photosynthetic assimilation occurred at
depths corresponding to between 25 to 50 percent
of incident radiation. When, on the other hand,
solar radiation was low (20 to 30 cal/cm^2/half-
light day) there was no evidence of photo-inhibition. The threshold of photo-inhibition for
antarctic phytoplankton was calculated to be in
the range of 40 to 50 cal/cm^2/half-light day.

(3)   Nutrient Concentration

The numerous observations on the nutrient salts in the Antarctic waters show that these salts appear to be in excess of phytoplankton requirements. This is primarily due to the mechanism of upwelling, which ensures abundant supply of these salts. Even at the peak of phytoplankton growth, the concentration of nutrients remains well above the limiting values. For instance, during the heavy phytoplankton bloom off the Ronne Ice Shelf, southwestern Weddell Sea, the nutrient salts still exhibited high concentrations e.g. phosphates: 2.02 µg at./l; nitrates: 24.9 µg at./l; and silicates: 68 µg at./l (El-Sayed, 1971). It is unlikely that these nutrient salts are sufficiently low at any one time to become limiting factors to the growth of phytoplankton.

While the concentration of nutrient salts in Antarctic waters is seldom low enough to limit productivity, there is some evidence that trace metals may, indeed, affect organic production in these waters (Volkovinsky, 1966). Unfortunately, however, the role these trace elements play in the productivity of the Antarctic waters has not been sufficiently studied.

As to the vitamin requirements of the Antarctic phytoplankton, some progress has been made in recent years. Thus Carlucci and Cuhel (in press) found that it is possible that the concentration of vitamin B_{12} may have important effects on the composition of the Antarctic phytoplankton. However, there does not seem to be any evidence that this vitamin affects primary productivity to any appreciable extent. The same authors also found that thiamin was usually lacking in detectable concentrations in Antarctic waters; however, they found that biotin was often present in high concentrations. Since only a few phytoplankton species require these vitamins, their concentrations are probably not of great ecological importance, (Holm-Hansen et al., in press).

(4)   Water Column Stability

Braarud and Klem (1931) were among the first to draw attention to the importance of instability

of surface waters as a factor affecting production. Their views have since been supported
by other investigators. Sverdrup (1953) discussed
the vernal blooming of phytoplankton in relation
to the critical depth and showed, theoretically,
that blooming takes place only if the depth of the
mixed layer is less than the compensation depth.
The depth of the mixed layer in the Southern Ocean
in general, is such that the phytoplankton is
carried below the euphotic zone and the average
amount of light received by the algal cells is
thereby reduced.

Hasle (1956) attributed the low productivity
of the sub-Antarctic water and at the Antarctic
Convergence to the comparatively low stability of
surface waters which prevents the phytoplankton
from remaining in the optimum light zone long
enough for extensive production. Similar findings
were also reported by El-Sayed et al. (1964), Hart
(1934) and Saijo and Kawashima (1964). These
authors suggest that areas of high primary productivity are those in which comparative stability
of the water column prevails (El-Sayed and
Mandelli, 1965). Thus, the high value of primary
production (1.56 $gC/m^2/day$) recorded during the
extensive Weddell Sea bloom mentioned above
(El-Sayed, 1971) may be due to the strong pycno-
cline produced by the melting of ice at the edge
of the shelf. This resulted in the formation of a
mixed layer shallower than the critical depth,
thus permitting the development of the bloom.

IV. ECOLOGICAL EFFICIENCY AND ESTIMATION OF
     POTENTIAL YIELD

In assessing the efficiency of the Antarctic
marine ecosystem, one is primarily interested in
estimating the net trophic efficiency starting
with the primary producers and on to the other
higher trophic levels. However, given the state
of our knowledge of the Antarctic marine ecosystem, this cannot be readily calculated. For
instance, although the primary production of the
Antarctic waters has been estimated, we have no
reliable figures for the secondary production.
The numerous attempts which were made to estimate
the annual production of, say, krill (Euphausia
superba) gave conflicting results due to major
sources of error in the methods used (Allen,1971;

Gulland, 1970; Hempel, 1968).

Thus, in the absence of reliable data on
biomass and production of the organisms at higher
trophic levels, an attempt is made to speculate
on the general overall biological productivity of
the Southern Ocean and to calculate, on theoret-
ical grounds, the potential yields of that system.
In so doing three different estimates of primary
production are used: (a) 100 $gC/m^2/year$ given by
Ryther (1963) which, incidentally, he calculated
using Hart's DISCOVERY data; (b) 43 $gC/m^2/year$,
calculated by Currie (1964) and (c) 16 $gC/m^2/year$,
calculated by Holm-Hansen et al.(in press). This
latter figure is based on an average primary production value of 0.134 $gC/m^2/day$ (see p. 5). As
for trophic efficiency, the following values: 10,
15 and 20 percent are used. The results of these
calculations are given in Table 1.

Table 1 shows that if we take the lowest
mean annual productivity value (16 $gC/m^2/year$) to
be representative of the Southern Ocean as a whole
and if we assume that the surface area of the
Antarctic waters is about 38.1 x 10^6 km^2, then the
annual primary production value is calculated at
610 x 10^6 tons of carbon. If we further assume
that the ratio between carbon and fresh weight is
1:10, then the total annual primary production
(in terms of fresh weight)is 6.1 x 10^9 tons. If
on the other hand, we take the two other figures
(i.e. 43 and 100 $gC/m^2/year$), the total annual
primary production (fresh weight) will be more
than twofold and sixfold, respectively, of the
values derived by Holm-Hansen et al.(in press)
estimates.

Table 1 further shows that if we increase
the ecological efficiency from 10 to 15 and 20
percent, this results in significant increases in
the estimates of the yields at the herbivores and
primary carnivores levels.

V. DISCUSSION

In this paper we have attempted to give a
brief summary of the distribution and magnitude
of the phytoplankton standing crop and phytoplankton production in the Southern Ocean based

TABLE 1

ESTIMATES OF POTENTIAL YIELD (PER YEAR) AT VARIOUS TROPHIC LEVELS IN METRIC TONS ($\times 10^9$) USING THREE ESTIMATES OF PRIMARY PRODUCTION IN THE SOUTHERN OCEAN

Annual Primary Production (gC/m²)	Trophic Level	Ecological Efficiency Factor					
		10%		15%		20%	
		Carbon (tons)	Wet Wt. (tons)	Carbon (tons)	Wet Wt. (tons)	Carbon (tons)	Wet Wt. (tons)
100*	Phytoplankton	3.80	38.0	3.80	38.0	3.80	38.0
	Herbivores	0.38	3.8	0.57	5.7	0.76	7.6
	Primary Carnivores	0.038	0.38	0.09	0.9	0.15	1.5
43**	Phytoplankton	1.63	16.3	1.63	16.3	1.63	16.3
	Herbivores	0.163	1.63	0.24	2.4	0.33	3.3
	Primary Carnivores	0.016	0.16	0.04	0.4	0.07	0.7
16***	Phytoplankton	0.61	6.1	0.61	6.1	0.61	6.1
	Herbivores	0.061	0.61	0.09	0.9	0.12	1.2
	Primary Carnivores	0.006	0.06	0.01	0.1	0.02	0.2

* (Ryther, 1963)
** (Currie, 1964)
*** (Holm-Hansen, El-Sayed, Franceschini and Cuhel, in press).

primarily on the investigations carried out during
the past fifteen years. The two most significant
findings resulting from these investigations are:
(a) that there is much greater variability in the
productivity parameters studied than had been previously thought; (b) that the productivity of the
Southern Ocean as a whole, perhaps, is not as high
as we were led to believe. Although this great
variability should not come as a surprise for a
region which covers slightly less than 10% of the
World Ocean, and is dominated by the circumpolar
current, with its high nutrient salt concentrations
and nearly homeothermic sea temperature (which
varies very little with depth or season), such
variations are, nevertheless, puzzling.

In discussing the factors which limit phytoplankton production in the Southern Ocean, Holm-
Hansen <u>et al</u>.(in press) found it difficult or impossible to deduce rate-limiting factors by the
direct comparison of any one parameter (e.g.
temperature) as many factors vary simultaneously,
including the species composition of the phytoplankton (where significant floral changes take
place as the Antarctic Convergence is crossed from
north to south). It would seem that Foster (1977)
is correct when he stated that the large seasonal
variations of light and sea ice cover, and especially the near freezing temperatures of the surface waters, may be more significant in controlling the productivity of these waters than upwelling and the regeneration of nutrients. Undoubtedly, there are other limiting factors which
we have not touched upon in this brief review, e.g.
zooplankton grazing, settling rates of algal cells,
respiration rates, etc. Unfortunately, however,
we do not have sufficient data regarding these
factors to make meaningful interpretation of their
role in productivity studies of the Southern Ocean.

The second significant finding - namely that
recently acquired data show that the primary productivity of the Southern Ocean is not as high as
originally believed, has far-reaching implications
with regard to the future exploitation of the
living resources of that ocean. For management
decisions regarding the exploitation of these
resources must be based on better estimates of
productivity (primary, secondary, and tertiary) of
that ecosystem. For this reason the calculations

shown in Table 1 are indeed instructive. In this
respect, it is interesting to compare the amount
of phytoplankton production (shown in Table 1)
with the amount of krill consumed by whales, seals,
birds, fish and squid shown in Table 2.

Table 2*

Estimates of krill consumption (in millions of
tons/year) prior to whaling and at present.

	Est. Predation Prior to Whaling (X 10^6 tons/yr)	Est. Predation at Present (X 10^6 tons/yr)
Whales	174	37
Seals	?	30 - 64
Birds	?	43
Fish	?	?
Squid	?	?
Total	> 174	> 140

*
Based on data available at the International
Conference on Marine Living Resources of the
Southern Ocean held August, 1976, at Woods
Hole, Mass.

Since estimates of the krill consumed by the
fish, squid and other predators are lacking in the
above table, we will assume that the amount of
krill consumed by the Antarctic animals is about
200 x 10^6 tons annually. In terms of krill consumed, and using the lowest figure of annual
primary production [Table 1] (16 gC/m^2), this
200 x 10^6 tons represents only about 4 percent of
the total annual production. In terms of food
chain dynamics this seems to be an acceptable
figure. With regard to the question posed at the
outset of this paper as to whether the system is
capable of supporting as it once did, large
catches of baleen whales and fur seals, the data
and calculations shown in Tables 1 and 2, would
indicate the system is capable of sustaining such
catches.

VI. REFERENCES CITED

Allen, K. R. (1971). Relation between production
and biomass. Journ. Fish. Res. Bd. Canada.
28: 1573-1581.

Braarud, T. and A. Klem. (1931). Hydrographical
and chemical investigations in the coastal
waters off Møre and in the Romsdalfjord.
Hvalradets Skrifter. 1: 1-88.

Bunt, J. S. (1968). Microalgae of the Antarctic
pack ice zone. Symposium on Antarctic
Oceanography,(ed.)R. I. Currie. pp. 198-218.
Scott Polar Research Institute, Cambridge.

Burkholder, P. R. and E. F. Mandelli. (1965).
Productivity of microalgae in Antarctic sea
ice. Science. 149(3686): 872-874.

Carlucci, A. F. and R. L. Cuhel. Vitamins in the
south polar seas: distribution and significance of dissolved and particulate vitamin
B_{12}, thiamine and biotin in the southern
Indian Ocean. Proc. Ant. Sympos. (in press).

Currie, R. I. (1964). Environmental features in
the ecology of Antarctic seas. Biologie
Antarctique, (eds.) R. Carrick, M. W.
Holdgate and J. Prevost. pp. 87-94. Hermann,
Paris.

El-Sayed, S. Z. (1967). Biological productivity
investigations of the Pacific Sector of
Antarctica. Ant. Journ. U.S. 11: 200-201.

_____ (1968a). On the productivity of
the Southwest Atlantic Ocean and the waters
west of the Antarctic Peninsula. Biology of
the Ant. Seas. III, (eds.) G. A. Llano and
W. L. Schmitt. Ant. Res. Ser. 11: 15-47.

_____ (1968b). Primary productivity
of the Antarctic and sub-Antarctic. In:
Primary productivity and benthic marine
algae of the Antarctic and sub-Antarctic.
Folio 10, Ant. Map Folio Ser. (ed.) V. C.
Bushnell. pp. 1-6. Amer. Geogr. Soc.

El-Sayed, S. Z.   (1970).   On the productivity of
the Southern Ocean (Atlantic and Pacific
Sectors).   In: Antarctic Ecology, (ed.)
M. W. Holdgate.   1: 119-135.

_____   (1971).   Observations on phytoplankton bloom in the Weddell Sea.   Biology
of the Ant. Seas IV, (eds.) G. A. Llano and
I. E. Wallen.   Ant. Res. Ser. 17: 301-312.

_____   (1976).   Living resources of the
Southern Ocean.   Ant. Journ. U.S. 6(1): 8-12.

_____   and H. R. Jitts.   (1973).   Phyto-
plankton production in the southeastern
Indian Ocean.   The Biology of the Indian
Ocean, (ed.) B. Zeitzschel.   3: 131-142.
Springer-Verlag, Berlin, Heidelberg, New York

_____   and E. F. Mandelli.   (1965).
Primary production and standing crop of
phytoplankton in the Weddell Sea and Drake
Passage.   Biology of the Ant. Seas II, (ed.)
G. A. Llano.   Ant. Res. Ser. 5: 87-106.

_____, E. F. Mandelli and Y. Sugimura.
(1964).   Primary organic production in the
Drake Passage and Bransfield Strait. Biology
of the Ant. Seas I, (ed.) M. O. Lee. Ant.
Res. Ser. 1: 1-11.

_____   and J. T. Turner.   Productivity
of the Antarctic and subtropical regions:
A comparative study.   (ed.) Maxwell Dunbar.
Proc. of SCOR/SCAR Polar Oceans Conference.
Montreal, Canada, May 1974.   (in press).

Fogg, G. E.   Aquatic primary production in the
Antarctic.   In: Proceedings, Symposium on
British Antarctic Research.   Royal Society,
U.K., May 1976. (in press).

Foster, T. D.   (1976).   The physical oceanography
of the Southern Ocean: key to understanding
its biology.   (unpublished report).

Gran, H. H.   (1932).   Phytoplankton: methods and
problems.   Journ. Cons. Int. Explor. Mer.
7(3): 343-358.

Gulland, J. A. (1970). The development of the resources of antarctic seas. In: Antarctic Ecology, (ed.) M. W. Holdgate. 1: 217-223.

Hart, T. J. (1934). On the phytoplankton of the southwest Atlantic and the Bellingshausen Sea, 1929-1931. DISCOVERY Rept. 11: 1-268.

Hasle, G. R. (1956). Phytoplankton and hydrography of the Pacific part of the Antarctic Ocean. Nature. 177: 616-617.

Hempel, G. (1968). Area reviews on living resources of the world's ocean. Antarctica. Preliminary Draft. Informal Communication. U.N.F.A.O. Fisheries Circular No. 109.

Holm-Hansen, O., S. Z. El-Sayed, G. A. Franceschini and K. Cuhel. Primary production and the factors controlling phytoplankton growth in the Antarctic seas. Proc. Ant. Sympos. (in press).

Horne, A. J., G. E. Fogg and D. J. Eagle. (1969). Studies in situ of the primary production of an area of inshore Antarctic Sea. Journ. Mar. Biol. Assoc. U.K. 49: 393-405.

Ichimura, S. and H. Fukushima. (1963). On the chlorophyll content in the surface water of the Indian and the Antarctic Oceans. Bot. Mag. Tokyo. 76: 395-399.

Jitts, H. R. and D. J. Carpenter. Responses of phytoplankton photosynthesis to variations in light and temperature. CSIRO Division of Fish. & Oceanogr., Cronulla, Sydney, Australia. (unpublished report).

Klyashtorin, L. G. (1961). Primary production in the Atlantic and Southern Oceans according to the data obtained during the fifth antarctic voyage of the diesel-electric, OB. Dokl. Akad. Nauk. USSR. 141(5): 1204-1207.

Mandelli, E. F. and P. R. Burkholder. (1966). Primary productivity in the Gerlache and Bransfield Straits of Antarctica. Journ. Mar. Res. 24: 15-27.

Ryther, J. H.   (1963).   Geographic variations in
    productivity.   In: The Sea, (ed.) M. N. Hill.
    2: 347-380.   John Wiley & Sons, New York,
    London.

Saijo, Y. and T. Kawashima.   (1964).   Primary pro-
    duction in the Antarctic Ocean.   Journ.
    Oceanogr. Soc. Japan. 19: 22-28.

Sverdrup, H. U.   (1953).   On conditions for the
    vernal blooming of phytoplankton.   Journ.
    Cons. Int. Explor. Mer. 18: 287-295.

Volkovinsky, V. V.   (1966).   Studies of primary
    production in the waters of the South
    Atlantic Ocean.   Abst. 2nd Int. Oceanogr.
    Congr. Moscow.   pp. 386-387.

Walsh, J. J.   (1971).   Relative importance of
    habitat variables in predicting the distri-
    bution of phytoplankton at the ecotone of
    the antarctic upwelling system.   Ecol.
    Monogr. 41: 291-309.

VII.   ACKNOWLEDGMENT

I am grateful to the Division of Polar
Programs, National Science Foundation, for the
financial support (OPP-7509288 and OPP-7680738)
which made this work possible.   I am also grateful to my colleagues Dr. G. A. Franceschini,
Meteorology Department, Texas A&M University, for
his interpretation of the solar radiation data
collected during ELTANIN Cruises 46 and 51, and
to Dr. O. Holm-Hansen and his associates, Scripps
Institution of Oceanography for their interpretation of the temperature and nutrients data
collected also during these two cruises.   Dr.
M. A. McWhinnie, Chief Scientist, ELTANIN Cruise
51 deserves much thanks for the success of that
cruise.   I also wish to thank Mrs. Isabel H.
Robbins for typing this manuscript.

Problems in the Conservation of Polar Marine Mammals

Donald B. Siniff, Ian Stirling, and L. Lee Eberhardt

Within the last decade, marine mammals have become both subjects of great popular interest, and objects of widespread concern. This paper is concerned with problems in research and management of marine mammals in polar regions. Few people have the knowledge and experience necessary to consider this group as a whole and we do not claim any such status. We have, however, been involved in research on several species of marine mammals in both polar regions and have struggled with their associated management problems. We have tried to focus on ideas and problems basic to the whole ensemble using particular species to illustrate points. We have attempted to consider four general areas: specific management problems: population research; the role and value of modeling; and aesthetics and recreational considerations in management.

MANAGEMENT

A. Economics of Exploitation

Clark (1973) pointed out the need to assign a "discount rate" to future profits when assessing the value of a renewable resource. He noted that the optimum course of events from an economic point of view would often be over-exploitation to the point of near extinction, since this maximizes present over future profits (marine mammals are especially vulnerable because of low reproductive rates and, hence, low annual increments in the population). From a conservation point of view, such management is not acceptable, and careful control over capital investment is needed in the initial stages of exploitation of a renewable resource. This lesson, so dramatically exemplified by the great whales, probably applies to most of the polar marine mammals since

their life history patterns are rather similar (Eberhardt and
Siniff, 1977). Thus regulations preventing over-investment
would seem to be essential management of polar marine mammals.
To date, however, such regulations seem not to be considered,
perhaps because limited entry policy is new and complicated
to administer. In the few available instances where limited
entry has been applied (mostly in fisheries) it was implemented either because over-utilization of the resource was
already evident or because of an aesthetic desire to preserve
a way of life.

B. Impact of Economic Development and Tourism
      Hydrocarbon and mineral exploration and eventual produc-
tion pose a threat to arctic marine ecosystems, and in the
near future will probably pose similar threats in the antarctic. Tourism is developing in both regions and although it
is not yet a major industry, it has the potential to be and
needs to be monitored carefully. Because of the damage that
can be caused by human activity in polar regions, spatial
separation of resource sites and rigid time schedules and
regulations for development of human activity are imperative.
Otherwise, ecological damage of large lake regions where
resources are concentrated seems a likely outcome. Guide-
lines for minimizing impacts at sites of development have
received considerable attention and we support these efforts.
Separation of impact areas by considerable distances seems
to receive little attention because there usually seems to be
great pressure to tap all the reserves the area holds. It
would seem proper scheduling would allow partial development
of large reserves and separation of sites both in time and
space. The major objection concerning minerals and petro-
chemicals seems to be that such a plan would hold reserves
untapped until their time for development arrives. However,
with the prospect of alternative energy sources and the widely advertised emphasis on energy conservation measures, this
approach would seem consistent with current philosophies.

      Habitat destruction is the single known factor that al-
most always causes permanent reduction in species abundance.
Equally important but less readily apparent, is chemical pol-
lution. For example, Helle et al. (1976 a and b) showed that
for ringed seals (Phoca hispida) in the Baltic Sea, there was
a marked increase in pathological changes in uteri with an
adult pregnancy rate of 27% compared to 80-90% in normal populations. This reduction was apparently because of exception-
ably high levels of PCB. Similar findings in the California
sea lion (Zalophus californianus) have been reported by De
Long et al. (1973). Specific legislation to prevent such
damage is imperative but the problem has not been properly
addressed to date. The only document we know of which

addresses this point directly is the Agreement on the Conservation of Polar Bears (1974) which states in part, "Each con-
tracting party shall take appropriate action to protect the
ecosystems of which polar bears are a part . . . "   Unfortunately, the act has no enforcement capability or regulations
defining how such protection might be ensured.

Instead, present actions seem to revolve around determination of "baseline" population levels and general conditions.
Often, the period of time allowed for such evaluations is inadequate as well but that is another problem. The pattern
then seems to be to allow development with certain modifications to minimize "impact." Unfortunately, often there is
little follow-up study to evaluate what in fact the extent
and significance of the impact really was. Such baseline
studies have only historical value once damage is done. Of
course, a careful monitoring program (with enforcement if required) should proceed simultaneously with development, so
that the effects can be documented and applied to the development of reliable predictive capability.

C. Conflicts Between Marine Mammals and Fisheries
        To date, significant conflicts between fisheries and ma-
rine mammal populations in the polar regions have probably
not been significant, but those that may have occurred
    are certainly not well documented. However, this situa-
tion is likely to change in the near future as attention of
world fisheries begins to center on the seas surrounding the
antarctic region, along with the substantial influence some
fisheries may now be having in the arctic waters. The major
problem is that, at present, we seem to have no real prospect
of being able to assess such effects even in a qualitative
way.

International attention is now directed towards a krill
fishery in the antarctic waters. However, it appears likely
that this fishery will be developed before serious attempts
are made to assess its impact. Although, we would not debate
the possible viability of a krill fishery, we do strongly
suggest that considerable caution is needed to assess possible changes in competitive interactions among species using
krill as a food base. Traditionally, the evaluation of such
consequences would call for monitoring of changes concurrent-
ly with fishery development or even after the fact.

It seems this tradition stems from a myriad of complex
excuses, which basically mean that scientists seldom agree
on how conservative to be and industry is forceful, influen-
cial and united in cause. Thus, the traditional procedure
is likely to always be the outcome. We do not like to be

pessimistic on this point but unless action is taken at high
levels in the governments of interested countries, the outcome seems certain. For the Antarctic krill fishery, this is
unfortunate as clearly this situation begs for creative thinking. One suggestion we feel is worth considering is restrict-
ing the first fishery to one region, preceded by detailed
evaluation of population parameters such as age at first reproduction, pregnancy rates by age class, growth rates, and
adult survival rates, for selected vertebrate species in the
ecosystem. The logic then is that concentrated harvest in
one region would cause that region's populations to react
quickly, much like the total system will react eventually.
Problems of stock identification and discreteness are trouble-
some and probably the strongest scientific argument against
such a scheme. Also, this suggestion suffers because of the
limitations in area and hence, is counter to free access to
the seas philosophy. However, whatever the scheme devised it
is clear a new approach and philosophy is needed and a chal-
lenge to responsible scientists and governments.

It has been variously suggested that great reductions in
whale abundance left a "surplus" of krill that might ultimately be reflected in increased abundance of marine mammals and
birds. Equally plausible is the hypothesis that other species
with an inherently higher rate of increase would respond more
quickly. If so, various fish populations may have long since
expanded in proportion to the "surplus." The influence of
possible increased numbers of fish or invertebrate predators
on marine mammals can only be speculated on.

A case where the impact of fisheries on marine mammals
is probably now extant as there exists a concern that fisheries
in the Bering Sea may well have reduced the carrying capacity
for the norther fur seal (<u>Callorhinus ursinus</u>). Sergeant
(1976) has mentioned a similar seal-fishery conflict with the
harp seal (<u>Pagophilus groenlandicus</u>) in the North Atlantic.
Recovery of that seal population to its former abundance may
be precluded by the fishery on its diet species, capelin.
Actual evidence of such effects is not available simply for
the want of adequate data. Such conflicts are bound to become more important in the near future which makes it even
more vital that management plans be designed to consider research needs. Only then will data become available which may
serve to prevent irreversible changes in competititve interactions and ecosystem structure and function.

MODELING

Present day ecosystem models deal with the kinetics of
an ecosystem (flow of energy and/or materials) or with the
dynamics of a specific population. Modelers seem, almost

automatically, to chose one or the other approach and to
largely ignore alternative views. It seems clear that because of issues like this dichotomy there is, as yet, a long
way to go before models come of age. Margalef (1973) has described a number of problems involved in the construction of
realistic ecological models. As he notes, "mathematical models are indispensable, but they must help to grow ideas and
not just to feed computers." Some other modeling issues associated with data analysis and statistical methods are discussed by Eberhardt (1977 b.).

    We suggest that modeling of polar marine ecosystems
should proceed initially through a series of species-specific
and site-specific process models with maximum utilization of
field studies and experimentation to update the modeling process. The major areas involved for understanding processes
include: interspecific and intraspecific competition for
food and breeding space; fluctuations in age of first repro-
ductions, reproductive success, and survival; predator-prey
interactions, and the effects of climatic variables. It is
uncertain how such factors influence each other; how they
vary with population density; how plastic the species are in
their ability to change; and the speed that such changes can
occur. It seems apparent, however, that many of these relationships are very sensitive and change quickly. How these interrelationships remain in balance in the face of an uncertain environment having "random" features is not so evident.
Regulation is discussed below.

    Modeling to date has been largely based on the assump-
tion of a static ecosystem and constant population parameters
with little emphasis on changes caused by shifts in, for example, competitive coefficients. We see this as a basic flaw
in most modeling processes to date and since predictive ability of such models is based on static assumptions, they have
little power in a changing system. Until better data bases
are developed such models will continue to be used and they
have value, but reliance upon them should be tempered accord-
ingly.

    The skeptical attitude expressed above should not be
taken to imply that models are not important. To the contrary, they provide one of the best, if not the only, suitable
means for organizing data and identifying what further steps
need to be taken to unravel the interactions of the system
under study. We thus endorse the need for additional modeling efforts on polar systems. Unfortunately, the present
data base leaves the construction of meaningful flow diagrams
and attempts to obtain crude estimates of the relevant parameters the major exercise for the near future.

RESEARCH ON POPULATIONS

A. Abundance
    At present the state-of-the-art in censusing marine mammals is rather primitive. In part, this is a consequence of inadequate technology, but the more important aspect is that resources in funding and in logistic support have usually been insufficient and even when support is possible, investigators seem reluctant to commit time and money, since the return is often disappointing because of features such as weather and logistical failure. To a large degree, these factors have precluded developmental research on techniques. One needs only to consider the few areas that have been visited for censusing purposes in the arctic and antarctic to gain a real appreciation of the magnitude of logistical problems.

    Two examples may serve to illustrate the present status of census methods. One is the recent "rediscovery" of a large population of hooded seals (Cystophora cristata) after an interval of 100 years (Sergeant, 1974). The other is the contrast between estimates of the total antarctic population of crabeater seals (Lobodon carcinophagus). Eklund (1964) estimated the population as 5 million to 8 million, while Erickson et al. (1971), assumed density estimates for one region to be true for the entire antarctic pack ice and proposed the range as being 50 million to 75 million. Gilbert and Erickson (1977) have since produced an intermediate estimate, but the point remains; with low and irregular coverage of the population, really satisfactory estimates are not feasible.

    Without adequate and repeated surveys of population abundance, there really is no firm basis for implementing management measures or for appraising any of the problems suggested above. Invariably it will be suggested that some relative measure of abundance, probably obtained from harvest data and generally based on catch per unit information, will suffice. However, there is reason to suppose that such index techniques may not be satisfactory. For example, consider the substantial controversy over status of harp seal stocks in the Northwest Atlantic (summarized in IUCN Bulletin Vol 8 (3), (1977). Such instances provide good evidence of the weaknesses of management procedures which depend solely on use of an index, rather than an actual estimate of numerical abundance.

    We now have over twelve years of experience with intensive censusing of Weddell seals (Leptonychotes weddelli) in part of McMurdo Sound (Stirling, 1971 a.b.c; Siniff et al. 1977). This data, combined with a longer span generated by

New Zealand and U.S. investigators at the same location, makes
it abundantly clear that any real accuracy in management will
call for a very substantial census effort over large regions.
An essential question that we have not yet been able to demonstrate experimentally in the McMurdo study, is how the "self-
regulatory" mechanism in Weddell seal populations functions.
Suitable management (in fact, legal management under the U.S.
Marine Mammal Protection Act of 1972) requires such knowledge
since it is becoming rather evident that management legislation invoking concepts such as "optimum sustainable population" levels first requires understanding of maximum sustainable yield level.

B. Population Dynamics
    Marine mammals are characterized by relatively low repro-
ductive rates, are correspondingly long-lived, and thus, are
particularly vulnerable to over-exploitation. Although the
importance of age-structure information is well known, few
sets of representative data of this sort actually exist for
marine mammals. In addition, one critical item, almost uni-
versally lacking for marine mammals, is survival for the first
few years of life. Thus, there is a need for studies of what
might be called the "mechanics" of population dynamics analyses. Preliminary efforts have been prepared by Eberhardt and
Siniff (1977).

    These studies are particularly needed for evaluation of
the crucial issues of "optimal" population levels. Thus far,
much of the work on the relevant issues has tended to be done
in the terms of reference of fisheries research and management. We seriously question whether the models derived from
deterministic population growth curves and "stock-recruitment"
curves (which are in effect growth-curve models) can be depended on for appraisal of marine mammal populations. Much
more complex and more realistic models are available, but can
only be applied if suitable data are obtained.

    Most of the required parameters for the analysis of pop-
ulation dynamics can only be estimated from quite intensive
long term studies. Studies such as this are very expensive
if done over large areas. Thus, a prospect of exploiting
antarctic seals may need to be preceded by a combination of
locally intensive studies employing such tools as capture -
recapture analyses, plus a rather extensive, but well planned
and monitored harvest aimed at securing other essentials,
such as age structure, reproductive rates, age at first breeding, growth rates, and longevity.

C. Population Regulation
    The key issue in research, in modeling, and in manage-

ment of marine mammal populations may very well be that of
determining which regulatory processes play important roles
in marine mammal populations and how, or if, these roles
change through time. One of the key problems is the difficulty of carrying out experiments which require manipulation of
either the animals or the habitat in order to test hypotheses.
Several different cases need to be evaluated: 1) species that
have never been exploited (mostly in the antarctic), 2) species that are under continuing exploitation (e.g. fur seals
and some whales) and 3) species that were excessively exploited in the past, eventually excluded from exploitation, and
now are increasing (Holdgate, 1970, provides a useful review
of antarctic ecosystems in this light). The three cases are
very different, and require different kinds of research. It
should be noted that the opportunities for new knowledge
about natural populations are of great potential importance
to both scientific knowledge and management applications.
Few opportunities remain anywhere for the study of undisturbed populations. Conversely, few populations have been driven
to very low levels, and then left almost untouched in an essentially "pristine" environment, as is particularly true in
the subantarctic regions. There are thus, certain unique research opportunities still available in these regions but,
which may literally never recur.

We believe that the conceptual and analytical machinery
now available for research on population regulation should be
carefully examined for its applicability to circumstances per-
taining to marine mammals. Three classes of approaches may
be considered. One is that of conducting large scale experiments and/or manipulations in the field to test general hypotheses about regulations and other ecological relationships
(e.g. food-limited, socially limited, predator limited, etc.).
A second is to apply mathematical analyses, such as that embodied in the Lotka-Volterra equations and the many derivi-
tives thereof, to life history patterns typical of marine
mammal species. The third is the practical application of
models of density-dependence phenomena, exemplified by the
stock-recruitment models of fisheries management, using parameters reflecting marine mammal life history patterns (Eberhardt and Siniff, 1977).

A general model has recently been proposed for the sequence of regulatory events as a population increases towards
its asymptotic value (Eberhardt, 1977a). The sequence is:

IMMATURE MORTALITY RATES CHANGES		AGE OF FIRST REPRODUCTION SHIFTS		REPRODUCTIVE RATE OF ADULT FEMALES CHANGES		ADULT MORTALITY RATE CHANGES
IMMATURE MORTALITY RATES CHANGES	>	AGE OF FIRST REPRODUCTION SHIFTS	>	REPRODUCTIVE RATE OF ADULT FEMALES CHANGES	>	ADULT MORTALITY RATE CHANGES

It is proposed that these various events reflect in sequence
the most significant density-dependent factor as the population increases in size. Thus, increases in immature mortality rates are the first effect to come into play, followed by
a delay in the age of first breeding and so on. Rationale
for the model is that for long lived species with low reproductive rates, security of the fully adult population is the
key to persistence (Mertz, 1971, Keith, 1973). Adult survival is thus the last parameter to change with increasing numbers. Reproductive success in adult females is closely correlated with physical condition, and thus, very likely declines just before conditions reach the point where adult survival declines. It is fairly well-established that immatures
are most vulnerable to unusual severe environmental conditions, and are the first to suffer as high population levels
are approached. It is also likely that reductions in growth
rates ensue from the factors that lead to increased juvenile
mortality, so that the age of first breeding is delayed. Further details appear in Eberhardt (1977).

Harp seals (<u>Pagophila groenlandicus</u>) in the northwest
Atlantic provide an example of the problems faced in managing
polar marine mammals. Many observers feel the northwest
Atlantic population has been seriously over-exploited. Sergeant (1976) gives some background and the harvest record.

Space prohibits any detailed analysis of the present status of harp seal populations, and there are both uncertainties as to various estimated, and a number of points of controversy. The data (Sergeant, 1976) suggest that the maximum
sustainable harvest has been exceeded, and it may well have
been that the relatively high kill of adults and "bedlamers"
in the late 1950s and early 1960s was responsible.

Traditionally, harp seals have been harvested as very
young juveniles ("pups") before weaning. As with many pin-
nipieds, preweaning mortality is very low, being probably 5%
or less. If the model suggested above is correct, it seems
likely that the maxiumum sustainable yield of pups may occur
at a population level much closer to the maximum (asymptotic)
population level than previously suspected. This is because
removal, by harvest, of very young animals may preclude or at
least reduce the influence of, the operation of the first two
stages of the model suggested above. If sufficient survivors
are left, recruitment to the adult population may nonetheless
be adequate to sustain that population at a high level. Population regulation may then depend on the last two stages of
the model, which are believed to operate very near asymptotic
population levels.

The scheme suggested here may be most effective when density-dependent factors operating on immature and adult segments of the populations are, in effect, "decoupled." Two ways that this may occur can be suggested. One is if the immature classes are spatially separated from the adults, as appears to be the case with harp seals, at least seasonally. As second may apply to species reproducing on islands or compact mainland rookeries. We postulate that the density-dependent effect on young may be set in motion prior to weaning when high populations produce social pressure during lactation (e.g. Bryden, 1968). Young are weaned in generally poorer conditions and thus, environmental factors after weaning have a greater than usual influence on survival. Also, the density-dependent effects may operate on young just after weaning during their first feeding attempts, just because there are too many young animals for the food resources in the immediate vicinity of the colony. It seems categorically true that our poorest understanding of polar marine mammals, is of events at the time of weaning and dispersal of young, followed by the period leading up to recruitment into the adult population. Considerable research is needed to support or refute the above postulates.

A model for pup harvesting can be constructed from the "Lotka equations" of population dynamics, in much the same way as they were used by Leslie (1966). As shown by Cole (1954), these equations can be used in discrete form when reproduction occurs in a single, relatively short period each year. For present purposes, we assume a stable age distribution and constant population size. Under these conditions, the essential equations are given by Eberhardt and Siniff (1977). Allen (1975) postulates a model of the kind suggested here, but assumes the density-dependent effect is on pregnancy rates, rather than on first-year survival. We note that there is a good deal of evidence for density-dependent effects operating on immatures (cf. the reviews by Huffaker, 1971 and by Keith, 1973). It is also true that an effect on pregnancy rates will call for rather complex analyses, inasmuch as the age-specific reproductive rates will then change with density (there is also reason to doubt that the density of pups will influence pregnancy rates of adult females as Allen postulates). At any rate, Allen's analysis seems to have a major flaw somewhere, since he calculates (p. 305) that "a sustained harvest from all age groups of 51% of the population" is possible. As Eberhardt and Siniff (1977) show, rates of increase of much more than 10% per year are not very likely for pinnipeds, so that sustainable yields beyond that level are improbable.

We have explored a model of the kind outlined above, and find that a linear density-dependent relationship between pup

numbers and pup survival rates to be unrealistic. Using a
non-linear function, modelled after the fur seal data discussed in Eberhardt and Siniff (1977), leads to the conclusion
that the structural details may not be particularly important.
What is crucial, of course, is to locate the population size
at which pup survival begins to decline sharply. This is the
determinant of the MSY point. Our major conclusion from such
an exercise is that it will be necessary to measure first-
year survival to obtain any practical harvesting scheme, if
this model holds. Such data are generally not available for
marine mammals. Probably it should be noted that the mere
observation of the growth rate of marine mammals will not
substitute for the kind of analysis discussed above.

RECREATIONAL AND AESTHETIC VALUES

One of the most popular issues in marine mammal management in recent years is an emphasis on aesthetic and recreational values. Ehrenfeld (1976) discusses the values connected with such concepts and further suggests approaches, incor-
porating these considerations in management plans. However,
this area is controversial because it requires value judge-
ments and each individual concerned with marine mammals may
emphasize different aspects when evaluating a particular situation. It seems to us that this is an area that needs extremely careful, objective attention by individuals with differing points of view. Some relevant questions that might be
included in this context are: are population size and aesthetic value related? If so, how? How does subsistence or
aboriginal hunting of marine mammals fit into the aesthetic
role and are the more primitive, but possibly less humane
methods of take, more or less aesthetic than modern techniques? In terms of the polar marine mammals, most of the
human population of the world will probably never observe
these animals in their natural state. Thus, should aesthetic
concepts for these populations have different connotations
than aesthetic values for populations which are observed daily
by thousands of people? Is a harvested population of more or
less aesthetic value than an unharvested population? These
questions open difficult areas which are in need of discussion
and understanding if aesthetic and recreational values are to
be seriously considered in management decisions.

We suggest that serious scientific research concerning
the values of and the likely impacts of tourism in polar
areas is long overdue, although some pragmatic aspects have
been suggested by Budowski (1976). What we have in mind,
however, is exemplified by our work with Weddell seals in
Southeastern McMurdo Sound. Before Scott base (New Zealand)
and McMurdo Station (United States) were built, the largest
Weddell seal pupping colony in McMurdo Sound was at Pram

Point and there were others nearby (Wilson, 1907). These
colonies are now gone. Stirling (1971b) suggested that the
Pram Point pupping colony was eliminated by overharvesting of
the adult component of the population and that recolonization
was precluded by continued harvesting at the same location.
An additional possibility is simply that continued human activity in the area has been adequate to discourage recolonization. Only through careful monitoring and experimentation
with such situations will we be able to determine the relative importance of such influences.

LITERATURE CITED

Allen, R.L. (1975) A life table for harp seals in the Northwest Atlantic. Rapp. P.V. Reun. Cins. Int. Explor. Mer 169: 303-311.

Bryden, M.M. (1968) Control of growth in two populations of elephant seals. Nature 217:1106-1108.

Budowski, G. (1976) Tourism and environmental Conservation: conflict, coexistence, or symbiosis? Environmental Conservation 3(1):27-31.

Cole, L.C. (1954) The population consequences of life history phenomena. The Quart. Rev. of Biology, 29:103-137.

Conference to Prepare and Agreement on the Conservation of Polar Bears. Oslo, Norway, 13-15, November, 1973. Final Act and Summary Record. Oslo, 1974. 50pp.

Clark, C.W. (1973) The economics of over exploitation. Science 181:630-634.

DeLong, R.L., W.G. Gilmartin and J.B. Simpson. (1973) Premature Births in California Sea Lions: Association with High Organochlorine Pollutant Residue Levels. Science 181:1168-70.

Eberhardt, L.L. (1977a) Optimal policies for conservation of large mammals with special reference to marine ecosystems. Environmental Conservation (In press).

Eberhardt, L.L. (1977b) Applied systems ecology: models, data and statistical methods. Simulation Councils (In press).

Eberhardt, L.L. and D.B. Siniff. (1977) Population dynamics and marine mammal management policies. Journal Fisheries Research Board Canada, 34(2):183-190.

Ehrenfeld, D.W. (1964) The conservation of non-resources, Am. Scientist 64:648-656.

Eklund, C.R. (1964) Population studies of Antarctic seals and birds. In: Biologie Antarctique, (R.Carrick, M. Holdgate and J. Prèvost, eds.) Hermann, Paris, pp 415-419.

Erickson, A.W., D.B. Siniff, D.R. Cline and R.J. Hofman.(1971) Distributional Ecology of Antarctic seals. SCAR Symposium on Antarctic Ice and Water Masses. Tokyo, Japan, Sept.1970.

Gilbert, J.R. and A.W. Erickson (1977) The biology and distribution of seals in Antarctic packice. In: Proc. 3rd Symposium on Antarctic Biology. Washington, D.C. G. Llano, ed. (In press).

Helle, E., M.Olson, and S. Jensen. (1976a) DDT and PCB levels in ringed seal from the Bothian Bay. Ambio, 5:188-189.

Helle, E., M. Olson, and S. Jensen. (1976b) PCB levels correlated with pathological changes in seal uteri. Ambio 5: 261-263.

Huffaker, C.B. (1971) The phenomenon of predation and its role in nature. In deBoer and Gradwell. (1971) Dynamics of Nos. in Populations. Proc. of the Adv. Study Instl, Oosterbeek, Netherlands, Sept. 1970.

Keith, L.B. (1973) Some features of population dynamics of mammals. Symposium: Population Ecology of Game Species. Stockholm, Sweden, 1972, pp. 19-57.

Leslie, P.H. (1966) The intrinsic rate of increase and the overlap of successive generations in a population of guillemots (Uria aalge Pont), J. Amm. Ecol. 35:291-301.

Margalef, R. (1973) Some critical remarks on the usual approaches to ecological modelling. Investigaciones Pesqueras 37(3):621-640.

Mertz, D.B. (1971) The mathematical demography of the California condor population. Am. Nat. 105:437-453.

Sergeant, D.E. (1974) A rediscovered whelping populations of hooded seals (Cystophora cristata Erxleben) and its possible relationship to other populations. Polarforschung 44(1):1-7.

Sergeant, D.E. (1976) History and present status of populations of harp and hooded seals. Biol. Conserv. 10:95-118.

Siniff, D.B., L.L., Eberhardt, D.P. DeMaster and R.J. Hofman (1977) An analysis of the dynamics of a Weddell seal population. Ecological Monographs (In press).

Stirling, I. (1971a) Population dynamics of the Weddell seal (Leptonychotes weddelli) in McMurdo Sound, Antarctica, 1966-68. Antarct. Res. Ser. Am. Geophys. Union 18:141-161.

Stirling, I. (1971b) Population aspects of Weddell seal harvesting in McMurdo Sound, Antarctica. Polar Record 15:653-667.

Wilson, E.A. (1907) Mammalia (seals and whales). In: National Antarctic Expedition, 1901-1904. National History, Zoology, Vol 2, p. 1-66.

The Physiology and Biochemistry of Low Temperature Adaptations in Polar Marine Ectotherms

8

Arthur L. DeVries

Visitors' impressions of the polar regions
are often those of great expanses devoid of life
and they are most impressed by the extremely low
temperatures, snow, ice and long periods of darkness. Close inspection of these regions even in
the wintertime reveals that life does exist, both
on the land as well as in the icy waters beneath
the thick sea-ice cover. Although the fauna of the
polar oceans are not as taxonomically diverse as
those of the temperate and tropical seas, they are
by no means lacking in numbers of organisms. The
numbers of individuals of certain species can be
enormous (Murphy, 1962; Andriashev, 1965) and in
some shallow water benthic communities the invertebrate fauna are relatively diverse (Dayton, et al.,
1974). From the relative abundance of certain
groups of marine organisms in the Arctic and
Antarctic Oceans, it is clear that they have adapted to the environmental extremes of low temperature,
ice and darkness. Those adaptations which have ensured survival of the polar forms at temperatures
near the freezing point of sea-water in some cases
are more readily apparent, and more easily studied
than in temperate counterparts which show seasonal
acclimatization to the cold. These low temperature
adaptations are the subject of this essay.

The mechanism of cold adaptation which permits survival of marine ectotherms at low temperatures can be divided into two general categories;
those which extend the lower temperature tolerances
of the organisms and, those which confer relatively
high levels of metabolism and growth on organisms.
The former are referred to as resistance adapta-

tions in contrast to the latter which are termed
capacity adaptations. Both of these types of
adaptations will be discussed.

The Polar Environments

In some respects the arctic and antarctic
polar marine environments are very similar. Both
are characterized by alternating periods of intense
light and darkness, low temperatures and thick ice
cover. However a number of interesting physical
distinctions can be made between the two areas
which have lead to different evolutionary responses
in the physiology and biochemistry of polar marine
organisms.

The Arctic Ocean is surrounded by several
relatively large and in some cases ice-free land
masses. The weather patterns over the near-shore
waters of this ocean are thus strongly influenced
by those of the adjacent land masses. Compared to
the antarctic, the climate of the terrestrial
arctic is rather temperate during the summer. As a
consequence the temperature of the coastal waters
of the Arctic Ocean are often several degrees warmer than those of the coastal waters of the
Antarctic Ocean. Ice cover near the shore is also
much reduced in the arctic during the summer and in
some ·of its areas the waters are ice-free.

Antarctica on the other hand is a land mass
surrounded by water on all coasts. Cold winds
generated on its high polar plateau blow toward
the coast with tremendous force and have a strong
cooling effect on the surrounding ocean. As a result, heat is continually being removed from the
water keeping it near its freezing point throughout the year, resulting in rapid growth of the
sea ice during the winter. The Antarctic Peninsula
however, is an exception to this generalization.
It is much warmer during both the summer and winter
because it extends well north of the Antarctic
Circle and is generally out of range of the cooling
effect of the winds from the polar cap. Thus, because of the geographical features, the climates of
the two polar marine areas are quite different.

The geography of the polar regions has a
tremendous effect on the climate which in turn affects the ice cover. The Arctic Ocean is covered

by a permanent floating thick ice sheet that drifts
around the Arctic Ocean during the winter and summer.   The coastline however is covered by fast ice
in general, only during the winter.   The coastal
areas of the antarctic are characterized by massive permanent ice shelves and thick sea-ice cover,
the latter which remains throughout the year except
for one or two of the warmest summer months.

A comparison between two polar marine stations
located at nearly the same latitude in the northern and southern hemispheres is useful for illustrating some of the more subtle differences between the two marine environments.   Point Barrow,
Alaska is north of the Arctic Circle and experiences 8,500 degree-days of cold per year (Lewis
and Weeks, 1971).   McMurdo Station, located on
McMurdo Sound, Antarctica is undoubtedly the coldest marine station in the world and experiences
13,300 degree-days of cold per year (Table 1).
The low temperatures of McMurdo Sound keep its
waters near the freezing point throughout the year.
The mean annual water temperature for the year of
1961 was $-1.86^{\circ}C$ and varied with depth and season
by only $0.1^{\circ}C$ (Littlepage, 1965).   The Sound is
ice-covered for 10 to 11 months out of the year
and by the end of the winter it is usually 3.0
meters thick.   At this time large aggregations of
ice crystals 2 mm in thickness and 10 to 15 cm in
diameter can be found frozen to the bottom at
depths down to 33 meters (Dayton, et al., 1969)
and have been termed anchor ice.   Ice platelet
aggregations also are found beneath the solid ice
where they form a continuous zone which often
grows to 3 meters in thickness.   Throughout the
winter congelation occurs in the upper part of
this crystal zone and it becomes indistinguishable
from the solid sea ice.   The water column is also
saturated with small ice crystals during much of
the winter and it is likely that in part the sub-
ice platelet layer results from the accumulation
of these small crystals.   During the late summer
the temperature of the water of McMurdo Sound
rises slightly, weakening the ice, and frequent
storms cause it to break into large flows that are
carried by currents into the Ross Sea.

The water temperatures near Point Barrow are
at their freezing point of $-1.7^{\circ}C$ during most of
the winter.   However the ice is thinner than that

Table 1. Physical data for marine environments at Point

Barrow, Alaska and McMurdo Sound, Antarctica.

Location	Water Temperature Summer Winter (°C)		Sea Ice Thickness (meters)	Months of Solid Ice Cover	Sub-ice Crystal Formations
Point Barrow, Alaska (71° 20'N)	+7	−1.7	2.0	6	reduced or absent
McMurdo Sound, Antarctica (77° 50'S)	−1.8	−1.9	3.0	10	thick mats of anchor ice and 3 meter thick sub-ice platelet layer

at McMurdo presumably because of year round warmer
temperatures. Anchor ice and sub-ice platelet
formations are greatly reduced or do not exist beneath the winter ice in the vicinity of Point
Barrow. The water temperature warms to +7°C during
the summer. Because of this large seasonal temperature variation in the arctic region, organisms
living there would be expected to exhibit somewhat
different physiological and biochemical responses
to thermal change over the course of the year than
their antarctic counterparts which live in a constant, near-freezing environment.

Resistance Adaptations

The temperatures of McMurdo Sound are cold
and there is little variation with season and although few studies have been done on the invertebrate and fish fauna, those that have been done
indicate that they are very stenothermal. The
large isopod, Glyptonotus antarcticus is reported
to have an upper incipient lethal temperature of
only +6°C (Menzies and George, 1968). Its lower
lethal temperature is only slightly less than the
freezing point of sea-water (-1.9°C, a temperature
at which its body fluids also freeze. In the absence of ice however, it can supercool to temperatures of -4 to -6°C without suffering any apparent
harm (Rakusa-Suszczewski and McWhinnie, 1976).
The same is true for several other benthic invertebrates such as the nemertinean, Lineus corrugatus,
the sea urchin Sterechinus sp. and the starfish,
Odontaster validus which inhabit McMurdo Sound.
The incipient lethal temperature of the small am-
phipod, Orchomene plebs is also similar to that of
the isopod (+6 to +8°C). No studies have been
done to demonstrate that warm acclimation leads to
changes in the upper thermal tolerances. Since
the upper lethal temperatures of some antarctic
fish do not change even after prolonged warm acclimation, it seems unlikely that warm acclimation
would alter the temperature tolerances of the invertebrates either. It is conceivable that
throughout the long evolutionary development in
the constantly cold waters of the antarctic these
marine ectotherms either lost or never developed a
capacity to compensate for thermal change.

The antarctic fish are some of the most stenothermal organisms in the animal world (Somero and

Table 2. Seasonal thermal tolerances of some arctic and
          antarctic ectotherms.

Species	Water Temp. and/or Thermal History (°C)	Incipient Lethal Temp. (°C)		Reference
		Lower	Upper	
ARCTIC				
Crustacea				
Gammaras locusta (amphipod)	0°	-1.7°	+20°	Scholander et al., 1953
Mesidothea entomon (isopod)	-1.7°	-1.7°	+20°	Scholander et al., 1953
Teleosti				
Eleginus gracilis	-1.7°	-1.8°	+15°	Raymond and DeVries, unpublished data
Boreogadus saida (summer)	+2° to +4°	-1.0°	+17°	Scholander et al., 1953
Pseudopleuronectes americanus (winter)	-1.7°	-1.5°	+18°	Duman and DeVries, 1974a
Pseudopleuronectes americanus (summer)	+18°	-0.7°	+27°	McCracken, 1963
ANTARCTIC				
Crustacea				
Orchomene plebs (amphipod)	-1.9°	-1.9°	+8°	DeVries, unpublished data
Glyptonotus antarcticus (isopod)	-1.9°	-1.9°	+6°	Menzies and George, 1968
Teleosti				
Rhigophila dearborni	-1.9°	-1.5°	+7°	DeVries, unpublished data
Rhigophila dearborni	Acclimated to +4°	-1.4°	+8°	DeVries, unpublished data
Trematomus borchgrevinki	-1.9°	-2.0°	+7°	DeVries, unpublished data
Trematomus borchgrevinki	Acclimated to +4°	-1.9°	+8°	DeVries, unpublished data

DeVries, 1967). The upper and lower thermal tolerances cannot be changed even after long periods of
cold or warm acclimation (Table 2). In the case
of the zoarcid fish, <u>Rhigophila</u> <u>dearborni</u>, this extreme stenothermy is especially interesting because
all the physiological studies done so far indicate
that it is not especially well adapted to the cold
in the sense that its resting metabolism is much
lower than that exhibited by the other antarctic
fish (Wohlschlag, 1964). However, Holeton (1974)
has pointed out that it is not clear how high
levels of oxygen consumption in the 'cold' confer
an advantage to organisms; this characteristic implies a high level of maintenance costs in terms
of energy. Freezing avoidance studies have also
shown that this zoarcid fish possesses only half as
much "antifreeze" as the endemic antarctic noto-
theniids which live at the same depth and temperature. It is interesting that Wohlschlag (1964)
noted that this species has greater geographical
affinities with the fish fauna of the temperate
oceans than with that of the Antarctic Ocean.
From this it can be inferred that this fish is
probably a recent immigrant to the antarctic. It
is possible that it has not been in the cold long
enough for the necessary physiological and biochemical changes to have evolved allowing it to
become completely cold adapted.

Variation in seasonal temperature in the arctic
marine environment is much greater than that in
the antarctic environment (Table 1) and intuitive-
ly one would expect arctic ectotherms to be less
stenothermal than their antarctic counterparts.
Scholander and colleagues (1953) have shown this
to be the case with the marine fauna near Point
Barrow. Most of the invertebrates they studied
were active down to their freezing point of -1.8°C
and upon supercooling some were still active.
Their response to low temperature is similar to
that of the antarctic forms in this respect.
Their responses to elevated temperatures are, however, different than those of the antarctic forms.
Amphipods and isopods collected from the ocean
near Point Barrow can tolerate temperatures as
high as 20°C, however they die at 25°C (Scholander
et al., 1953). Although the upper lethal tempera-
tures have not been well defined for many of these
species their upper thermal tolerances are clearly
much higher than those reported for the antarctic
forms.

Fish in the arctic region also show much higher upper temperature tolerances. The saffron cod, Eleginus gracilis taken from $-1.7°C$ water in the winter has an upper incipient lethal temperature of approximately $+12°C$. After warm acclimation they are able to tolerate temperatures of approximately $+16°C$ (Raymond, 1976). Other species of fish taken from $-1.0°C$ water of the Bering Sea such as the sculpin, Myoxocephalus verrucosus can be transferred directly to $+13°C$ water and appear normal after 48 hours (Table 2). However, if transferred to $+15°C$ it will die in several hours. After several weeks acclimation to $+10°C$, its upper thermal tolerance rises and it can survive in $+17°C$ water (DeVries, 1976). Although the winter flounder, Pseudopleuronectes americanus and the atlantic tomcod, Microgadus tomcod are not strictly arctic forms they do experience thermal regimes similar to fish living in the arctic. In the winter these fish also live beneath the ice at the freezing point of seawater and both have lower upper and lower temperature tolerances than they do in the summer. For the flounder the thermal tolerance limits have been reasonably well defined and during summer the upper limit is $+19°C$ but after acclimation to $+18°C$ the upper limit rises to $+27°C$ (McCracken, 1963).

Freezing Avoidance

Marine ectotherms of polar oceans, like those from any other habitat, do not conserve their metabolic heat as heat loss occurs rapidly at their respiratory surfaces as well as through the body wall (Stevens and Sutterlin, 1976; Spigarelli et al., 1977). As a consequence, body temperatures of marine ectotherms are essentially the same as that of the surrounding environment (Smith, 1972). Because of this the use of elevated body temperatures as a mechanism for avoiding freezing is precluded and, an imperative adaptation for them is one that lowers the freezing point of their body fluids to, or below that, of the seawater in which they live. For the invertebrates, danger from freezing exists only in special circumstances because their body fluids contain as much or sometimes more salt than is present in seawater, although in slightly different proportions. The circumstances that lead to freezing in invertebrates are when they become trapped in the anchor

ice masses in the shallow waters of McMurdo Sound.
Others are in danger when they become exposed to
low air temperatures in the intertidal regions of
the arctic at low tide. The intertidal region in
Antarctica is poorly developed because it is usually covered by a thick layer of ice that persists
throughout the year (Hedgpeth, 1969). Entrapment
of invertebrates in the ice in McMurdo Sound usually occurs only when large masses of anchor ice
break away from the bottom and float to the under-
side of the solid sea ice. Here solidification of
the uplifted ice eventually occurs and it becomes
part of the solid sea ice. The less mobile invertebrates such as the pynogonids, sponges and
molluscs associated with the bottom where these
ice formations occur, cannot escape and eventually
freeze. Starfish and worms being somewhat more
mobile generally escape from the interstices of
the uplifted anchor ice and fall back to the bottom. Fish, being very motile, apparently are
seldom trapped and frozen in the uplifted anchor
ice in this manner.

The concentration of ions in body fluids of
fish is about one-third that found in body fluids
of the invertebrates or that of seawater, and
therefore it would appear that they would be in
danger of freezing at temperatures below -0.7° C.
The fact that many antarctic fish can rest on
large ice crystals at the freezing point of seawater indicates that they have developed a mechanism for avoiding freezing (Fig. 1). So far in all
of the fish observed living in ice-laden seawater
that have been thoroughly studied, freezing occurs
only when the temperature is lowered a few tenths
of a degree below the freezing point of seawater.
The solutes responsible for low freezing points
are not entirely due to sodium chloride, the major
blood salt present in all vertebrate blood, (Table
3), although such fish do have higher levels of
sodium chloride in their blood than do their temperate relatives. The solutes responsible for
most of the lowering of freezing points in polar
fish are macromolecules which possess unique antifreeze properties. These "antifreezes" act in a
non-colligative manner by lowering the freezing
point without affecting the melting point
(Scholander and Maggert, 1971; DeVries, 1971). In
the case of antarctic notyotheniids the antifreezes
are glycopeptides while in northern fish which

Table 3. The effect of temperature on blood freezing points

Species	Thermal History (°C)	Organismal Freezing Point (°C)
North Temperate & Arctic		
Winter		
Pseudopleuronectes americanus	-1.2°	-1.4°
Eleginus gracilis	-1.7°	-2.0°
Myoxocephalus scorpius	-1.2°	-1.7°
Pseudopleuronectes americanus	Acclimated to 14°C, 35 days	-0.7°
Summer		
Pseudopleuronectes americanus	+17°	-0.7°
Eleginus gracilis	+4°	-0.9°
Antarctic		
Winter		
Trematomus borchgrevinki	-1.9°	-1.9°
Rhigophila dearborni	-1.9°	-1.5°
Trematomus borchgrevinki	Acclimated to 4°C, 60 days	-1.8°
Rhigophila dearborni	Acclimated to 4°C, 60 days	-1.4°

and on levels of antifreeze in cold-water fish.

Blood Freezing Point (°C)	Cl⁻ mM/L	Freezing Point of Colloidal Fraction (°C)	Reference
-1.37°	178	-0.65°	Duman and DeVries 1974a
-2.1°	240	-1.0°	Scholander and Maggert, 1971
-1.7°	200	-0.79°	Duman and DeVries 1974a
-0.7°	150	0°	Duman and DeVries 1974a
-0.7°	147	0°	Duman and DeVries 1974a
-0.9°	180	0°	Raymond, 1976
-2.7°	238	-1.3°	DeVries, unpublished data
-1.9°	243	-0.7°	DeVries, unpublished data
-2.5°	216	-1.3°	DeVries, unpublished data
-1.6°	205	-0.6°	DeVries, unpublished data

Figure 1. The naked dragon fish, *Gymnodraco acuticeps*, resting on bottom of McMurdo Sound in 10 meters of water. The ice crystals of the anchor ice mat provide a safe refuge in which this fish can escape predaceous seals and wait for small juvenile fish to swim by.

have been examined they are glycopeptides in some
species and peptides in other species (Raymond, et
al., 1975; DeVries, 1976). In antarctic nototheni-
ids the glycopeptide antifreezes account for slightly more than half of the observed freezing point
depression of the blood. They are also present in
other body fluids, such as coelomic fluid, peri-
cardial fluid and intracellular fluid, but they are
not present in bile, vitreous humor or urine. They
are not present in urine because these fish have
kidneys lacking glomeruli (Dobbs, et al., 1974;
Dobbs and DeVries, 1975a) and urine formation
therefore involves only secretion (Dobbs and
DeVries, 1975b).

The glycopeptides are very simple compounds.
They are composed of the two amino acids, alanine
and threonine and the two sugars, galactose and
N-acetylgalactosamine (DeVries, et al., 1970).
Their structure is shown in Figure 2. The glyco-
peptides occur in blood in several sizes ranging in

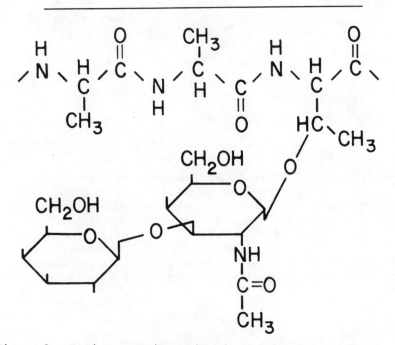

Figure 2. Basic repeating unit of glycopeptide antifreeze
molecules. The peptide backbone is composed of two amino
acids, alanine and threonine in the sequence of -ala-ala-
thr- with a disaccharide of galactose and N-acetylgalactosamine attached to every threonine.

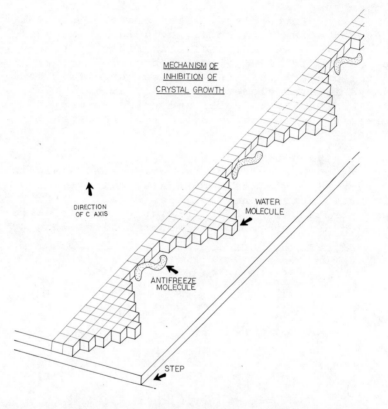

Figure 3. A model illustrating adsorbed antifreeze molecules at the step on the face of an ice crystal. The
bound antifreeze molecules force water molecules to join the
ice lattice between the adsorbed molecules resulting in
growth in the form of areas of high curvature. In order for
ice to grow in an area of high curvature, the temperature
must be lowered. This is the same as lowering the freezing
point. Water molecules are diagramatically illustrated as
cubes.

molecular weight from 2,600 to 33,000 daltons (Lin, et al., 1972). The different sizes can be account- ed for by the presence of different numbers of the basic repeating unit,

-alanyl-threonyl-alanyl-

O

disaccharide

as shown (Fig. 2). The smaller ones not only dif- fer in size but also have proline residues replac- ing some of the alanine residues in the repeating subunit (Lin, et al., 1972). These glycopeptides are expanded molecules and appear to have a structure which presents a large surface area that can interact with ice or water (DeVries, 1974). The mechanism by which the glycopeptides lower the freezing point of water as well as prevent ice from forming in fluids of the fish is not fully understood. However, studies of their freezing and melting behavior indicate that they probably exert their effect at the ice-water interface (Raymond and DeVries, 1972). Recent work with an in vitro system has demonstrated that binding to the surface of ice occurs, and that it is an im- portant requirement for antifreeze activity, Lin, et al., (1976). Recently a model (Fig. 3) has been proposed whereby binding to the surface of ice inhibits ice growth by forcing the ice to grow in areas of high curvature (Raymond and DeVries, 1977). The effect of such constraint on the pat- tern of crystal growth is that a lower temperature is required for growth to occur. In other words the freezing point is lowered.

In arctic and north-temperate fish both glyco- peptide and peptide antifreezes have been identi- fied. In the saffron cod, E. gracilis, a group of glycopeptides with antifreeze properties have been isolated and characterized and they are in many respects similar to those isolated from antarctic nototheniid fish (Raymond, et al., 1975). They differ in being less potent antifreeze agents and in composition. These agents contain significantly more of the amino acids proline and arginine than do the antarctic glycopeptides. In the arctic sculpin, Myoxocephalus verrucosus, the antifreeze is a group of different sized peptides composed of only 12 different amino acids. Alanine accounts for sixty percent of the amino acid residues pres-

ent (Raymond, et al., 1975). Both the winter
flounder, P. americanus, and the alaskan plaice,
Pleuronectes quadrituberculatus, have peptide
antifreezes (Duman and DeVries, 1976; DeVries,
1976). They are the simplest of the peptide antifreezes consisting of only 7 amino acids with
alanine making up two-thirds of the residues.
Most of the remainder are the polar amino acid
residues threonine, serine, aspartic and glutamic
acid (Duman and DeVries, 1976). The structure of
the peptide antifreeze has recently been determined and is given in Figure 4. It is of interest
because of the repeating sequence of leu-thr-ala-
ala-asp-(ala)$_6$. The spacing between the two polar
residues threonine and aspartic acid is equal to
some of the spacings between the oxygen atoms in
the ice lattice. As with the glycopeptides, the
peptides are small (average molecular weights are
approximately 6,000) and they have expanded structures. Circular dichroism studies indicate that the
peptide antifreeze from winter flounder exists as
a rod that has a helical content of 90 percent
(Ananthanarayanan and Hew, 1977; Raymond and
DeVries, 1977). Although it has been demonstrated
that glycopeptide antifreezes are expanded structures it is not possible to establish with certainty
whether they have helical conformations with repeat
distances represented in the ice lattice (Raymond
and DeVries, 1977). Despite the fact that the
peptides and glycopeptides are structurally very
different, they appear to lower the freezing point

NH$_2$-ASP-THR-ALA-SER-ASP-ALA-ALA-ALA-ALA-ALA-ALA-LEU
-THR-ALA-ALA-ASP-ALA-ALA-ALA-ALA-ALA-ALA-LEU
-THR-ALA-ALA-ASP-ALA-ALA-ALA-COOH

Figure 4. The primary structure of the peptide antifreeze
isolated from the blood of the winter flounder,
Pseudopleuronectes americanus. Most of the amino acid
residues are alanines and the polar residues threonine,
serine and glutamic acid.

of water in the same way (Raymond and DeVries, 1977).

Isolation and characterization of different types of antifreezes employed by fish to avoid freezing has only recently begun. Structural investigations of the different types of antifreeze and elucidation of how the different types function to produce the same effect on the freezing point of water are potential areas for further research.

Seasonal Patterns of Freezing Avoidance

The effects of elevated temperatures on the freezing points of southern and northern polar fish are quite different. A few antarctic fish experience temperatures as high as $+1^{\circ}C$; however these fish inhabit the northern-most part of the Antarctic Peninsula region and one would expect that they might lack, or have reduced levels of, antifreeze during this period. Few studies have been done with these fish and the extent to which elevated temperatures affect their levels of antifreeze is not known. In contrast fish inhabiting McMurdo Sound do not experience water temperatures above $-1.0^{\circ}C$ and therefore the presence of an antifreeze is always necessary for survival. Thermal acclimation in the laboratory has little affect on their freezing points as well as on the amount of antifreeze present in their blood. Acclimation to $+4^{\circ}C$ for 60 days raises the freezing point of the antarctic nototheniid and zoarcid fish blood by only 0.2 to $0.3^{\circ}C$ (Table 3). Almost all of the observed changes can be attributed to decreases in the concentration of sodium chloride in blood. The levels of glycopeptide antifreeze do not appear to change as indicated by similar freezing points of the colloidal fraction (non-dialyzable fraction) of blood before and after acclimation. Thus the levels of antifreeze in the fish of McMurdo Sound appear to be genetically fixed and cannot be modulated by thermal change. There is one possible explanation for the lack of change with warm acclimation that should be mentioned; namely, the antifreeze molecules may turn over so slowly that 60 days of warm acclimation is not sufficient time to observe a measurable loss in concentration of antifreeze even though elevated temperatures may have "turned off" synthesis of the molecules. Direct measurement of

the turnover rate of glycopeptides should yield
information as to whether the latter possibility
is the case.

In arctic and northern temperate fish the
presence of peptide and glycopeptide antifreezes
and their ability to avoid freezing are seasonal
(Gordon et al., 1962). In summer the blood of
winter flounder, P. americanus freezes at $-0.7^{\circ}C$
while during winter it freezes at $-1.4^{\circ}C$ (Duman
and DeVries, 1974a). If flounder collected during
the winter are acclimated to $+12^{\circ}C$ their freezing
point rises to $-0.7^{\circ}C$ in approximately 10 days
(Duman and DeVries, 1974b). The rise in freezing
point can be correlated with a slight decrease in
the concentration of blood sodium chloride and the
complete loss of antifreeze peptides. Similar
changes also occur in the blood of saffron cod, E.
gracilis during summer or upon warm acclimation of
fish collected in winter (Raymond and DeVries,
1977).

The seasonal glycopeptide and peptide antifreeze system present in northern fish appears to
be a system that has much potential for future
studies, especially in the field of control of
protein synthesis. The characteristics of this
system that make it attractive for study are the
fact that gene products (peptides and glycopeptides) are present in very high concentrations in
blood and therefore their m-RNAs should also be
present in high concentration in liver, the site
of their synthesis. Since low temperature appears
to "turn on" synthesis of the antifreezes in
northern fish, it should be possible to establish
whether temperature affects protein synthesis at
the level of transcription or translation. Because of the ease with thich appearance of the
gene product is measured and the presence of large
amounts of its m-RNA, it should be possible to determine whether low temperatures lead to changes
in the amount of antifreeze m-RNA present, or only
to changes in the rate at which amino acids are
translated into protein from the m-RNA.

Capacity Adaptation

Low environmental temperatures pose unique
problems for marine ectotherms because with the
reduction of chemical and kinetic energy that oc-

curs, rates of biochemical reactions are significantly reduced. Despite the rate-depressing effects of low temperatures on biochemical reactions, numerous ectotherms are still very active at temperatures down to the freezing point of the ocean. By this we mean that they are sufficiently active to obtain food which they metabolize producing energy and substrates for growth and reproduction. Generally high rates of oxygen consumption are indicative of high rates of growth and reproduction. Comparison of the rates of metabolism of tropical, temperate and polar fish at similar temperatures indicates that polar fish have managed to adjust their biochemical machinery to compensate for the rate depressing effects of low temperatures (Fig. 5). At $5^{o}C$ the arctic forms show an upward displacement in their metabolic rate of about 3 times that found in temperate forms at the same temperature. In the antarctic nototheniid fish the upward displacement at $5^{o}C$ is about 5 times.

In polar fish this high degree of metabolic cold adaptation is not only characteristic of the whole organism (Scholander et al., 1953; Wohlschlag, 1964) but also of isolated tissues (Peiss and Field, 1950; Somero et al., 1968; Lin et al., 1974). The biochemical mechanisms underlying these high levels of cold adaptation have not been elucidated. However they most surely involve changes at the enzymatic level, because the metabolism of an organism arises from the sum total of the activities of its enzymes. In antarctic fish the high level of cold adaptation extends down to the molecular level as evidenced by the fact that at $-2^{o}C$ the enzymes of Trematomus appear to be more efficient catalysts than enzymes from temperate fish (Somero 1969a). The way in which some of these biochemical adjustments might occur have recently been reviewed (Hochachka and Somero, 1973). The changes suggested include evolution of enzyme variants whose activities are less affected by decreases in temperature, increases in the amount of a given enzyme present, and alteration in the control of activities of enzymes. Thus far, there are few studies that give reliable data which permit one to distinguish which of these three changes are responsible for cold adaptation at the enzymatic level in polar marine forms.

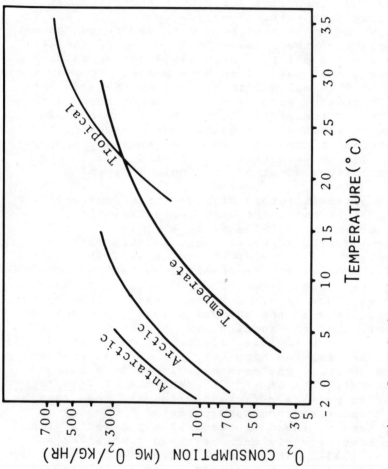

Figure 5. Relationship between temperature and metabolic rate (oxygen consumption) of tropical, temperate and polar marine fish (Modified after Wohlschlag, 1964).

Other changes in metabolic pathways appear to have taken place during the evolution of antarctic ectotherms in their near-freezing environments. One notable change is that carbohydrate substrates are metabolized principally via the hexose mono-phosphate shunt rather than predominantly through the glycolytic pathway (McWhinnie et al., 1975). The hexose monophosphate shunt produces less energy and is also a strictly oxidative pathway. Use of this pathway results in production of the coenzyme NADPH, a form of reducing power needed for synthesis of lipids. This pathway also yields pentose sugars which are important starting materials for the synthesis of cell membranes and genetic materials. Although definitive data are wanting, it is possible that the observed metabo-lism of carbohydrate via the hexose monophosphate shunt has little to do with cold adaptation and is instead, a response to requirements for synthesis of lipid and genetic material for reproduction in organisms which derive energy primarily from oxi-dation of ingested food which is very rich in lipid. The large lipid depots in antarctic fish and its occurrence in large amounts in tissues of many members of the antarctic food chain suggests that lipids are the primary substrate metabolized for production of energy. In the case of antarctic fish, lipids not only appear to be the major energy source, but they also play a role in buoyancy. Pelagic antarctic fish lack swim blad-ders and in order to maintain their position in the water column, they must overcome the negative buoyancy resulting from the presence of carbohy-drate, protein and skeletal structures which have densities greater than seawater. In some of these pelagic fish depots of lipid have been identified in strategic locations and appear to compensate for the absence of lift usually supplied by the presence of gas filled swim bladders. In the antarctic smelt, <u>Pleuragramma antarcticum</u>, lipid sacs occur beneath the integument in the region of the pectoral fins and in muscle masses at the base of the dorsal and anal fins (DeVries and Eastman, 1977). These sacs contain pure triglyceride and their size and distribution are such that they make a substantial contribution to the buoyancy of this fish allowing it to feed in the midwaters of the Antarctic Ocean--an under-utilized ecological niche.

Effect of Warm Acclimation
on Metabolic Compensation

Antarctic fish are notable as they do not show
metabolic compensation upon warm acclimation.
Oxygen consumption levels of fish maintained at environmental temperatures and after warm acclimation
have been shown to be very similar when determined
at the same temperature (Wohlschlag, 1964). The
lack of compensation after warm acclimation has
also been noted at the tissue level. Rates of
oxygen consumption of gill and brain tissue from
warm acclimated Trematomus fish are similar to
those of environmental fish when both are measured
at $-2^{\circ}C$ (Somero, et al., 1968). Although no
studies have been done with arctic forms it is
likely that they will show seasonal adjustments in
their levels of metabolism because of the seasonal
thermal variation experienced in their environments.

In studies of temperate species that show metabolic compensation it appears that the effects of
changing temperature on metabolism have been in
part circumvented by evolution of different forms
of the same enzyme (isozymes) that are specialized
for function at different temperatures. When ocean
temperatures are cold molecular forms of the enzyme
which function best at low temperatures predominate
while when water temperatures are high another form
of the same enzyme predominates. Each form of the
enzyme appears to be less influenced by the rate-
depressing effects of temperatures in a temperature
range corresponding to its environmental temperature (Somero, 1969b). In antarctic ectotherms
there would be no requirement for high temperature
variants of enzymes because they always live in the
cold. If the antarctic fauna evolved from temperate ancestors that possessed "warm" and "cold" isozymes, then it appears that during the course of
evolution the capacity for elaborating "warm" isozymes was lost. The inability of zoarcid fish to
function at elevated temperatures and their failure
to acclimate to elevated temperatures seems consistent with the idea that loss of the capacity to produce isozymes can occur rapidly, if indeed this
fish is only a recent immigrant to the antarctic.

The lack of biochemical capabilities for thermal adjustments in antarctic forms leads one to suggest that these organisms may possess less genetic

material than those that have had to elaborate more
complex systems to accommodate seasonal temperature
changes. For example, as far as is known, temperature change has no effect on the rate of synthesis
or degradation of glycopeptide antifreezes in
antarctic fish, whereas its synthesis and degradation is a seasonal event in northern fish which
presumably is caused by temperature change. It
would seem that the latter system with its temperature sensitive control mechanisms would require
more biochemical machinery and associated genetic
material for its elaboration.

   The obligate stenothermy in antarctic ectotherms is of interest and the mechanisms underly-
it deserve further comment. The fact that these
forms cannot live at elevated temperatures implies
that their physiology and biochemistry differ
markedly from that of temperate forms which survive
low temperatures in winter and high temperatures
in summer. Although the biochemical basis of differences between the antarctic and temperate forms
have not been elucidated, it would seem likely
that enzymes and cell membranes of antarctic forms
are heat labile. Some data suggest that at elevated temperatures ($+7^{\circ}$C) lipids in cell membranes
of the central nervous system of antarctic fish
become liquid which results in cellular breakdown,
(Somero and DeVries, 1967). Loss of membrane in-
tegrity would certainly result in disruption of
ion concentration gradients that exist across them
and may be the basis of the heat death observed in
these forms. Similar changes do not appear to
take place in temperate forms over such a narrow
temperature range.

References

Ananthanarayanan, V.S. and Hew, C.L. (1977) Structural studies on the freezing-point-depressing protein of the winter flounder Pseudopleuronectes americanus. Biochem. Biophy. Res. Comm. 74:685-689.

Andriashev, A.P. (1965) A general review of the Antarctic fish fauna. Biogeography and Ecology in Antarctica, ed. J. Van Mieghem and P. van Oye, Junk, The Hague, pp.

Dayton, P.K., Robilliard, G.A. and DeVries, A.L. (1969) Anchor ice formation in McMurdo Sound, Antarctica, and its biological effects. Science 163:273-274.

Dayton, P.K., Robilliard, G.A., Paine, R.T. and Dayton, L.B. (1974) Biological accommodation in the benthic community at McMurdo Sound, Antarctica. Ecol. Monogr. 44:105-128.

DeVries, A.L. (1971) Fish glycoproteins as biological antifreeze in antarctic fish. Science 172:1152-1155.

DeVries, A.L. (1974) Survival at freezing temperatures. In Biochemical and Biophysical Perspectives in Marine Biology. eds. J. Sargent and D.C. Malins, Vol. I. pp. 289-330. Acad. Press, London.

DeVries, A.L., Komatsu, S.K. and Feeney, R.E. (1970) Chemical and physical properties of freezing-point-depressing glycoproteins from antarctic fish. Jour. Biol. Chem. 245:2901-2908.

DeVries, A.L. (1976) Antifreezes in cold-water fish. Oceanus 19:23-31.

DeVries, A.L. (1977) Unpublished data.

DeVries, A.L. and Eastman, J.T. (1977) Lipid sacs as a buoyancy adaptation in an antarctic fish. (submitted for publication).

Dobbs, G. H., Lin, Y. and DeVries, A. L. (1974) Aglomerularism in antarctic fish. Science 185:793-794.

Dobbs, G. H. and DeVries, A. L. (1975a) The aglomerular nephron of the antarctic teleosts: a light and electron microscopic study. Tissue and cell 7:159-170.

Dobbs, G. H. and DeVries, A. L. (1975b) Renal function in antarctic teleost fish: serum and urine composition. Marine Biol. 29:59-70.

Duman, J. G. and DeVries, A. L. (1974a) Freezing resistance in winter flounder Pseudopleuronectes americanus. Nature 247:237-238.

Duman, J. G. and DeVries, A. L. (1974b) The effect of temperature and photoperiod on antifreeze production in cold water fish. Jour. Exp. Zool. 190:89-97.

Duman, J. G. and DeVries, A. L. (1976) Isolation, characterization, and physical properties of protein antifreezes from the winter flounder, Pseudopleuronectes americanus. Comp. Biochem. Physiol. 54B:375-380.

Gordon, M. S., Amdur, B. N. and Scholander, P. F. (1962) Freezing resistance in some northern fish. Biol. Bull. 122:52-62.

Hedgpeth, J. W. (1969) Preliminary observations of life between tidemarks at Palmer Station, 64°45'S, 64°05'W. Antarct. Jour. U.S. 4:106-107.

Hochachka, P. W. and Somero, G. N. (1973) Strategies of Biochemical Adaptation. W.B.Saunders Company, Philadelphia.

Holeton, G. F. (1974) Metabolic cold adaptation of polar fish: fact or artifact? Physiol. Zool. 47:137-152.

Lewis, E. L. and Weeks, W. F. (1971) Sea ice: some polar contrasts. In Symposium on Antarctic Ice and Water Masses. ed. G. Deacon, pp. 23-34. Scientific Committee on Antarctic Research, Cambridge, England.

Lin, Y., Duman, J. G. and DeVries, A. L. (1972)
Studies on the structure and activity of low
molecular weight glycoproteins from antarctic
fish. Biochem. Biophys. Res. Commun. 46:87-
92.

Lin, Y., Dobbs, G. H. and DeVries, A. L. (1974)
Oxygen consumption and lipid content in red
and white muscles of antarctic fish. Jour.
Exp. Zool. 189:379-385.

Lin, Y., Raymond, J. A. and DeVries, A. L. (1976)
Compartmentalization of NaCl in frozen solutions of antifreeze glycoproteins. Cryobiol.
13:334-340.

Littlepage, J. L. (1965) Oceanographic investiga-
tions in McMurdo Sound, Antarctica. In
Biology of the Antarctic Seas. ed. M. O. Lee,
Vol. 2, pp. 1-37. Amer. Geophys. Union,
Washington, D.C.

McCracken, F. D. (1963) Seasonal movements of
winter flounder, Pseudopleuronectes americanus
(Walbaum), on the Atlantic Coast. Jour. Fish.
Res. Bd. Canada 20(2):551-586.

McWhinnie, M. A., Rakusa-Suszczewski, S. and
Cahoon, M. D. (1975) Physiological and metabolic studies of antarctic fauna, austral
1974 winter at McMurdo Station. Antarctic
Jour. of U.S. X:293-297.

Menzies, R. J. and George, R. Y. (1968) Investigations of isopod crustaceans of Erebus Bay,
McMurdo Sound. Antarctic Jour. of U.S. 3:129.

Murphy, R. C. (1962) The oceanic life of the
antarctic. Scientific American 207:186-210.

Peiss, C. N. and Field, J. (1950) The respiratory
metabolism of excised tissues of warm and
cold adapted fish. Biol. Bull. 99:213-224.

Rakusa-Suszczewski, S. and McWhinnie, M. A. (1976)
Resistance to freezing by antarctic fauna:
Supercooling and osmoregulation. Comp. Bio-
chem. Physiol. 54A:291-300.

Raymond, J. A. and DeVries, A. L. (1972) Freezing behavior of fish blood glycoproteins with antifreeze properties. Cryobiol. 9:541-547.

Raymond, J. A., Lin, Y. and DeVries, A. L. (1975) Glycoprotein and protein antifreezes in two alaskan fish. Jour. Exp. Zool. 193:125-130.

Raymond, J. A. (1976) Adsorption inhibition as a mechanism of freezing resistance in polar fish. Ph.D. dissertation, University of California, San Diego.

Raymond, J. A. and DeVries, A. L. (1977) Adsorption inhibition as a mechanism of freezing resistance in polar fish. Submitted for publication.

Scholander, P. F., Flagg, W., Walters, V. and Irving, L. (1953) Climatic adaptation in arctic and tropical poikilotherms. Physiol. Zool. 26:67-92.

Scholander, P. F. and Maggert, J. E. (1971) Supercooling and ice propagation in blood from arctic fish. Cryobiol. 8:371-374.

Smith, R. N. (1972) The freezing resistance of antarctic fish: I. Serum composition and its relation to freezing resistance. Br. Antarct. Surv. Bull. 28:1-10.

Somero, G. N. (1969a) Enzymic mechanisms of temperature compensation: immediate and evolutionary effects of temperature on enzymes of aquatic poikilotherms. American Naturalist 103:517-530.

Somero, G. N. (1969b) Pyruvate kinase variants of the alaskan king crab: evidence for a temperature-dependent interconversion between two forms having distinct and adaptive kinetic properties. Biochemical Jour. 114:237-241.

Somero, G. N. and DeVries, A. L. (1967) Temperature tolerance of some antarctic fish. Science 156:257-258.

Somero, G. N., Giese, A. C. and Wohlschlag, D. E.
    (1968) Cold adaptation of the antarctic fish
    <u>Trematomus</u> <u>bernacchii</u>.   Comp. Biochem.
    Physiol. <u>26</u>:223-233.

Spigarelli, S. A., Thommes, M. M. and Beitinger, T.
    L. (1977) The influence of body weight on
    heating and cooling of selected Lake Michigan
    fish.   Comp. Biochem. Physiol. <u>56A</u>:51-57.

Stevens, D. E. and Sutterlin, A. M. (1976) Heat
    transfer between fish and ambient water.
    Jour. Exp. Biol. <u>65</u>:131-145.

Wohlschlag, D. E. (1964) Respiratory metabolism
    and ecological characteristics of some fish
    in McMurdo Sound, Antarctica.   In, Biology of
    the Antarctic Seas.   ed. M. O. Lee, Vol. 1,
    pp. 33-62.   Amer. Geophys. Union.   Washington,
    D.C.

9

Terrestrial Adaptations in Polar Regions

Bruce C. Parker

Introduction

This paper presents (1) a non-comprehensive review of the terrestrial and aquatic (non-marine) biota of polar regions, (2) investigations conducted toward identifying and understanding adaptations of these biota, and (3) the trends in research which should lead to future directions in this area of polar biology. A select supplemental bibliography also is included.

Adaptations are properties of organisms which favor survival in a specific, usually stressful, environment (Prosser, 1964). Adaptations thus can be environmentally determined, as is any acclimation to an environmental variable by an organism. Also, adaptations can be genetically based variations; that is, permanent changes inherited through the genetic code (Prosser, 1964). Finally, adaptations can be at the subcellular (e.g., enzyme), cellular, tissue, organ, organism, or community and ecosystem levels.

While this paper includes the Arctic and Antarctic, one should not view these polar regions as identical or completely different. Indeed, often there is too little information to draw valid comparisons. Numerous nations with their indigenous human populations in or bordering on the Arctic have stimulated a vastly greater terrestrial biology information base than for the Antarctic, and undoubtedly this thrust in Arctic research will continue to out-distance that in the Antarctic at least in the near future. Also, year-round investigations have been and will continue to be common in the Arctic and rare in Antarctica where few biologists winter-over or find the logistic support adequate for year-round studies. Antarctic terrestrial biology is appreciably smaller in total effort than that of the Arctic, even more so because only about 4% of Antarctica has terrestrial life.

Table 1. List of Features of Arctic and Antarctic Terrestrial Ecosystems

	ARCTIC	ANTARCTIC
1. Temperature	Cold in winter	Colder in winter
2. Moisture	Relatively wet	Relatively dry
3. Radiation	Drastic seasonal fluxes	Drastic seasonal fluxes
4. Salinity	Lakes and soils not pronouncedly saline	Lakes and soils usually highly saline
5. Nutrient Limitations	Often nitrogen	Often nitrogen
6. Geography	Connected to non-polar regions	Disjoined from other land masses
7. Glaciation History	Quite recent (1–2 million years	Not recent (over 20 million years)
8. Diversity of Biota	Relatively high	Relatively low
9. Complexity of Communities & Ecosystems	Relatively high	Relatively low
10. Mechanisms of dispersal, colonization, productivity, energy flow, and evolution	Relatively more numerous, more complex, reflecting a shorter period of evolution	Relatively fewer, simpler, having evolved longer and closer to a steady state

Thus, despite some similarities, the environments of the two polar regions are quite different. The Antarctic continent lies within the Antarctic Circle (66°30'S), while only small parts of Alaska, Canada, Norway, the USSR and a larger part of Greenland lie within the Arctic Circle (66°30'N). In other words, McMurdo Station, Antarctica, is truly Antarctic, while Point Barrow, Alaska, tends more toward subarctic (Dunbar, in press). The Arctic resembles an ocean surrounded by fringes of continents, and Antarctica is a nearly totally ice-covered continent surrounded by the largest uninterrupted ocean on Earth. The Arctic ocean is a positive source of heat much of the year and a warm current. The continents extending into it also warm during the summer. In contrast Antarctica, with 90% of its solar energy re-radiated back into the atmosphere, is a heat sink. Antarctica's mean elevation (ca. 2000 m), as well as its generally higher southerly latitudes, dictate that it will be colder than the Arctic. Winters are longer in the Antarctic and summers colder. The Arctic has no sea barrier to the dispersal of biota. These points, in addition to those listed in Table 1, substantiate that important differences in terrestrial adaptations of the two polar regions will be found.

The Committee on Polar Research (1970) noted, "Research on any systematic basis into polar biology and medicine could be said to date back only twenty years or so, having been initiated under the impetus of World War II..." Thus, we are reviewing essentially 25-30 years of research for the Arctic and really only 20 years for Antarctica, representing the post-International Geophysical Year (1957-58) period. It may be added that, as far as antarctic science goes, biology was a minor by-product of the more than 150 pre-IGY expeditions (Heywood, 1972).

Terrestrial and Aquatic Biota
in Polar Regions

Table 2 summarizes the major groups and relative abundance of biota found on land and in aquatic environments (non-marine) of the arctic and antarctic. A major observation arising from this list is that the diversity of species and often their biomass in the arctic usually greatly exceeds that for Antarctica. Entire major groups are absent from Antarctica, such as, ferns, gymnosperms, fishes, amphibians, reptiles, and mammals (man included). As noted previously, only approximately 4% of the antarctic land mass supports even a sparse biota. These areas occur on the Antarctic Peninsula and adjacent islands, along the continental coast, in some inland mountain ranges and isolated mountain peaks, and within "oases" or "dry valleys" such as the Bunger Hills

Table 2. Comparison of Major Groups of Terrestrial and
Aquatic Biota Found in the Arctic and Antarctic

GROUP	ARCTIC	ANTARCTIC
I. Algae and Fungi		
Prokaryote bacteria	Abundant	Common
Bluegreen algae	Uncommon	Abundant
Euglenoids	Abundant	Rare
Green algae	Abundant (esp. conjugatae)	Common (conjugatae rare)
Diatoms & other chrysophytes	Abundant	Common
Dinoflagellates	Common	Essentially absent
Red algae	Uncommon	Essentially absent
Slime molds	Common	Rare
Fungi	Abundant	Common-Rare (yeasts abundant)
II. Land Plants		
Bryophytes	Abundant (high biomass)	Common in select areas of high moisture: low species diversity and biomass
Lichens	Abundant (high biomass)	Common in select areas of high moisture: low species diversity and biomass
Ferns	Common	Absent
Gymnosperms	Common	Absent
Angiosperms	Abundant (esp. perennial herbs)	Only two native and one introduced
III. Animals		
Protozoa	Abundant	Common
Rotifers	Abundant	Common in aquatic environments
Nematodes	Abundant	A few species common in aquatic environments
Annelids	Abundant	Essentially absent (except Peninsula)
Tardigrades	Abundant	Several species common in aquatic environments
Fishes	Common (in deeper lakes)	Absent
Amphibians	Rare	Absent
Reptiles	Rare	Absent
Birds	Abundant	Abundant (lower diversity)
Mammals	Abundant	Absent

and parts of South Victoria Land. Within these ice-free
areas one finds beach sands and gravels, rocky cliffs, glacial moraines, lakes with permanent, seasonal, or no ice
cover, totally frozen lakes, ponds and pools, summer melt-
streams generally of small size and varying seasonality. In
some of these environments the biota of terrestrial Antarctica, namely Microbiota, Cryptogamia, Arachnida, and Insecta
develop luxuriantly. However, in a number of locations no
trace of life can be detected (Greene et al., 1967).

The Arctic, by contrast, is wet and biologically luxuri-
ant over vast areas which have been aptly described by
Wiggins (1953) in reference to Alaska:

> The tundra is carpeted with a dense growth of low
> perennial vegetation, composed mostly of prostrate
> shrubs, herbs, grasses, sedges, mosses, and lich-
> ens. The ponds, lakes and wet surfaces of the
> soil support a large number of algae. Thousands
> of birds nest on the tundra, myriads of insects and
> mites inhabit the peaty "active layer," and popu-
> lations of small mammals as lemmings, foxes,
> weasels, and shrews occur in varying numbers near
> Point Barrow. Farther inland, particularly in the
> rolling foothills of the Brooks Range (between 68°
> and 69° N), such additional mammals as the barren-
> ground grizzlies, caribou, arctic squirrels, voles,
> wolves, marmots and wolverines occur.

This great variety of biota in the arctic and the considerably less diversified selection in Antarctica have,
thus, been the sources and focuses of studies of adaptations
in polar regions. Of course, no organism has been so intensively studied that all details of its adaptation mechanism,
from genetic code -- to adaptation -- to result of adaptation, can be told. Nevertheless, progress has been significant in both polar regions, especially adaptations to such
stresses as limiting moisture or desiccation, high salinity,
low temperature, high radiation (e.g., ultraviolet), prolonged darkness, nutrient deficiencies, and possibly toxic
trace elements.

Adaptations of Antarctic Dry Valley
Soil Microorganisms

Investigations of soil microbial ecology in Antarctica
have placed considerable emphasis on the dry valleys of
South Victoria Land within easy reach by helicopter from
McMurdo Station where an adequate microbiology laboratory
facility exists. In contrast, other antarctic dry valley
areas such as the Bunger Hills, Schirmacher Ponds, or the
Vestfold Hills, have received less attention.

Table 3.   Contributions to Antarctic Dry Valley
Soil Microbial Ecology

---

1. Some soils abiotic, lacking detectable organisms.

2. NH_4-N often dominant N source.

3. Boron perhaps toxic in some soils.

4. Psychrophilic bacteria and psychrophilic halophiles isolated (some claim).

5. One Antarctic halophile behaved as a xerophile.

6. Viable soil microorganisms increase during austral summer.

7. Chromogenic bacteria dominate near surface, non-chromogenic forms dominate below.

8. Bluegreen and green algae from Antarctica have higher rates of viability on freezing than similar species from Wisconsin.

9. Greatest numbers of organisms occur at ice-cemented surface.

10. Bluegreen algae are chief primary producers in soils.

11. Best isolation medium so far contains peptone and yeast extract.

12. Numerous viable microorganisms occur in ice-cemented permafrost.

13. Diesel fuel-contaminated soils develop vastly different microbial communities. $CaCl_2$ contaminated soils exhibit low diversity.

14. Semitransparent orthoquartcite rocks often have internal spaces colonized by bluegreen algae.

15. Limiting factors are moisture, salts, temperature, and organic substrate.

The soils of South Victoria Land exhibit wide variations in their physical, chemical, and microbiological character- istics. The climate of this region (lat. 77°10' S, long. 161° E) is that of a frigid desert: mean annual temperature, -18°C; total annual precipitation, 15.0 cm of water; mean summer temperature, -3.1°C (Heywood, 1972). The microcli- mate, however, is extremely variable from site to site, based on such variables as orientation of major slopes, exposure, extent of incline, solar radiation, wind direction and hu- midity content, drainage, proximity to glaciers, etc.

Soils in the youngest moraines often are grey to pale yellow, possess a coarse sandy texture, are low in salts and free iron oxides, contain 15% moisture by weight during the austral summer, and have ice-cemented permafrost at shallow depths (i.e., 8.0 cm). At the other extreme are soils of the older moraines; these are brown, sandy but with some clay (6%), high in soluble salts and with some carbonates, 1% free iron oxide, a moisture content of 1.5%, and an ice-cemented permafrost perhaps 70 cm below the surface (Ugolini, 1970). In such locations often the salts are visible at the surface and include such evaporite minerals as mirabilite, $Na_2SO_4.10H_2O$ (thenardite, Na_2SO_4), antarctocite ($CaCl_2.6H_2O$), and/or gypsum, $CaSO_4.2H_2O$ (anhydrite, $CaSO_4$). In summer, South Victoria Land soils can warm to about 13°C at the sur- face and can reach above freezing temperatures down to 15 cm, which if within the depth of the ice-cemented layer, provides moisture for the upper dry soil (Ugolini, 1970).

Highlights of research on antarctic dry valley soils and their microbial ecology are listed in Table 3. Information in this table suggests a number of adaptations to such stresses as the paucity of moisture or desiccation, high salt accumulations, low temperature and freeze-thaw cycles, low organic matter or humic content, high intensity radiation, and perhaps toxic substances. On further investigation, it may be shown that many of these adaptations represent natural inherent plasticity (broad tolerance limits) by the organisms rather than specific adaptive mechanisms. For example, Cameron et al. (1970) have shown that certain groups of ter- restrial dry valley organisms are more tolerant to unfavor- able environmental conditions than others (their Figure 6). Table 3 also reveals that there is contradiction as to wheth- er halophiles represent true, obligate halophiles rather than halotolerant forms (Hall, 1968; Benoit and Hall, 1970; Imshenetsky et al., 1973), or whether obligate psychrophiles occur in antarctic dry valley soils (Boyd et al., 1966; Hall, 1968; Benoit and Hall, 1970; Cameron in press). Apparently no one has investigated the reason for the apparent adapta- tion which involves a dominance of pigmented (chromogenic)

Table 4. Comparison of Some Properties of Arctic and Antarctic Lakes

	ARCTIC	ANTARCTIC
1. Numbers of lakes	Abundant	Relatively few
2. Morphometry	High diversity	Low diversity
3. Associated streams, rivers	Numerous	Few, small
4. Thermal regime	Often ice cover in winter, surface water 10-16°C in summer	Ice-covered permanently, partially, or never: few reaching 10°C
5. Allochthonous matter	Many receive, humic	Rarely receive
6. Summer thermal stratification	Common	Uncommon
7. Salinity	Few highly	Many highly
8. Permafrost melt regime	More deeply, fresh	Shallow or not at all, saline
9. Biota in general	Richer	Poorer
10. Attached macrophytes	Numerous	Mosses in a few lakes only
11. Algae	Rich, great diversity	Poor, planktonic forms often absent
12. Attached algae	Conjugatae common, bluegreens scarce	Bluegreens common, conjugatae seldom present
13. Phytoplankton	Nannoplankton dominate, adapted to low light beneath ice	Nannoplankton dominate, probably adapted to low light beneath ice
14. Productivity	Generally very low	Generally very low
15. Fauna	More diverse. Incl. fishes	Low diversity, low biomass, often practically absent

bacteria in the surface layers of dry valley soils and their
paucity to virtual absence in deeper layers; it is intriguing, however, to postulate here some form of adaptation to
the high ultraviolet radiation fluxes which occur in this
region during the austral summer. Yet another adaptation
largely overlooked is the inherent ability of an organism in
its vegetative stage to "shut down" metabolically, that is
to enter periods of prolonged inactivity and thus conserve
energy sources. The often lengthy lag phase for visible
growth of many Antarctic soil microorganisms suggests this
adaptation does indeed exist (Parker, unpublished).

As with the antarctic, no doubt numerous studies on
arctic soil microorganisms will continue. However, in the
Arctic, studies should have broader focus. They will include
the growing interest in nitrogen fixation, as exemplified by
Alexander et al. (1974) and Alexander and Schell (1973). The
higher moisture, high organic matter content, generally
milder climate and current land use of the Arctic also will
encourage further studies of nutrient cycles and decomposition rates (Bunnel, 1973) and increasing studies of crude oil
spill effects (Campbell, Harris, and Benoit, 1973).

Adaptations in Polar Lakes

Fewer lakes occur in Antarctica and generally less is
known of them relative to the Arctic although the generalizations cited in Table 4 are probably quite accurate. Regarding Antarctic lakes Bardin (1963) notes that Russian field
parties discovered lakes in mountains protruding through the
continental ice sheet in areas of Dronning Maud Land many
miles from the coast. These lakes apparently did not freeze
solid during winter even though the region has an annual mean
temperature of -55°C. Apparently ice cover is too thick on
these lakes to permit their study. Instead, lakes which have
been studied are found within the continental inland ice-free
"oases" or "dry valleys," continental coastal areas and adjacent islands, or the Antarctic Peninsula and adjacent
islands (Heywood, 1972). Lake Bonney is one of the several
more interesting lakes which has been investigated (Craig
et al., 1975, 1976; Fortner et al., 1976; Hoehn et al., *in*
press; Parker et al., *in* *press*; Weand et al., 1976). It
is a permanently ice-covered lake in South Victoria Land
(lat. 77°45' S., long. 160°20'-163°00' E) and reveals a number of organism adaptations which, most likely, occur in
other lakes in both polar regions. These adaptations involved microorganisms; in fact, the most complex organisms in
Lake Bonney are a few tardigrades, rotifers, and nematodes.

Chromatic Adaptation by Algae in Lake Bonney

Lake Bonney contains a large biomass of attached benthic algal mats dominated by certain blue-green algae. Now,
the phenomenon of chromatic adaptation in bluegreen algae is
well-known throughout the world. However, it achieves a
high level of development in this lake. The best developed
algal mats in Lake Bonney are up to 3.0 cm thick and about
5 years old (Sugg and Parker, unpublished). During the early
austral summer as these mats initiate growth, they often become pink on the upper surface and a deep bluegreen beneath
progressing to black on the anaerobic bottom surface. The
predominant pink pigment apparently is phycoerythrin, an accessory pigment in photosynthesis which absorbs green light
more efficiently than chlorophyll and, therefore, enhances
the photosynthesis of these surface algal mats under early
season, low light conditions. By the peak of the austral
summer, a large number of mat pieces exhibit an orange pig-
mentation on the upper surface. This is a second type of
chromatic adaptation where bright light has induced the
production of an excess of carotenoid pigment which acts to
shield the chlorophyll from light injury. In both instances,
the algal species involved are essentially the same.

Chromatic adaptation also has been observed by others in
polar regions (Fogg and Horne, 1970). Llano (1967) observed
the end result of this phenomenon in antarctic green snow algae at Wilkes Station (now Casey), Antarctica. The green
algae, apparently in response to increasing light intensity,
developed an excess of red (probably carotenoid) pigment and
flourished for some weeks in the snow. The physiological
ecology of this form of chromatic adaptation has not been
examined in detail. However, we know that the red-pigmented
snow algae on the Antarctic Peninsula occupied snow at 2-3°C,
while green snow algae in the same snow bank measured only
1°C (Samsel and Parker, unpublished). This observation supports the theory that the red pigment may be an adaptation
to aid warming of the snow such that the algae can obtain
nutrient and grow more rapidly.

Adaptations of Aquatic Microorganisms to Cold Temperature

Lane (1975) isolated two psychrophilic bacteria from
Lake Bonney; these may not have been obligate psychrophiles.
However, Stanley and Rose (1967) isolated psychrophilic bac-
teria, yeasts, and fungi from pools on Deception Island, one
of the South Shetland Islands associated with the Antarctic
Peninsula which are really subantarctic or maritime.

Adaptation by Lake Algae to Winter Darkness

Several investigators have suggested that antarctic and arctic lake algae may possess special adaptations to polar night, such as the ability to excrete organic matter during photosynthesis and reabsorb and utilize it during subsequent darkness or twilight. Baker (1967) proposed that dense layers of algae living at some depth in Lake Miers, South Victoria Land, might be adapted for heterotrophic growth during the approximately 4 months of antarctic winter night. In their studies of phytoplankton algal productivity in lakes on Signey Island, Fogg and Horne (1970) supported a modified version of this theory which also has been voiced extensively for arctic lakes. They demonstrated that 23-40% of the total carbon fixed photosynthetically into organic matter was excreted or released as extracellular products. They postulated that this extracellular photosynthate might serve as a reservoir of organic matter to enable continued growth of the algae during dim light conditions (i.e., photo-assimilation). We have suggested the same for Lake Bonney located at still higher latitude (Parker et al., in press).

Adaptations of Microorganisms to High Salinity Waters

Meyer et al. (1962) isolated three bacteria from Don Juan Pond, South Victoria Land. This pond is nearly 12 times the salinity of seawater and its predominant solute is calcium chloride. Later, Cameron (1972) could find only one organism in Don Juan Pond which had adapted to be able to grow at such high salinities (Achromobacter parvulum).

Adaptations by Rotifers to Environmental Stresses

Murray (1910) pioneered in studying adaptations in antarctic rotifers, namely collections from Ross Island. Adult rotifers during dormancy tolerated repeated freezing and thawing for several months, temperatures down to -40°C, desiccation and ablation. Philodina gregaria survived -78°C for hours, lived one month in seawater and became active immediately on return to freshwater. Some Adineta grandis even survived +100°C.

Adaptations by Arthropods

As with the rotifers above, often only one specific stage is capable of surviving the stress. Arthropods often hibernate or enter a phase which suspends feeding, growth, reproduction, mobility, and perhaps even metamorphose to the quiescent stage. Such is a genetic-based adaptation. An environmentally-based or acclimation type of adaptation is illustrated by cold temperature adaptation of stone flies, ants, beetles, and mosquitoes in the arctic (Mellanby, 1939). In all cases, the chill-coma temperatures of these mature arthropods were lowered through acclimation, whereas the aquatic larvae of the stone fly and two mosquitoes could not so acclimate.

The arctic crustacean, Mysis relicta, shows an interesting metabolic adaptation. Lasenby and Langford (1972) found the organism had no metabolic compensation over its geographic range. In Char Lake, Cornwallis Island (Canadian Arctic) the species took two years to reach maturity and exhibited higher respiration rates compared with the species in Stony Lake (Ontario) where it took one year to reach maturity. The point, however, is that the females in both lakes used the same number of calories for growth and respiration to reach maturity. This theory that species use the same amount of energy to become mature may well be an adaptive mechanism in some, but not all polar organisms, according to Dunbar (in press). Kinne (1964) and Salt (1964) discuss other details of arthropod adaptations relevant to aquatic environments.

Adaptations of Select Land Invertebrates, Land Plants, Birds and Mammals

Invertebrates

Antarctic mites belonging to the genera Tydeus and Nanorchestes have been studied at several locations on the antarctic continent (Block, 1976; Matsuda, in press; Rounsevell, in press). These arachnids which graze on algae, seem poorly adapted to low temperature and moisture except for their ability to survive prolonged inactivity in freezing sands.

Kinne (1964) reports that Crustacea in general are poorly adapted to a non-aqueous environment. They have no effective protection against surface evaporation (no wax layer in the epicuticle); respiration is still accomplished by gills which have been modified only slightly; the eggs still are carried by the parent and are by no means cleidoic (i.e., enclosed); excretion is still primarily ammonotelic; osmotic changes are tolerated rather than controlled; and high ambient temperatures are suffered only at the expense of increased transpiration. With respect to polar regions, most of this work must, by necessity, be accomplished in the arctic where Crustacea are abundant.

According to Bullard (1964), annelids and molluscs adapt to Arctic cold temperatures primarily by increased respiration rates. Respiration of stenothermal Antarctic springtails, Cryptopygus antarcticus, may involve a quite different adaptive mechanism (Block and Tilbrook, 1975).

Land Plants

Relative to animals, the research effort on adaptations for polar vascular plants has been small. Several years ago, the microclimate of Hallett Station, Antarctica, was assessed to be compatible with the two flowering plants native to Antarctica but found only at relatively low latitudes on the Antarctic Peninsula. An attempt to transplant these plants to Hallett Station failed primarily due to no follow-up research.

Callaghan (in press) undertook studies of adaptive mechanisms of grasses on South Georgia Island in the maritime or subantarctic. It is noteworthy that he found a number of similarities with the adaptations there and in the Arctic: protracted life cycles and flowering phases; predominance of long-lived perennial species which enable accumulation of biomass over extended periods; and vast vegetative clones with tillers which can translocate organics and, thereby function to conserve energy.

Birds and Mammals

Studies of adaptations in birds offer the field of terrestrial polar biology many opportunities, especially as numerous birds occur in both arctic and antarctic regions and because the adaptations are many which sometimes may even be followed from an evolutionary standpoint. A common example is the adaptation complex which is associated with the evolution of flightless, swimming and diving birds which, in Antarctica however, have total dependence for food on the non-terrestrial marine ecosystem.

Parmelee (in press) reports that the Arctic tern (Sterna paradisea) which is migratory to Antarctica and the antarctic tern (S. vittata) which is essentially non-migratory differ markedly in their ecology. Arctic terns are among the last bird species to arrive and breed at high latitudes in the north polar region, while antarctic terns are among the first. Parmelee suggests that the early breeding of the antarctic tern and its rather uniquely selected nesting area with high colony density represent adaptations to predation from antarctic skuas. The skuas take increasing numbers of eggs and chicks only after their own eggs have hatched. By contrast, arctic terns in Antarctica occupy the pack ice where they feed, rest, and moult in an environment essentially free from predators and interspecific competition.

The voluminous literature on adaptations in birds cannot be included here. Considerable emphasis has been placed on cold temperature adaptations. In large arctic birds, such as the arctic glaucous gull, the numbers, sizes, and arrangements of feathers often are adapted to high efficiency insulation. Smaller birds like redpolls and chickadees, however, apparently survive the cold stress by increased production of metabolic heat (Irving, 1964b).

The extensive literature on adaptations in mammals also exceeds the bounds of this paper's objectives. Numerous studies on fur thickness and insulation, heat regulation, behavior, and hibernation physiology and biochemistry on polar mammals, all arctic of course, have been published (Irving, 1964a,b; Hoffman, 1964). Studies of this sort often have a close biomedical affiliation.

Future Directions in Research on Polar Adaptations - The Next Decade

Investigations concerning adaptations in polar terrestrial environments already seem to have entered a new phase, one which instead of studying select organisms removed from their ecosystem, attempts rather to study the organism within its ecosystem. Indeed, the trend appears to be one in which the biologist views adaptations as just another interesting component to the ecosystems being studied. In addition to this approach, however, it is certain that investigations will penetrate more deeply into the genetic, physiological and biochemical mechanisms which underlie adaptation. Only by this latter approach can we expect ultimately to understand the feedback systems involved between organisms and their environments which lead to the ultimate adaptations.

In the arctic, biologists already have entered another phase, one of retesting certain principles of ecology, physiology, genetics, evolution, etc. initially formulated on the basis of temperate and tropical ecosystems. Interestingly, some but not all of these biological principles hold for the arctic, and it is likely that they will be re-examined also, where possible, for the antarctic. Dunbar (1968) and Van der Spoel (1971) have suggested that high-latitude fauna contained significantly more intraspecific variation than the tropics. Thus, the high diversity in the stable tropics represents the end product of long-term evolution of variants (ecotypes, subspecies) to the specific level. Contrastingly, they claim that the communities in the Arctic which have high intraspecific variation are immature and still evolving rapidly. This idea is intriguing and deserves further testing on plants, algae, fungi, invertebrates as well as birds and mammals in both polar regions. The picture certainly differs for antarctic dry valley microorganisms. As was noted, the diversity of soil microorganisms was lowest in the older moraines, not the younger ones. Studies of this sort in the antarctic will be useful in that there are barriers to dispersal, invasion, and colonization by lower organisms which are lacking in the Arctic.

Adaptations, not merely of organisms, but by communities and ecosystems have been mentioned as a potential new thrust in research. Whittaker and Woodwell (1972) state, "....communities must change and may diverge in structure and function from ancestral communities through evolutionary time. Communities, like species, should be related to one another by phylogenies."

Another example of a principle being tested is that of Lack (1966) who states, "...only those predatory species which have not exterminated their prey survive today, hence we observe in nature only those systems which have proved sufficiently stable."

It would be presumptuous to end this paper with a list of all the areas of research on terrestrial adaptations which, (1) should be conducted and, (2) should be funded. This has been done in great detail by the Committee on Polar Research (1970). CPR has discussed areas of research weakness, such as limnology, work on streams, psychrobiology and cryobiology, adaptations, etc. The only criticism which might be leveled at CPR's report is that it is perhaps too long and too detailed. However, it covers nearly everything. The only area which may have cropped up since that report is the growing emphasis on global monitoring and environmental impact, prediction, and assessment. By better coordinating efforts in the polar regions, hopefully many of these biological studies which address adaptations can be more readily accomplished. Such coordination to enable comparative studies in the polar regions will be facilitated by the research supported by the Division of Polar Programs of the National Science Foundation --the only agency concerned with both arctic and antarctic.

References

Alexander, V., M. Billington, and D. M. Schell (1974) The influence of abiotic factors on nitrogen fixation rates in the Barrow, Alaska, arctic tundra. Report Kevo Subarctic Research Station 11. 11:3-11.

Alexander, V. and D. M. Schell (1973) Seasonal and spatial variation of nitrogen fixation in the Barrow, Alaska tundra. Arctic & Alpine Res. 5:77-78.

Baker, A. N. (1967) Algae from Lake Miers, a solar-heated Antarctic lake. New Zealand Jour. Bot. 5:453-468.

Bardin, V. I. (1963) Ozera v gorakh Antarktidy (o novom tipe ozer)(Lakes in the mountains of Antarctica (a new type of lake)). In: Antarctika. Ed. Bugaev, V. A. Doklady komissii 1962. Moskva, Izdatel'stvo Akademii Nauk SSSR, 49-59. (Antarctica, Commission reports 1972. Jerusalem, Israel Program for Scientific Translations, 1969, 49-59).

Benoit, R. E. and C. L. Hall, Jr. (1970) The microbiology of some dry valley soils of Southern Victoria Land, Antarctica. In: Antarctic Ecology. Ed. Holdgate, M. W. Academic Press, New York, pp. 697-701.

Block, W. (1976) Oxygen uptake by Nanorchestes antarcticus (Acari). Oikos 27:320-323.

Block, W. and P. J. Tilbrook (1975) Respiration studies on the Antarctic collembolan Cryptopygus antarcticus. Oikos 26:15-25.

Boyd, W. L., J. T. Staley and J. W. Boyd (1966) Ecology of soil microorganisms of Antarctica. Antarctic Res. Series, U.S. Geophys. Union, 8:125-259.

Bullard, R. W. (1964) Animals in aquatic environments. Annelids and molluscs. In: Adaptation to the Environment. Ed. Dill, D. B. Handbook of Physiology, Section 4, American Physiol. Soc., Wash. D.C., pp. 683-695.

Bunnell, F. (1973) Decomposition: models and the
real world. Bull. Ecological Res. Comm.
(Stockholm) 17:407-415.

Callaghan, T. V. Adaptation strategies in the life
cycles of South Georgian graminoid species.
In: Adaptations Within Antarctic Ecosystems.
Ed. Llano, G. A. 3rd Internat. Antarctic Biol.
Symp. (SCAR)(In Press).

Cameron, R. E. Evolution of polar ecosystems --
Discussion. In: Adaptations Within Antarctic
Ecosystems. Ed. Llano, G. A. 3rd Internat.
Antarctic Biol. Symp. (SCAR)(In Press).

Cameron, R. E., J. King and N. C. David (1970)
Microbiology, ecology, and microclimatology
of soil sites in dry valleys of Southern
Victoria Land, Antarctica. In: Antarctic
Ecology. Ed. Holdgate, M. W. Academic Press,
New York, pp. 702-716.

Cameron, R. E., F. A. Morelli and L. P. Randall
(1972) Aerial, aquatic, and soil microbiology
of Don Juan Pond, Antarctica. Antarct. Jour.
U.S. VII:254-258.

Campbell, W. B., R. W. Harris and R. E. Benoit
(1973) Response of Alaskan tundra microflora
to crude oil spill. In: Proc. of Symp. on
the Impact of Oil Resource Development on
Northern Plant Communities. Occasional Publ.
on Northern Life, No. 1, Univ. of Alaska,
pp. 53-62.

Committee on Polar Research (1970) Polar Research.
A Survey. National Academy of Sciences,
Publ. and Print. Off., Washington, D.C.
pp. 9-10 and pp. 178-184.

Craig, J. R., J. F. Light, B. C. Parker and M.
Mudrey (1975) Identification of hydrohalite.
Antarct. Jour. U.S. X:178-179.

Craig, J. R., R. D. Fortner and B. L. Weand (1976)
Halite and hydrohalite from Lake Bonney,
Taylor Valley, Antarctica. Geol. 1:389-390.

Dunbar, M. J. The evolution of polar ecosystems.
    In: Adaptations Within Antarctic Ecosystems.
    Ed. Llano, G. A. 3rd Internat. Antarctic
    Biol. Symp. (SCAR)(In Press).

Dunbar, M. J. (1968) Ecological Development in
    Polar Regions: A study in Evolution.
    Prentice-Hall, Englewood Cliffs, New Jersey.

Fogg, G. E. and A. J. Horne (1970) The physiology
    of Antarctic freshwater algae. In: Antarctic
    Ecology. Ed. Holdgate, M. W. Academic Press,
    New York, pp. 632-638.

Fortner, R. D., B. L. Weand, R. C. Hoehn, and B.C.
    Parker (1976) Revaluation of ortho-phosphorus
    and inorganic nitrogen levels in an Antarctic
    meromictic lake. Hydrogiol. 49:229-232.

Greene, S. W., J. L. Gressitt, D. Koob, G.A. Llano,
    E. D. Rudolph, R. Singer, W. C. Steere and
    F. C. Ugolini (1967) Terrestrial Life of
    Antarctica. Antarctic Map Folio Series,
    Folio 5, Amer. Geograph. Soc.

Hall, C. L., Jr. (1968) Isolation of psychrophilic
    halophiles from the Antarctic polar desert.
    M.S. Thesis, Virginia Polytechnic Inst. and
    State Univ., Blacksburg, 56 pp.

Heywood, R. B. (1972) Antarctic limnology: A re-
    view. British Antarct. Survey Bull., No. 29:
    35-65.

Hoehn, R. C., B. C. Parker, R. Fortner, B.L. Weand,
    J. A. Craft, L. S. Lane, R. Stavros, H. Sugg,
    and J. Whitehurst. Nitrogen and phosphorus
    availability to plankton and benthic communi-
    ties in Lake Bonney, Southern Victoria Land,
    Antarctica. In: Adaptations Within Antarctic
    Ecosystems. Ed. Llano, G. A. 3rd Internat.
    Biol. Symp. (SCAR)(In Press).

Hoffman, R. A. (1964) Terrestrial animals in cold:
    Hibernators. In: Adaptation to the Environ-
    ment. Ed. Dill, D. B. Handbook of Physiolo-
    gy, Section 4, American Physiological Soc.,
    Washington, D. C., pp. 379-403.

Imshenetsky, A. A., L. A. Kouz yurina, and V. M.
Jakshina (1973) On the multiplication of xero-
philic micro-organisms under simulated Martian
conditions. In: Life Sciences and Space Research XI, Akademie-Verlag, Berlin, Ed.
Sneath, P. H. A., pp. 63-66.

Irving, L. (1964a) Terrestrial animals in cold:
Introduction. In: Adaptation to the Environment. Ed. Dill, D. B. Handbook of Physiology, Section 4, Amer. Physiol. Soc.,
Washington, D.C., pp. 343-347.

Irving, L. (1964b) Terrestrial animals in cold:
Birds and mammals. In: Adaptations in the
Environment. Ed. Dill, D. B. Handbook of
Physiology, Section 4, Amer. Physiol. Soc.,
Washington, D.C., pp. 361-377.

Kinne, O. (1964) Animals in aquatic environments.
Crustaceans. In: Adaptations to the Environment. Ed. Dill, D. B. Handbook of Physiology, Soc., Washington, D.C., pp. 669-682.

Lack, D. (1966) Population Studies of Birds.
Clarendon Press, Oxford, England, pp. 341.

Lane, L. S. (1975) A study of the planktonic
bacterial population fluctuations in Lake
Bonney, Antarctica, including physiological
characterization and identification of select
members. M.S. Thesis, Virginia Polytechnic
Inst. & State Univ., Blacksburg, 102 pp.

Lasenby, D. C. and R. R. Langford (1972) Growth,
life history and respiration of Mysis relicta
in an Arctic and temperate lake. Jour. Fish.
Res. Bd. Canada 29:1701-1708.

Llano, G. A. (1967) Photograph of snow algae
(Plate 11), In: Greene, S. W., J. L. Gressitt,
D. Koob, G. A. Llano, E. D. Rudolph, R.
Singer, W. C. Steere and F. C. Ugolini (1967)
Terrestrial Life of Antarctica, Antarctic Map
Folio Series, Folio 5, Amer. Geograph. Soc.

Matsuda, T. Ecological investigation on free-
living mites near Syowa Station, Antarctica.
In: Adaptations Within Antarctic Ecosystems.
Ed. Llano, G. A. 3rd Internat. Biol. Symp.
(SCAR)(In Press).

Mellanby, K. (1939) Low temperature and insect
    activity. Proc. Roy. Soc. London 127B:473-
    487.

Meyer, G. H., M. B. Morrow, O. Wyss, T. E. Berg
    and J. L. Littlepage (1962) Antarctica. The
    microbiology of an unfrozen saline pond.
    Science 138:1103-1104.

Murray, J. (1910) Antarctic Rotifera. In: British
    Antarctic Expedition, 1907-1909. Ed. Murray,
    J. Reports on the scientific investigations.
    Biology Vol. 1, London, William Heinemann,
    41-65.

Parker, B. C., R. C. Hoehn, R. A. Paterson, J. A.
    Craft, L. S. Lane, R. Stavros, H. Sugg, J.
    Whitehurst, R. Fortner and B. L. Weand. In:
    Adaptations Within Antarctic Ecosystems. Ed.
    Llano, G. A. 3rd Internat. Biol. Symp.
    (SCAR)(In Press).

Parmelee, D. F. Adaptations of Arctic terns and
    Antarctic terns within Antarctic ecosystems.
    In: Adaptations Within Antarctic Ecosystems.
    Ed. Llano, G. A. 3rd Internat. Biol. Symp.
    (SCAR)(In Press).

Prosser, C. L. (1964) Perspectives of adaptation:
    theoretical aspects. In: Adaptation to the
    Environment. Ed. Dill, D. B. Handbook of
    Physiology, Section 4, Amer. Physiol. Soc.,
    Washington, D.C., pp. 11-25.

Rounsevell, D. E. The ecology of the Pan
    Antarctic mite Nanorchestes antarcticus
    (Strandtmann). In: Adaptations within
    Antarctic Ecosystems. Ed. Llano, G. A.
    3rd Internat. Biol. Symp. (SCAR)(In Press).

Salt, R. W. (1964) Terrestrial animals in cold:
    arthropods. In: Adaptation to the Environ-
    ment. Ed. Dill, D. B. Handbook of Physi-
    ology, Section 4, Amer. Physiol. Soc.,
    Washington, D.C., pp. 349-355.

Stanley, S. O. and A. H. Rose (1967) Bacteria and
    yeasts from lakes on Deception Island. In:
    A discussion on the terrestrial Antarctic
    ecosystem. Organizer, Smith, J. E. Phil.
    Trans. Roy. Soc. 252B:199-207.

Ugolini, F. C. (1970) Antarctic soils and their
ecology. In: Antarctic Ecology. Ed.
Holdgate, M. W. Academic Press, New York,
pp. 673-692.

Van der Spoel, S. (1971) Some problems in intraspecific classification of holoplanktonic
animals. Z. Zool. Syst. Evolutionsforsch.
9(2):107-138.

Weand, B. L., B. C. Parker and R. C. Hoehn (1976)
Trace element distributions in an Antarctic
meromictic lake. Hydrogiol. Bull. 10(2):
104-114.

Whittaker, R. H. and G. M. Woodwell (1972) Evolu-
tion of natural communities. In: Ecosystem
Structure and Function. Ed. Wiens, J. A.
Proc. 31st Ann. Biol. Colloq., Oregon State
Univ. Press, Corvallis, pp. 137-159.

Wiggins, I. L. (1953) The organization and facili-
ties of the Arctic Research Laboratory.
Stanford Univ. Publ. Biological Sciences.
No. 11:3-6.

Additional References

Allessio, M. L. and L. Tieszen (1975) Patterns of
carbon allocation in an arctic tundra grass
Dupontia fischeri gramineae at Barrow, Alaska
U.S.A. Am. Jour. Bot. No. 8, 62:797-807.

Atlas, R. M., E. A. Schofield, F. A. Morelli and
R. E. Cameron (1974) Interactions of microorganisms and petroleum pollutants in the
Arctic. Ann. Meet. Amer. Soc. Microbiol.
74:64 (Abstr.).

Barsdate, R. J. (1972) Ecologic changes in an
arctic tundra pond following exposure to
crude oil. Sci. Alaska Proc. Alaskan Sci.
Conf. 23:118.

Batzli, G. O. (1975) The role of small mammals in
Arctic ecosystems. In: International Bio-
logical Programme, No. 5, Small Mammals:
Their Productivity and Population Dynamics,
Eds. Golley, F. B., K. Petrusewicz and L.
Ryszkowski, pp. 243-268.

Behrisch, H. W. (1973) Molecular mechanisms of
    temperature adaptation in arctic ectotherms
    and heterotherms. In: <u>Effects of Temperature
    on Ectothermic Organisms: Ecological Implica-
    tions and Mechanisms of Compensation</u>. Ed.
    Wieser, W. Symp. Obergurgl, Austria,
    Sept. 4-8, 1972, pp. 123-137.

Block, W. and P. J. Tilbrook (1975) Respiration
    studies on the Antarctic collembolan
    <u>Cryptopygus</u> <u>antarcticus</u>. Oikos <u>26</u>(1):15-25.

Booth, T. and P. Barrett (1976) Taxonomic and
    ecologic observations of zoosporic fungi in
    soils of a high Arctic ecosystem. Can. Jour.
    Bot. <u>54</u>(5-6):533-538.

Cameron, R. E., G. H. Lacy, F. A. Morelli and J.B.
    Marsh (1971) Farthest south soil microbial
    and ecological investigations. Antarct.
    Jour. U.S. <u>6</u>(4):105-106.

Corbet, P. S. (1972) The micro-climate of Arctic
    plants and animals on land and in fresh
    water. Acta Arct. <u>18</u>:1-43.

Craig, P. C. and J. Wells (1976) Life history
    notes for a population of slimy sculpin
    <u>Cottus</u> <u>cognatus</u> in an Alaskan U.S.A. Arctic
    stream. J. Fish. Res. Bd. Canada <u>33</u>(7):1639-
    1642.

Dunbar, M. J. (1973) Stability and fragility in
    Arctic ecosystems. Arctic <u>26</u>(3):170-185.

Fogg, G. E., M. F. Burton and S. J. Coughlan
    (1975) The occurrence of glycolic acid in
    Antarctic waters. British Antarct. Surv.
    Bull. <u>41-42</u>:193-195.

Gjessing, Y. T. and D. O. Ovstedal (1975) Energy
    budget and ecology of two vegetation types in
    Svalbard, Norway. Astarte <u>8</u>(2):83-92.

Greene, D. and A. Holtom (1971) Studies in
    <u>Colobanthus</u> <u>quitensis</u> M and <u>Deschampsia</u>
    <u>antarctica</u> M. Part III: Distribution habi-
    tats and performance in the Antarctic
    botanical zone. British Antarct. Surv. Bull.
    <u>26</u>:1-29.

Grotnes, P. E. and A. Klemetsen (1974) The consequences of impoundment on an Arctic char lake
system - and analysis by simulation modeling.
XIX Cong. Internat. Assoc. Limnol. Winnipeg,
Canada. Fresh Water Inst., Dept. of Environment: Winnipeg, p. 71.

Guard, C. L. and D. E. Murrish (1975) Effects of
temperature on the viscous behavior of blood
from Antarctic birds and mammals. Comp. Biochem. Physiol. 52(2):287-290.

Haag, R. W. (1974) Nutrient limitations to plant
production in two tundra communities. Can.
Jour. Bot. 52(1):103-116.

Haftorn, S. (1972) Hypothermia of Tits in the
Arctic winter. Ornis. Scand. 3(2):153-166.

Hanna, B. M., J. Hellebust and T. C. Hutchinson
(1974) Field studies on the phyto-toxicity of
crude oil to Arctic aquatic vegetation. XIX
Cong. Internat. Assoc. Limnol. Winnipeg,
Canada. Fresh Water Inst., Dept. of Environment: Winnipeg, p. 77.

Henshaw, R. E., B. A. Henshaw, L. S. Underwood and
S. Zervanos (1971) Energetic efficiency of
large Arctic terrestrial mammals due to peripheral thermo regulation. Proc. Alaska Sci.
Conf. 22:11.

Hodge, R. P. (1972) Arctic herps. Animals (Lond.)
14(2):74-76.

Holeton, G. F. (1973) Respiration of Arctic char
Salvelinus alpinus from a high Arctic lake.
Jour. Fish. Res. Bd., Canada 30(6):717-723.

Ingham, J. D., R. E. Cameron and D. D. Lawson
(1974) Microbial abundance and thermolumin-
escence of antarctic Dry Valley soils. Soil
Sci. 117(1):46-57.

Jasiski, A. (1973) Structural adaptation of
mammals to extreme environmental temperatures.
Wszechswiat 5:122-126.

Johnson, D. A. and M. M. Caldwell (1976) Water potential components stomatal function and liquid phase water transport resistances of four Arctic and alpine species in relation to moisture stress. Physiol. Plant. 36(3):271-278.

Johnson, D. A. and M. M. Caldwell (1975) Gas exchange of four Arctic and alpine tundra plant species in relation to atmospheric and oil moisture stress. Oecologia (Berl.) 21(2): 93-108.

Kalff, J., H. E. Welch and S. K. Holmgren (1972) Pigment cycles in two high Arctic Canadian lakes. In: Internat. Assoc. Theoret. & Appl. Limnol. Ed. Sladecek, V. 18(1&2):250-256.

Kalff, J. (1971) Nutrient limiting factors in an Arctic tundra pond. Ecol. 52(4):655-659.

Kalff, J., S. K. Holmgren, H. Kling and H.E. Welch (1974) Phytoplankton biomass cycles in an unpolluted and in a polluted polar lake. XIX Cong. Internat. Assoc. Limnol. Winnipeg, Canada. Fresh Water Inst., Dept. of Environment. Winnipeg, p. 99.

Kallio, P. S. Suhonen and H. Kallio (1972) The ecology of nitrogen fixation in Nephroma arcticum and Solorina crocea. Ann. Univ. Turk. Ser. A(II) 49:7-14.

Kislyuk, I. M. and E. I. Den'ko (1976) Thermostability of cells in Arctic and boreal plants and its significance for adaptation to the conditions of the north. Bot. Zh. (Leningr.) 61(4):488-498.

Kolpakov, M. G. (1975) Rhythmology in chronic pathological processes. Vestn. Akad. Med. Nauk. SSSR 10:36-39.

Krasnozhenov, E. P., N. V. Vasil'ev, E. S. Smol'yaninov, and T. I. Fomina (1974) Dynamics of bactericidal properties of human saliva and blood serum during adaptation to conditions of the transpolar region. Byull. Eksp. Biol. Med. 78(10):72-74.

Krasnozhenov, E. P., N. V. Vasil'ev, E. S.
    Smol'yaninov and T. I. Fomina (1974) Dynamics
    of bactericidal properties of human saliva
    and blood serum during adaptation to Arctic
    conditions. Bull. Exp. Biol. Med. 78(10):
    1165-1167.

Kuzmin, L. L. (1976) Free living nematodes in the
    tundra of western Taimyr USSR. Oikos 27(3):
    501-505.

Latter, P. M. and O. W. Heal (1971) A preliminary
    study of the growth of fungi and bacteria
    from temperate and Antarctic soils in rela-
    tion to temperature. Soil Biol. Biochem.
    3(4):365-379.

Leblanc, J., J. Dulac, J. Cote and B. Girard
    (1975) Autonomic nervous system and adapta-
    tion to cold in man. Jour. Appl. Physiol.
    39(2):181-186.

Lindholm, G. R., S. McGee and S. A. Norrell (1972)
    Seasonal and perturbational changes in deni-
    trification in Arctic soils. Ann. Mtg. Amer.
    Soc. Microbiol. 72:14 (Abstr.).

Lyakh, S. P. and S. S. Abyzov (1976) Some aspects
    of the microflora in the Antarctic depending
    on specific extreme environmental conditions.
    Izv. Akad. Nauk SSSR Ser. Biol. 2:252-262.

Lyakh, S. P. and S. S. Abyzov (1974) Adaptation of
    Antarctic microflora to frost and dryness as
    the basic extreme factors of the environment.
    Izv. Akad. Nauk SSSR Ser. Biol. 5:688-698.

McCown, B., L. Tieszen, D. Vietor, J. Brown and P.
    Murrmann (1971) Influence of oil spills on
    Arctic ecosystems. U.S. I. B. P. Anal. Eco-
    syst. Program Interbiome 1(4):294 (Abstr.).

McWhinnie, M. A., M. O. Cahoon and S. Rakusa-
    Suszczewski (1976) Some metabolic character-
    istics of Antarctic aquatic fauna. Amer.
    Zool. 16(2):210.

Nikulina, V. M. (1974) Photosynthetic activity of
    individual algal species of the plankton of
    Lake Krivoye USSR. Ekologiya 5(4):101-104.

228   *Bruce C. Parker*

Norrell, S. A. and M. H. Johnston (1974) Seasonal
    changes in ammonification and its relation-
    ship to bacterial biomass in arctic tundra
    soils. Ann. Meet. Am. Soc. Microbiol. 74:4
    (Abstr.).

Opalinski, K. W. (1974) Standard routine and act-
    ive metabolism of the Antarctic amphipod
    Paramoera walkeri. Pol. Arch. Hydrobiol.
    21(3-4):423-430.

Parker, B. C., J. T. Whitehurst and R. C. Hoehn
    (1974) Observations of in situ concentrations
    and production of organic matter in an
    Antarctic meromictic lake. Va. Jour. Sci.
    25(3):136-140.

Percy, J. A. (1974) Thermal adaptation in the
    boreo arctic echinoid Strongylocentrotus
    droebachiensis. Pt. 4: Acclimation in the
    laboratory. Physiol. Zool. 47(3):163-171.

Richards, K. W. (1973) Biology of Bombus polaris
    and Bombus hyperboreus at Lake Hazen north-
    west-territories Hymenoptera: Bombini. Quaest.
    Entomol. 9(2):115-157.

Roberts, R. A. (1971) Preliminary observations on
    the ionic regulation of the Arctic char
    Salvelinus alpinus. Jour. Expl. Biol. 55(1):
    213-222.

Roff, J. C. and J. C. H. Carter (1972) Life cycle
    and seasonal abundance of the copepod Limno-
    calanus macrurus in a high Arctic lake.
    Limnol. Oceanogr. 17(3):363-370.

Savile, D. B. O. (1972) Arctic adaptations in
    plants. Can. Dep. Agric. Res. Branch Monogr.
    6:7-81.

Savile, D. B. O. (1971) Arctic adaptations in
    fungi. Amer. Jour. Bot. 58(5/2):485.

Sexstone, J. A., C. Winter and R. M. Atlas (1976)
    Response of microorganisms in Arctic tundra
    soils to application of crude oil. Ann. Meet.
    Amer. Soc. Microbiol. 76:Q22 (Abstr.).

Shurley, J. T. (1971) New directions in Antarctic biomedical research. In: Research in the Antarctic. Ed. Quam, L. O. Am. Assoc. Adv. Sci. Publ. 93. Symp., Dallas, Texas, Dec., 1968, pp. 277-287.

Sjostrand, F. S. (1974) A search for the circuitry of directional selectivity and neural adaptation through three dimensional analysis of the outer plexiform layer of the rabbit retina. Jour. Ultrastruct. Res. 49(1):60-156.

Skreslet, S. (1973) The ecosystem of the Arctic Lake Nordlaguna, Jan-Mayen Island. Pt. 3: Ecology of Arctic char Salvelinus alpinus. Astarte 6(2):43-54.

Stross, R. G. and S. W. Chisholm (1974) Maternal reaction to self regulation and competition in Arctic populations of Daphnia. XIX Cong. Internat. Assoc. Limnol. Winnipeg, Canada. Fresh Water Inst., Dept. of Environment. Winnipeg, p. 204.

Teeri, J. A. (1973) Polar desert adaptations of a high Arctic plant species. Sci. 179:496-497.

Tieszen, L. L. (1972) The seasonal course of above ground production and chlorophyll distribution in a wet Arctic tundra at Barrow, Alaska. Arct. Alp. Res. 4(4):307-324.

Tomilin, B. A. (1974) Adaptation of fungi to living conditions in the Arctic and mycoflora of the tundras. Mikol Fitopatol 8(6):465-471.

Vishniac, H. S., P. Farrell and W. P. Hampfling (1976) Correspondence between predicted and determined characteristics of Antarctic Dry Valley yeasts. Ann. Meet. Am. Soc. Microbiol. 76:185 (Abstr.).

Wang, L.C.H., D.L. Jones, R.A. MacArthur and W.A. Fuller (1973) Adaptation to cold energy metabolism in an atypical Lagomorph, the Arctic hare Lepus arcticus. Can. Jour. Zool. 51(8): 841-846.

Welch, H.E. (1974) Metabolic rates of Arctic lakes. Limnol. Oceanogr. 19(1):65-73.

10

Polar Logistic Support:
The United States Navy

Gene C. Valentine

The U.S. Navy holds a distinguished place in
the history of man's exploration and investigation
of polar regions. Since the days of naval
explorer-scientists the role of the Navy evolved
to defense related research in the Arctic and
logistic support of the United States research
programs in Antarctica.

Arctic

Between 1825 and 1840 Matthew Fontaine Maury,
Superintendent of the U.S. Navy Depot of Charts
and Instruments, compiled nautical data and charts
from observations provided by captains of ships
sailing in high latitudes. In 1850-1851 and again
in 1853-1855 the United States government sponsored the Navy-Grinnell Arctic Expedition. Between
1879 and 1882 the JEANNETTE (under Navy LT George
Washington DeLong) was commissioned to travel
through the Bering Strait and westward of the
Chukchi Sea to investigate the existence of an
open arctic sea, (DeLong, 1884). The ship was
lost to the crushing forces of ice in the Laptev
Sea. Commanded by Army LT Adolphus W. Greely, the
Lady Franklin Bay Expedition (1881-1884) was part
of the U.S. participation in the First International Polar Year; a U.S. Station was built at
Point Barrow, Alaska where arctic research was
directed by Army LT P. H. Ray. Later civilian
engineers and Navy LT Robert T. Peary led a journey (1886) from Disco Bay eastward into Greenland.
The experience of ice travel and observations of
Eskimo habits during this expedition provided background understanding for later exploration.

In 1925, Commander Richard E. Byrd made pioneer-
ing flights for the Navy in northwestern Greenland
and Ellesmere Island. On May 9, 1926, he flew from
Spitsbergen to the North Pole and return in 16
hours establishing the successful use of airplanes
in exploration of the arctic. This precedent was
later transferred to Antarctica when Byrd made his
historical flight to South Pole, on November 29,
1929.

The next phase of arctic history was dominated
largely by the submarine. The possibility of a
submarine traverse, beneath the Polar Ice Cap, was
suggested as early as 1648 by the British mathematician, Bishop John Wilkins. Two and one-half
centuries later Simon Lake developed the first
modern submarine and held a similar view. The
strongest proponent of this concept was Vihjalmur
Stefansson, who was born in Canada, educated in the
United States, and later served as the U.S. Defense
Advisor for polar operations during World War II.
The first under-ice submarine voyage was attempted
by Sir George Hubert Wilkins, an Australian arctic
explorer. Sailing NAUTILUS, Wilkins and Chief
Scientist Harold U. Sverdrup left Spitsbergen in
August 1931 on a voyage under the ice but failure
of diving gear allowed only brief excursions from
the ship. Although several short submarine voyages
were made under the margins of polar ice after
World War II, serious attempts at navigation in
arctic waters were not considered feasible until
atomic-powered vessels had been built. The USS
NAUTILUS (SSN-571), launched in 1954, was the first
of these ships and its success on long distance
voyages resulted in arctic trials in August 1957
but due to ice conditions NAUTILUS failed to reach
the pole by some 180 miles (Anderson, 1959). However, the same vessel reached the North Pole August
3, 1958 after submerging near Point Barrow, Alaska,
and using a "canyon" at the edge of the continental
shelf as a route toward the pole. Two days later
NAUTILUS emerged in ice-free water between Iceland
and Spitsbergen. Scientific data were recorded
throughout the 96 hour voyage of 1,830 miles
(Weems, 1960).

A second nuclear-powered submarine, SKATE
studied the possibility of surfacing through openings in polar pack ice. This operation would provide diverse marine capabilities including oceano-

graphic studies. During a 10-day voyage from the Atlantic side (August 1958) SKATE travelled 3,093 miles circling the North Pole while submerged and visiting the floating Ice Station Alfa which was established as part of the International Geophysical Year. In March 1959 submarine navigation in polar waters was studied under maximum ice thickness during a 3,100 mile and 12-day voyage under the ice. These studies demonstrated that polar submarine work could be conducted on an annual basis.

The role of the Navy in the arctic today remains different from its support function in the antarctic.

The principal objective of its polar research and engineering studies is to acquire multidisciplinary knowledge for surface and submarine vessel capabilities in arctic seas. A major goal is to understand the qualitative and quantitative characteristics of environmental systems, their variations, interrelationships, periodicities and time-based changes and processes. The physical and chemical interrelationships of the ocean, atmosphere, and maritime lands provide the framework of investigations. Emphasis is on determining features and influences of the peripheral lands and the continental shelf on oceanic phenomena, as well as the adaptation of mammals to cold, (Stringer, 1976).

The data obtained through this program provide a technological base that is essential for operating submarine vessels in sea ice conditions, and the operation of equipment and facilities on snow and ice.

Current research falls into several categories including acoustics, geology and geophysics, environmental prediction, snow, ice and permafrost engineering, polar material systems, and human adaptation to cold. In applied research and technology, emphasis is on ocean prediction as it affects submarine operations. This is important as effectiveness of submarine work in arctic and marginal ice-zones is diminished by inadequate knowledge of ice-water-air interactions.

Antarctic

The first formal exploration into the antarctic, supported by the U.S. Government, was led by Navy LT Charles Wilkes of the U.S. Exploring Expedition, 1838-1842. Departing the United States late in 1838, Wilkes reached the antarctic south of Cape Horn early the following year. After skirting the ice pack along a westward course, he reached Australia and returned to the antarctic, south of Australia, in December 1839. Sailing again in a westerly direction he sighted land at numerous points over a distance of 1,500 miles. By the time Wilkes returned, the existence of a southern continent, Antarctica, had become accepted.

For years the United States demonstrated little interest in antarctic exploration. After the early expeditions only occasional efforts were made to learn more about the southern-most ice-covered continent, although sealers and whalers from the United States had based their operations on islands in the vicinity of the Antarctic Convergence until about 1880.

The next major activity of the U.S. in Antarctica occurred when Rear Admiral Richard E. Byrd led his first expedition there between 1928-1930. Accompanying Commander Byrd as science leader was Dr. Laurence M. Gould under whose direction significant scientific discoveries were made and landmarks were identified, including the Ford Range, the Rockefeller Mountains, and Marie Byrd Land. Based at Little America, on the Bay of Whales, Byrd established the effectiveness of the airplane as a tool of exploration.

Byrd's Second Antarctic Expedition (1933-1935) concentrated on scientific work and used tracked vehicles more extensively than any previous expedition. The use of aircraft, tracked vehicles, radio, and diverse scientific instruments by this party gradually made private financing of expeditions increasingly prohibitive. With Congressional authorization, the United States Antarctic Service Expedition was organized and carried out 1938-1941. Under the command of Byrd, the responsibility for antarctic research was shifted from the private sector to the government. The last privately financed expedition was

under Commander Finn Ronne although it too, received assistance from the U.S. Government.

The United States Antarctic Service established
two permanent bases; East and West Base. Each
year a new group of men were to replace those who
had stayed through the winter. However, as War
broke out in Europe these bases were closed in
1941. Thus, the United States was the first
nation to plan permanent stations, and this was
pursued sometime after World War II. In the interim it authorized expeditions for limited
periods. The first of these was named Operation
Highjump, 1946-1947. Rear Admiral Byrd was the
Officer-in-Charge, and Rear Admiral R. H. Cruzen
commanded the Navy's Task Force 68. With 13 ships
including a submarine and over 4,000 men, it remains the largest expedition ever sent to the
antarctic, (NSFA, 1969).

An outstanding event in the operation was the
flight of six twin-engine C-47 transport planes
from an aircraft carrier to their base of operations at Little America IV, on the Bay of Whales.
Another innovation in antarctic exploration was
the successful use of icebreakers, with helicopter
support to break a path through the ice pack. Seaplanes operating from the aircraft carrier photographed large areas never seen before this time;
flights by seaplanes and C-47's resulted in discovery of more of Antarctica during Operation
Highjump than in all previous expeditions (NSFA,
1969).

Construction of accurate maps from aerial
photographs requires precise relations to definite
ground points. Unfortunately, Operation Highjump
had not obtained sufficient ground control points,
and the icebreakers EDISTO and BURTON ISLAND were
sent to the antarctic in 1947-1948 to provide this
information. This expedition, under Commander
Gerald L. Ketchum, was knicknamed "Operation Windmill" because of extensive use of helicopters used
to move observers ashore in order to obtain mapping references and other scientific observations,
(NSFA, 1969), (Fig. 1).

On returning from Antarctica the icebreakers
called at Marguerite Bay, where they freed the
ship of a private United States expedition that

Figure 1. Icebreaker at work to open McMurdo Sound for re-supply ships.

had occupied the old East Base on Stonington
Island. Led by Commander Finn Ronne, a veteran of
two expeditions with Admiral Byrd, this group
greatly extended the work begun by the United
States Antarctic Service Expedition in 1940 and
1941. Among the members of the wintering over
party were Commander Ronne's wife Edith and Tennie
Darlington, wife of an aircraft pilot. These were
the first women to experience the hardships of an
antarctic winter, (NSFA, 1969).

Admiral Byrd described Antarctica as a "great
white continent for peace" where men of all
nations could work together to expand the frontiers of human knowledge. He lived long enough to
see his dream on its way to accomplishment. When
he died in 1957, a dozen nations were engaged in
scientific studies to elucidate the secrets of
Antarctica's icy mass. Through the joint efforts
established during the IGY, the complimentary
roles of the U.S. Navy and the scientific community developed further (NSFA, 1969). Today the
National Science Foundation funds and manages the
overall U.S. national program in Antarctica.

Since the beginning of Operation DEEP FREEZE in
1955, the Department of Defense has been responsible for logistic activities in Antarctica. The
U.S. Navy has assumed a major share of the responsibility while significant contributions have
been made by the U.S. Coast Guard, the U.S. Army,
the U.S. Marine Corps and the U.S. Air Force.
Personnel of the U.S. Public Health Service also
have participated in some operations. Support
activities conducted on behalf of science since
DEEP FREEZE I fall into 4 areas: station construction and operation, ship operations, and air
operations. In addition, meteorological data are
provided for world-wide use, (Fig. 2).

Navy support of the U.S. Antarctic Research
Programs begins in the continental United States.
Equipment and supplies prepared for shipment leave
the Naval Support Force, Antarctica base at Port
Hueneme, California for transit by ship, while
support and scientific personnel fly to New
Zealand and subsequently to Antarctica. The prin-
cipal United States operating area for eastern
Antarctica lies directly south of New Zealand
where the air and port facilities of that country

Figure 2.   Instrumented weather balloon being
released on the icecap in Antarctica.

are used. The advance headquarters of the Navy's
support organization are at Christchurch, on New
Zealand's South Island, 2,400 miles north of
McMurdo Station. In contrast, Palmer Station,
located in western Antarctica on Anvers Island
near the Antarctic Peninsula, is south of South
America and is supplied by the British ship, RRS
BRANSFIELD, via South American ports.

The largest scientific station is at McMurdo
which has both air and deep water port facilities
and serves as the primary United States research
and supply base in Antarctica. To McMurdo come
ships with fuel, fresh foods, and high priority
cargo. Incoming material is sorted, and some of
it is prepared for further shipment inland. Until
1959, the United States shipped much of its
material from the coast to interior stations on
sleds drawn by tracked vehicles; since then all
supplies are moved inland by aircraft.

Station Construction

Since 1957, the number of year-round stations
operated by the United States has varied between
4 and 7 (Table 1). With the closing of Plateau
Station on January 29, 1969, and the conversion of
Byrd Station to a summer-only station after 1971,
there are currently four: McMurdo at $77^{O}53'S$,
$166^{O}40'E$, Amundsen-Scott South Pole Station at the
geographic South Pole, Palmer Station at $64^{O}46'S$,
$64^{O}03'W$, and Siple at $75^{O}56'S$, $84^{O}15'W$. Hallett
Station was occupied on a year-round basis from
1957 to 1965, after which it was manned only in
the summer until February 1973 when it was closed.

Throughout the IGY, most expeditions planned to
remain in Antarctica for only a year or two, and
drifting snow was not a great concern in station
construction; in fact, it could be turned to advantage. Admiral Byrd did this by placing his
buildings on the surface and connecting them with
enclosed passageways made of lumber covered with
wire and burlap. Drifting snow soon turned these
corridors into tunnels in which supplies could be
stored and movement within the Station was made
easier without exposure to weather. However, over
the years, snow builds up gradually turning to ice
which crushes the roof and also moves against the
sides and floors; the result resembles closing a

Table 1

ANTARCTIC STATION LOCATION AND CLIMATE SUMMARY*

Data	McMurdo	Amundsen-Scott South Pole	Byrd Summer Only	Eights Closed	Ellsworth Closed	Hallett Closed
Latitude	77°51'S.	90°00'S.	80°01'S.	75°14'S.	77°39'S.	72°18'S.
Longitude	166°37'E.		119°31'W.	77°10'W.	44°08'W.	170°18'W.
Elevation Feet	102	9,184	5,012	1,483	131	16
Meters	31	2,800	1,530	452	40	5
Temperature°C. Annual Mean	-17.3	-49.3	-28.1	-25.6	-22.9	-15.3
°F.	0.8	-56.6	-18.6	-14.0	-9.2	4.5
Temperature°C. Extreme Low	-50.6	-80.7	-63.2	-50.0	-55.6	-47.8
°F.	-59.1	-113.3	-81.8	-58.0	-68.1	-54.0
Recorded	Jul 60	Jul 65	Jul 58	Jun 64	May 58	Aug 59
Temperature°C. Extreme High	6.7	-14.7	2.2	2.2	2.4	8.3
°F.	44.0	5.5	36.0	36.0	36.3	46.9
Recorded	Jan 71	Jan 58	Jan 73	Dec 64	Dec 60	Jan 59
Wind Knots	12.7	12.2	16.7	10.1	12.5	7.1
Direction	East	NNE	NNE	South	South	SW
Air Mileage from McMurdo Nautical Miles		730	801	1,325	1,426	338
Statute Miles		840	922	1,554	1,641	389
Officially Opened	16 Feb 56	23 Jan 57	13 Feb 62	27 Jan 63	11 Feb 57	9 Jan 57
Operation as U.S. station Discontinued				Closed 15 Nov 64,	Transferred 2 Jan 59, Argentina	

* Data source, NSFA, 1965

Table 1 (Continued)

Data	Little America V (Closed)	Palmer	Plateau (Closed)	Wilkes (Closed)	Siple
Latitude	78°11'S.	64°46'S.	79°15'S.	66°15'S.	75°56'S.
Longitude	162°10'W.	64°05'W.	40°30'E.	110°31'E.	84°15'W.
Elevation Feet	141	26	11,890	30	3,458
Meters	43	8	3,264	9	1,054
Temperature°C.	-23.3	-3.2	-56.4	-9.8	N.A.
Annual Mean°F.	-9.9	26.2	-69.5	14.4	N.A.
Temperature°C.	-60.6	-28.1	-85.2	-37.8	N.A.
Extreme Low°F.	-77.0	-18.6	-121.4	-36.0	N.A.
Recorded	Aug 56	Oct 65	Aug 66	Jul 58	N.A.
Temperature°C.	3.3	9.8	-20.3	8.0	N.A.
Extreme High°F.	38.0	49.6	-4.5	46.4	N.A.
Recorded	Jan 57	Feb 65	Dec 66	Jan 58	N.A.
Wind Knots	11.0	6.3	9.3	11.2	N.A.
Direction	SE	NNE	North	East	N.A.
Air Mileage Nautical Miles from McMurdo	383	1,832	1,224	1,179	1,306
Statute Miles	440	2,108	1,409	1,356	1,504
Officially Opened	4 Jan 56	25 Feb 65	30 Jan 66	16 Feb 57	
Operation as U.S. station Discontinued	Closed 6 Jan 59			Transferred 4 Feb 59 Australia	

Table 1 (Continued)

Station	Origin of Name
Amundsen-Scott South Pole Station	Roald Amundsen (Norwegian) and Capt. Robert F. Scott (British); first men to reach the South Pole.
Byrd Station	Rear Admiral Richard E. Byrd, USN, famed polar aviator and explorer.
Eights Station	James Eights, Scientist aboard Nathaniel Palmer's ANNAWAN, U.S. expedition of 1829-1831.
Ellsworth Station	Lincoln Ellsworth, an American who in 1935 was first to fly across Antarctica.
Hallett Station	Location on Cape Hallett, named in 1841 for purser aboard Ross' EREBUS.
Little America V	Continuation in the sequence of U.S. stations occupied on the Ross Ice Shelf.
McMurdo Station	Located on McMurdo Sound, named in 1841 for LT Archibald McMurdo of Ross' TERROR.
Palmer Station	Capt. Nathaniel B. Palmer American ship captain who sighted the Antarctic Peninsula on 17 November 1820.
Plateau Station	Location on polar plateau. Camps and stations are often named for the area in which they are located.
Wilkes Station	LT (later R. Adm.) Charles Wilkes, USN, commander, U.S. Exploring Expedition, 1838-1842.
Siple Station	Paul Siple, a boyscout with Admiral Byrd's first expedition. Later, antarctic geologist and geographer.

giant vise. Built in 1955-1956, Little America V
had to be closed in 1959 before it collapsed,
(NSFA, 1965).

   Most of the stations built on ice shelves or on
the polar plateau during the IGY were constructed
in this fashion, and many have been abandoned or
replaced. To avoid the problem of snow accumulation, several designs have been developed, both in
Antarctica and Greenland, where similar conditions
prevail. Some expeditions placed buildings into
ice trenches based on the hypothesis that the snow
would blow across the covered trench with minimum
accumulation. The U.S. Army adopted an elaborate
form of this technique in building Camp Century on
the Greenland ice cap. When the original Byrd
Station threatened to collapse after four years of
use, the Navy duplicated this type of construction
in building a new station. Deep trenches were
covered with metal arches, and finally snow was
blown back across the arches creating a level surface over the tunnels. Insulated buildings were
erected in the tunnels with surrounding space for
walkways, thus creating a veritable village under
the snow. Only exhaust stacks, radio antennas,
and scientific observatories appeared above the
surface. A variation of this technique was used
to prolong the life of the first Amundsen-Scott
South Pole Station, which was also being threatened by accumulating snow, (NSFA, 1969).

   An approach developed for Greenland involves
elevating the building on columns above the surface. Even though most of the snow blows past and
beneath the building, some does accumulate gradually. When this happens, the building can be
raised by extending the columns using elevating
support with jacks. This type of construction is
expensive and worthwhile only where snow accumulation is very acute; its rate of accumulation in
Antarctica varies considerably from place to
place. In 1929, Admiral Byrd installed a 75-foot
radio tower at the Bay of Whales. Thirty years
later to the month, only four feet remained above
the surface. On the other hand, at the Soviet's
Vostok Station on the plateau, there has been
virtually no snow accumulation in 15 years,
(NSFA, 1969).

   Prefabricated buildings are commonly used in

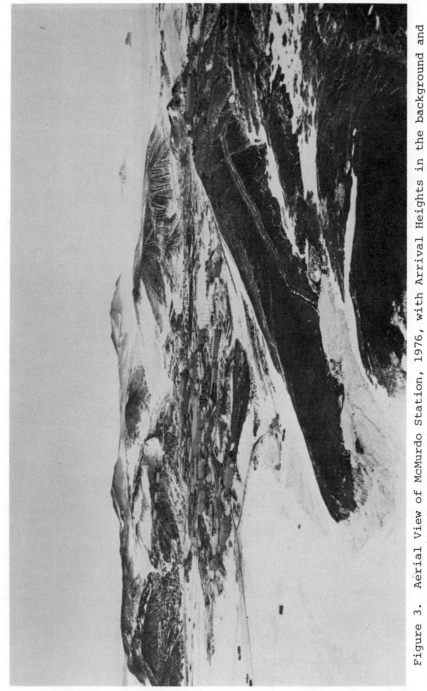

Figure 3. Aerial View of McMurdo Station, 1976, with Arrival Heights in the background and Hut Point in the background left.

Antarctica, and for small stations vans called
"Wanigans" have been used often. Resembling house
trailers on skis, they are pulled into place by
tracked vehicles. Vostok is an example of this
construction, as was Little Rockford, a United
States summer weather station established in 1958,
and abandoned early in 1965. Because the Wanigans
can be moved, it is possible to relocate them on
the surface as the snow piles up, (NSFA, 1969).

The van concept continued for station construction during DEEP FREEZE 63 (1962-1963) when
Eights Station was built.   Vans that could be
joined together at the construction site were
built to fit into an LC-130F cargo plane. Units
were fully furnished for their intended use before
being flown from McMurdo Station to a site near
the base of the Antarctic Peninsula. There, eight
such units, mounted on skids, were pulled by
tractor into parallel rows; the whole complex was
roofed over to form a large building of eight
rooms around a central hallway, (NSFA, 1969).

Bases made of vans are easy to construct, to
disassemble and move. This was not done at Eights
but a similarly constructed summer weather station
was returned to McMurdo in 1966 for relocation the
following season. Two other stations were built
in DEEP FREEZE 66 (1965-1966). One, called
Longwire, was a small substation about 12 miles
from Byrd Station. The other, Plateau Station,
built on a featureless snow plain at an altitude
of 12,000 feet, was the most remote U.S. station,
600 miles beyond the South Pole from McMurdo
Station. Plateau Station was closed on January
29, 1969, (NSFA, 1969).

Over the years of antarctic exploration and research, experience has greatly improved the quality
of living and working in polar areas. However,
nowhere is the contrast between past and present
more evident than on Ross Island, on McMurdo Sound.
Here, only a short distance from McMurdo Station,
stands the camps built by Scott in 1902 and
Shackleton in 1908. They are little more than
wooden shacks, once briefly occupied and then
abandoned while, in contrast, McMurdo has become a
small city (Fig. 3). Today, it has several
laboratories, a church, store, movies, and a
gymnasium, among nearly 100 buildings. Its summer
population averages over 800 and approximately 70

people spend the winter there. As a result, support personnel are amplified by the peculiar conditions of Antarctica, especially the scarcity of
water, (NSFA, 1969).

Station Operations

Today, water, the most important commodity in
Antarctica is still difficult to obtain, even
though 95 percent of the continent is covered with
snow and ice. In the few areas where natural
melting occurs in summer, it is possible to obtain
water from ponds, but in winter, it must be obtained by using a snow melter or a water desalination
plant.

Often the snow melter is built around the exhaust pipes from the electric generating engines
using heat that would otherwise be wasted. This
method, however, is not sufficient for a station
the size of McMurdo. A water desalination plant
produces 21,000 gallons per day for use at this
large Station. Additionally, a storage tank hold-
ing 110,000 gallons is maintained to supply the
difference between production and usage. As a
rule, small stations can handle the problems of
water supply and sanitation without elaborate
equipment, but there are exceptions. For example,
Hallet Station (now closed) is located on a sand
spit that is also the site of an Adelie penguin
rookery. The snow, therefore, is often contaminated. Since its construction in 1957, Hallet had
fuel-evaporators to desalinate seawater, as well
as conventional snow melters. The French at Dumont
D'Urville Station, 66°40'S, 140°01'E, had the same
problem and in 1967 installed a distillation plant.
On ice shelves and on the polar plateau, there is
unlimited snow and little or no source of con-
tamination.

Water from the snow melters is carefully
rationed. Digging and carrying snow is arduous
work, especially in harsh weather. Moreover, all
fuel to melt snow, heat buildings, generate
electricity, power vehicles must be imported into
Antarctica over great distances and at considerable expense; fuel is the largest single item in
the shipping of all expeditions. During DEEP
FREEZE 77, for example, over 1.9 million gallons
of diesel and automotive fuels were delivered to

United States stations; another 2.5 million
gallons of aviation fuel (JP-4) were delivered.

The scarcity of water makes fire perhaps the
greatest single danger in Antarctica, with the
potential loss of shelter and food. For this
reason, antarctic stations usually consist of
separate buildings, and supplies are stored where
they will not catch fire. Many bases have a
refuge hut some distance from the main living
quarters. If chemical extinguishers do not control the fire and the base is destroyed, a refuge
with food is near. Personnel would be crowded and
have to ration their food carefully, but they
could survive until a plane or ship came to their
rescue; U.S. stations maintain at least a 15 month
supply of food, (NSFA, 1969).

In addition to producing water and electricity,
the Public Works Department maintains the many
different vehicles which build and maintain the
annual ice runways, both at McMurdo and the various field camps as established. They also provide
engineering guidance and information in addition
to acting as city planners. Other support
functions provided by the Navy at several stations
include communication services with the rest of
the world through the Defense Communications
Agency (DCA). The Navy also provides medical and
dental care for residents of the various stations.
Stations without complete dental or medical
facilities may send patients to McMurdo where a
complete health facility is maintained. Patients
with serious illness or life-threatening conditions can be removed from the continent using
the Department of Defense Medical Evacuation
System (MEDEVAC). The management of the port and
air terminals in the United States at Port Hueneme,
California, Christchurch, New Zealand, and in the
various stations is the responsibility of the Army
Transportation Corps assigned to Operation DEEP
FREEZE.

One of the last two stations to be built by the
Navy Seabees was Siple Station which is used primarily for upper atmosphere studies located near
the Antarctic Peninsula; construction was initiated on January 25, 1973 and is of the wonder-arch
type.

One of the most innovative types of antarctic

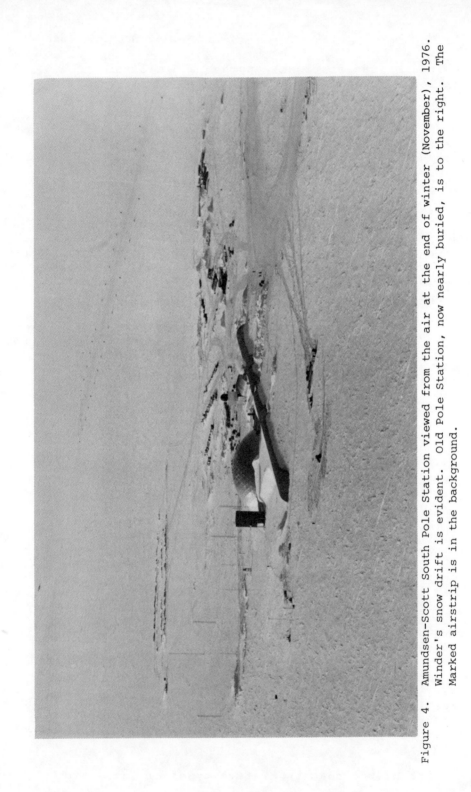

Figure 4. Amundsen-Scott South Pole Station viewed from the air at the end of winter (November), 1976. Winter's snow drift is evident. Old Pole Station, now nearly buried, is to the right. The Marked airstrip is in the background.

architecture is to be found at the new Amundsen-
Scott South Pole Station, (Fig. 4). Erected between DEEP FREEZE 71 and DEEP FREEZE 75, this station consists of a 16 meter high geodesic dome.
The dome covers three rectangular modular buildings; air between the dome and buildings is kept
at ambient temperature to avoid ice build-up as
well as melting of the snow and ice below. Attached to the dome are two wings built under steel
wonder-arches which are 14 meters wide, 24 meters
long.

The geodesic dome, first conceived by
Buckminster Fuller, was engineered by the Navy
Facilities Engineering Command and the Navy Civil
Engineering Laboratory. The design was chosen to
minimize snow build-up, which increases the ef-
fective life of the station.

The construction of the new South Pole Station
took the Seabees over 11,000 direct man-days,
18,000 including indirect and overhead requirements attributable to the project; a civilian con-
tractor expended 1,052 man-days on the project.

A 1972 study evaluated the desirability of
transfering the logistic support functions of
antarctic stations to civilian contractors. It
was determined that while it was cost effective to
transfer responsibility for the Amundsen-Scott
South Pole, Siple and Palmer Stations to civilian
contractors, McMurdo station should continue to be
operated principally by the Navy. However, the
Navy still provides resupply to the inland stations. Palmer Station is resupplied by the
British research vessel BRANSFIELD through an ar-
rangement with the National Science Foundation to
transport supplies from Naval Station, Mayport
Florida, and Naval Air Station, Jacksonville,
Florida.

Ship Operations

Fuel and most dry cargo are brought to
Antarctica by ship. In recent years, the United
States has had a tanker and a cargo ship plying
the route to Winter Quarters Bay at the foot of
McMurdo Station. Late in the season, a channel is
cut for these ships by Coast Guard icebreakers,
(Fig. 5). Ideally, the V-shaped channel is several

Figure 5.   Re-supply ships following a lead in
the sea ice cut by icebreakers.

miles wide at its entrance and gradually narrows
to several hundred yards at McMurdo's harbor, but
varying conditions of ice and weather often change
the plan, (NSFA, 1969).

To cut a channel, an icebreaker steams forward
and rides up onto the ice so that her weight can
break it; the engines are quickly reversed to
avoid getting stuck atop the ice. This is repeated to the left and right of the first cut. Often
a second icebreaker weaves back and forth across
the channel to keep the broken ice, called brash,
from refreezing. Man may design ships to break
the ice, but he must depend on nature to blow it
out to sea. Cutting a channel to McMurdo may take
three or more weeks but this can be done later in
the summer season because of an 18 month supply of
fuel stored at McMurdo. This time schedule spares
icebreaker effort as ice conditions grow less difficult and dangerous with the advance of summer.
This also allows the Coast Guard to schedule icebreakers for escort duties and other tasks, such
as oceanographic surveys.

Aircraft Operations

The first flight of any type of aircraft in the
antarctic was made in February 1902 in a captive
balloon by the British explorer, Captain Robert F.
Scott, of the Royal Navy. On the same day, one of
Scott's officers, LT Ernest H. Shackleton, went
aloft and took the first aerial photographs of
Antarctica. Since the days of Scott use of the
airplane has come to prevail and the types of aircraft vary widely, (Table 2).

While ships have always been essential components of logistic and research efforts in
Antarctica, wheeled and ski-equipped airplanes and
helicopters have revolutionized travel. The airplanes (Hercules, LC-130) and turbine powered
helicopters have significantly increased logistic
support and scientific research capabilities.

When the U.S. built a station at the South Pole
during DEEP FREEZE II (1956-1957), it depended
solely upon airdrops for the delivery of supplies
and equipment. For construction of Byrd Station,
however, it relied mainly on tractor trains operating from Little America V which was closed in

Table 2

Aircraft Used in Antarctic 1955-1975
(Taken from NSFA Aircraft in the Antarctic, 1971)

DEEP FREEZE I
1955-1956
7 HO4S-3
2 P2V
2 R4D
2 R5D-3
4 UC-1

DEEP FREEZE II
1956-1957
8 C-124
10 HO4S-3
7 HTL-5
4 P2V
4 R4D
2 R5D-3
10 UC-1

DEEP FREEZE III
1957-1958
8 C-124
6 HO4S-3
3 HUS-1A
5 HUL

DEEP FREEZE 60
1959-1960
2 C-54
10 C-124

4 P2V
4 R4D
2 R4D-8
2 R5D-3
9 UC-1

DEEP FREEZE IV
1958-1959
10 C-124
2 HO4S-3
2 HRS-3
4 HUL-1
3 HUS-1A
4 P2V
2 R4D
4 R4D-8
1 R5D-3
1 R7V-1
8 UC-1

7 C-130D
1 HO4S-3
1 HRS-3
1 HUL-1
4 HUS-1A

DEEP FREEZE 61
1960-1961
2 C-54
10 C-124
4 HO4S-3
4 HUL-1
4 HUS-1A
4 LC-130BL
3 P2V
1 R4D
3 R4D-8
1 R5D-3
1 R7V-1
5 UC-1

DEEP FREEZE 62
1961-1962
2 C-54

9 C-124
4 C-130BL
5 HRS-3
1 HTL-7
1 HUL-1
4 HUS-1A
2 HU-1B
3 P2V
1 R4D
3 R4D-8
1 R7V-1
4 UC-1

DEEP FREEZE 63
1962-1963
1 C-54Q
9 C-124
4 CH-19E
1 C-121J
3 HU-1B
3 LC-47
2 LC-117D
4 LC-130F
4 LH-34D

2 LP-2J
2 TH-13N
6 U-1B
1 UH-13P

DEEP FREEZE 64
1963-1964
1 C-54Q
1 C-121J
1 C-124
3 P2V
2 R4D
4 R4D-8
1 R5D-3
1 R7V-1
6 UC-1

DEEP FREEZE 65
1964-1965
2 C-121J
1 C-124
3 C-130E
5 CH-19E
5 LC-47

Table 2 (Continued)

2 LC-117D
4 LC-130F
5 LH-34D
4 U-1B
3 UH-1B
2 UH-13P

DEEP FREEZE 66
1965-1966

2 C-121J
2 C-124
4 C-130E
4 CH-19E
2 HH-52A
4 LC-47
2 LC-117D
4 LC-130F
5 LH-34D
4 U-1B
3 UH-1B
2 UH-13P

DEEP FREEZE 67
1966-1967

2 C-121J
2 C-130E

1 C-141
1 CH-19E
2 HH-52A
1 LC-47
2 LC-117D
4 LC-130F
5 LH-34D
3 UH-1D
2 UH-2A
2 UH-2B
1 UH-13P

DEEP FREEZE 68
1967-1968

2 C-121J
3 C-130E
5 CH-19E
5 LC-47
1 LC-117D
4 LC-130F
4 LH-34D
1 TH-13N
4 U-1B
3 UH-1B
2 UH-13P

DEEP FREEZE 69
1968-1969

2 C-121J
2 C-141
4 LC-130F
1 LC-130R
4 LH-34D
3 UH-1D
4 UH-2A
4 UH-2B

DEEP FREEZE 70
1969-1970

2 C-121J
2 C-141
4 LC-130F
1 LC-130R
4 LH-34D
3 UH-1D
6 HH-52A

DEEP FREEZE 71
1970-1971

4 LC-130F

1 LC-130R
2 C-121J
5 LH-34D
3 UH-1D

DEEP FREEZE 72
1971-1972

3 LC-130F
1 LC-130R
6 UH-1N

DEEP FREEZE 73
1972-1973

2 LC-130F
1 LC-130R
4 UH-1N

DEEP FREEZE 74
1973-1974

2 LC-130F
3 LC-130R
4 UH-1N

Figure 6. Fueling a Hercules LC-130 airplane from storage fuel bladders on the annual ice runway about two miles from McMurdo Station, Antarctica.

1959; subsequently, aircraft provided full support
of Byrd Station as well. Parachuting and free-
dropping cargo from the air was effective, but
with certain drawbacks. Notably, it placed a
heavy burden on the small groups of personnel who
had to recover scattered material, haul it to the
station, and store it. Also, the same lack of
ski-equipped airplanes that forced the use of airdrops meant that expensive parachutes and other
drop gear usually could not be recovered and re-
used.

In January 1960, the U.S. Air Force brought the
first ski-equipped C-130 cargo planes to Antarctica
and operated them out of McMurdo Station. These
aircraft, capable of landing on flat areas anywhere
in the antarctic, were so useful and versatile
that the Navy obtained four ski-equipped Hercules
later that year. Brought into service during DEEP
FREEZE 61, these LC-130's were at first used to
resupply South Pole and Byrd Station with dry
cargo while Air Force C-124's continued air-drop-
ping petroleum products to these inland stations.
Such airdrops continued through DEEP FREEZE 63
(1962-1963), after which there was no direct Air
Force support to the inland stations until operations at Dome Charlie during DEEP FREEZE 76 (1975-
1976). This operation necessitated an inland air
drop due to problems with the Hercules aircraft
operating in the area prior to preparation of skiways.

Since DEEP FREEZE 64 (1963-1964), Navy LC-130's
have flown fuel inland in metal tanks of 3,600
gallon capacity. At the stations, the fuel can be
pumped directly from these fuselage tanks into
rubber storage bladders in minutes, (Fig. 6).

The logistic usefulness of the Hercules was
also demonstrated during DEEP FREEZE 61 (1960-1961)
when five LC-130 flights carried all the building
materials, equipment, and supplies needed to establish Sky Hi, a summer scientific station, more
than 1,500 miles from McMurdo. It was this success
which led to the development of air transportable
van-type stations such as Eights and Plateau,
(NSFA, 1969).

Earlier, the LC-130 had revolutionized field
party support. On December 10, 1960, two of these

aircraft placed a party of nine men with 10 tons
of equipment, including vehicles, 1,300 miles distant from McMurdo. When recovered at the end of
the season, such parties may either leave their
supplies and camp where it plans to resume work
the following year, or have them returned to a
station for overhaul and repair, (NSFA, 1969).

Besides helping in the field, airplanes make
the scientist's work year more productive. Formerly, a scientist wishing to do field work arrived
in Antarctica one season, spent the winter at a
station, and went to the field the following
spring. Now, scientists leave the U.S. in October,
reach the field early in November, conduct studies,
and return in February, accomplishing in four or
five months that which had previously required 18.
In 1967, the United States experimented with fly-
ing a small group of scientists to McMurdo Station
in June, in the depth of the antarctic night,
bringing them back in August or early September,
at the conclusion of the summer vacation of northern hemisphere colleges and universities. This
permitted antarctic research by scientists who
could not otherwise have studied in Antarctica,
(NSFA, 1969). This experiment has not been repeated due to the difficulty of night-time
antarctic aviation.

Helicopters were introduced into the antarctic
in 1947 as part of Operation Highjump. Working
from ships, they were used for ice reconnaissance
and ship-to-shore transports. During the IGY and
later years, additional shore-based helicopters
have been employed to place biologists and geologists in the ice-free areas around McMurdo Sound
and to move them from one place of scientific interest to another. Piston-powered helicopters,
however, could not fly a sufficient distance or
elevation to support remote field investigations
in mountainous areas, or on the polar plateau.
During DEEP FREEZE 62 (1961-1962), however, the
U.S. Army sent two turbine-powered UH-1 helicopters to Antarctica. These vehicles could land at
heights up to 13,000 feet, thus overcoming the
altitude restriction of piston motors; furthermore, they could be transported in LC-130's, thus
extending their range. They were first used in
making topographic surveys and later adopted for
geological investigation. From 1965 to 1969, the

Army annually provided a detachment of three such
helicopters to support field surveys of up to 20
scientists. In April 1969, the detachment's three
UH-1's were transferred to the Navy for operation
beginning in DEEP FREEZE 70 (1969-1970), (NSFA,
1969).

Although airplanes and helicopters have opened
vast areas of the antarctic to man's scientific
curiosity, they do have their limitations. They
must have good weather in a region notorious for
bad weather. Even with skis, airplanes cannot
land everywhere; most helicopters, which can, lack
the range. Compared with the size of Antarctica,
even the range of the LC-130 is small, and trans-
porting fuel to extend its range, consumes vast
quantities of it. Finally, aircraft must have
many facilities on the surface if they are to operate dependably and safely. Despite all of this,
aircraft have clearly established themselves as a
most valuable resource of the United States
Antarctic Research Program, (NSFA, 1969).

The other aircraft used currently by the United
States is the Air Force C-141 Starlifter transport.
First tested in a November 1966 flight to McMurdo,
the giant pure-jet transport was put into regular
use in DEEP FREEZE 69 (1968-1969). It shuttles
cargo and passengers between the United States and
McMurdo Station each season. Because it lands on
wheels, it requires a prepared ice runway on the
annual sea ice about two miles from McMurdo. This
runway usually lasts until mid-December before it
becomes an unsafe platform for C-141 operations.
Thereafter all aircraft operations, on and off the
continent, are conducted with ski-equipped
LC-130's.

The United States has made great use of aviation in the antarctic (Table II), but it has not
been alone. A few other nations' expeditions em-
ploy light planes and helicopters carried aboard
ships while some use large airplanes. Argentina,
Great Britain, and Chile have operated aircraft
around the Antarctic Peninsula, and Argentine aircraft have twice visited the South Pole. On the
second of these flights, one Argentine C-47 continued across the continent and landed at McMurdo.
The Soviet Union supplements tractor-train support
of its inland stations with aircraft, (NSFA, 1969).

Figure 7. Preparing to tractor-haul a disabled Hercules LC-130 at Dome Charlie, Antarctica.

Aircraft accidents have spotted the history of antarctic aviation. However, not all aircraft accidents ended on a somber note. DEEP FREEZE 77 (1976-1977) saw the successful completion of one of the most challenging engineering endeavors to be attempted in the antarctic and it now provides another successful chapter in naval aviation history.

The Navy was asked to pick up a field party of five persons from the International Antarctic Glaciological Project (IAGP). Dome "C" (74°30'S, 123°10'E) is one of three ice domes which rise out of the antarctic plateau, the other two are designated "A" and "B". Dome C is of particular interest to glaciologists because it marks a point of some of the world's thickest known ice.

On January 15, 1975 the aircraft had an accident while making a jet assisted take-off (JATO) after picking up a field party. The JATO bottle became detached from the fuselage, fired through the starboard wing, aborting the takeoff; there were no personal injuries. Four hours later a second aircraft was dispatched to pick up the crew and passengers from the first. During its take-off the nose ski collapsed; within four hours two aircraft, representing approximately 18 million dollars, were stranded at this remote location (Fig. 7).

It was determined that repair of the aircraft in the field was feasible and that it would be cost effective to do so. During the salvage operation the following season, a third aircraft accident occurred when again a JATO bottle detached from the fuselage and was propelled forward to shatter the number three engine propeller. Salvage operations were continued and by the end of DEEP FREEZE 76 two of the three aircraft were recovered and returned to operation. The third was recovered during DEEP FREEZE 77 and, with a capital investment of approximately 2.5 million dollars and much ingenuity the three aircraft were returned to active support operations at a replacement savings of about 27 million dollars.

Even with the increased use of aircraft some scientific work, such as taking closely spaced seismic soundings, is best done on a traverse with tracked vehicles pulling sleds across the contin-

ent. Traverses have been used as recently as 1976
for the supplying of the various remote scientific
field camps within about 70 miles of McMurdo.

Regardless of the mode of travel in the
antarctic, weather is still the single most significant factor to be dealt with. A condition
known as "white-out" occurs all too frequently.
During a white-out condition the horizon loses all
definition and travel becomes extremely dangerous
if not impossible; accurate weather information in
Antarctica is of the greatest importance.

Meteorology

With only some 20 stations in Antarctica reporting weather observations (there are over 600
weather reporting stations in the continental
United States), meteorologists are anxious to use
Automatic Weather Stations (AWS). AWS are currently being tested in Antarctica. These units are
nuclear-powered, using thermocouples to convert a
part of the heat produced by the decay of radio-
isotopes to electrical energy. Currently, one of
these experimental units is located at Marble
Point on McMurdo Sound. Units of this type have
been under development since February 7, 1962, but
are still largely experimental. During DEEP FREEZE
77 (1976-1977) a battery powered AWS was located
at the Dufek Massif by a field research party.
The unit powered by twelve D-type dry cells
functioned for approximately two months. It is
anticipated that in the future these units can be
refined to allow increased accuracy in obtaining
weather data at uninhabited areas.

Automatic picture transmission (APT) to receive
satellite photographs was installed in late 1965
at McMurdo Station and DEEP FREEZE Advance Headquarters, Christchurch, New Zealand. These show
large-scale atmospheric phenomena such as the jet
stream and major storms. McMurdo's location
allows reception of photographs from part of every
satellite transit in polar orbit providing coverage of the entire continent. Analysts can distinguish clouds from snow-covered surfaces by
locating shadows of clouds or known landmarks.
Such shadows are most visible in photographs taken
at low sun angles which a satellite encounters
when passing from the dark hemisphere to the sun-

lit side of the earth. Higher sun angles make
pictures harder to interpret, except for ice reconnaissance, since ice contrasts sharply with
dark water, (NSFA, 1965).

Satellite photography has been a great asset in
polar meteorology. Forecasts based on APT data
were used to plan highly successful photomapping
flights during DEEP FREEZE 67 (1966-1967); among
areas photographed were the Belleny Islands south
of New Zealand where bad weather had blocked photomapping efforts for seven years. The first DEEP
FREEZE ship to have this equipment was USCGC
GLACIER, which was equipped with an APT receiver
for use during DEEP FREEZE 68 (1967-1968).

Additional meteorological support is provided
by the Navy Fleet Weather Facility (Suitland,
Maryland). This support includes specialized ice
reconnaisance utilizing very high resolution
satellite imagery. Daily satellite analyses of
weather systems over oceanic areas surrounding the
continent are transmitted to assist forecasters in
areas beyond local satellite receiving capabilities. Currently, McMurdo's Weather Center acts as
the central collecting agency for all antarctic
station observations and forecasts which are for-
warded to international weather networks.

McMurdo Weather Center supplies all field parties from either the United States or New Zealand
with field kits for making and recording meteorological observations if they request this equipment. Further support to field camps includes
severe weather warnings, daily forecasts for the
station and its environs, as well as aviation
forecasts in support of all aircraft operations in
the field.

The major focus, however, is providing enroute
and terminal weather forecasts for all inter- and
intracontinental LC-130 and UH-1N flights.

At both polar regions the Navy has had a significant role in the past and, if indeed history
is a valid teacher, the partnership between the
Navy and the scientific community seems very likely to continue into the future.

References

Anderson, Commander W.R. and Clay Blair Jr. 1959.
NAUTILUS 90 NORTH. World Publishing Company,
Cleveland, Ohio.

DeLong, Emma, 1884. The Voyage of the JEANNETTE,
Houghton Mifflin Company, Boston, Massachusetts.

Ley, Willy, 1962. The Poles, Time-Life Books,
Inc., New York, New York.

Naval Support Force, Antarctica (NSFA) September
1965. Support for Science:Antarctica. Superintendent of Documents, U.S. Government Printing Office, Washington, D.C.

Naval Support Force, Antarctica (NSFA) 1969.
Introduction to Antarctica. History and Re-
search Division, U.S. Naval Support Force,
Antarctica, Washington, D.C.

Naval Support Force, Antarctica (NSFA) April 1971.
U.S. Aircraft in the Antarctic:Basis of Modern
Exploration. (Monograph number three in a
series, History and Research Division). U.S.
Naval Support Force, Antarctica, Washington,
D.C.

Stringer, Jerry R., Capt. USAF (Ed.) 1976. Inter-
agency Arctic Research Coordinating Committee,
Arctic Bulletin 2(8). Information Service
Division of Polar Programs, National Science
Foundation, Washington, D.C.

Weems, John Edward, 1960. Race for the Pole.
Henry Holt and Company, New York, New York.

11

Polar Research:
Status and Prospectus

Robert H. Rutford

Nine years ago the American Association for the Advancement of Science sponsored a symposium at the 1968 meeting in
Dallas and published in a volume entitled "Research in the
Antarctic" (Quam, 1971). Seven years ago the Bulletin of
Atomic Scientists (1970) devoted an issue to the review of
progress in science and international cooperation in the
Antarctic. It is well worth reviewing the articles found
in those two volumes as background for a look at the status
of polar science today. What is most striking from such a
review is that, despite the pessimistic pronouncements of
some, the conduct of science in these less hospitable portions of the earth's environment continues to pay dividends.

This symposium has provided an opportunity to describe
to a broader audience than normal the accomplishments and
also the problems of polar science. Until recently there
has been a tendency to ignore the importance of the polar
regions in the development of many global models. This is
not surprising, since most of us grew up looking at the maps
of the world on Mercator projections that by construction
do not include the poles. Computers have found it difficult
to handle the rapid convergence of the lines of longitude
close to the poles, and even the automatic navigation
systems in aircraft cry "tilt" when forced to calculate
positions in the high polar regions.

Most of these technical problems have now been resolved.
Maps with polar projections are now more readily available.
Those who would model the earth's atmosphere or oceans are
aware they cannot ignore the seasonal growth and decay of
the sea ice around Antarctica or the thin ice cover of the
Arctic ocean. Navigation systems have been modified to
accomodate the special needs of the polar regions.

Previous authors have dealt with the specifics of their scientific discipline and have indicated some of the contribution that further studies can make. It is not my intent to reiterate their remarks, but rather to look at the matrix of outside influences that impact on the conduct of polar science. The antipodal geography of the two polar areas has been mentioned. I would note also to a very great degree, this could as well be applied to their social, political, and economic aspects as well.

The Arctic is an ocean basin with a thin ice cover surrounded by lands controlled by some of the major industrial nations of the world. The land masses surrounding the Arctic ocean basin have long been occupied by man, and only recently has the native culture been intruded upon by the influence of the industrial nations as the rich resources of these lands were exploited. The Antarctic is a land mass with a thick ice cover, over three kilometers thick, surrounded by the Southern Oceans. There is no record of an indigenous human population, and the only active political interest in territorial claims has been quite recent and has focused on the appendage extending north toward South America, the Antarctic Peninsula.

There is a tendency to think of the development of the Arctic as an historical event, yet it is only a century ago that the gold rush in Alaska took place, the event that opened up the interior of that state, and just over 75 years ago that the famous Klondike gold rush brought thousands of people to the north to seek their fortunes. World War II probably had a greater and more lasting impact on the semi-permanent to permanent settlement of the true Arctic than any other event.

Territorial claims had largely been settled prior to economic development in the Arctic. The driving force for development was the exploitation of the rich mineral and living resources of the area, and little attention was paid to conservation, environmental protection, or the impact of such activities on the native peoples and their culture.

In the Arctic today we have an extension of the industrial complex with all of its advantages, problems, and tensions. Commercial airline flights to Barrow, Prudhoe Bay, and Soviet arctic communities occur daily, but to some names such as Sondrestromfjord (Greenland) and Longyearbyen (Svalbard) in airline schedules may come as a surprise. We are all aware of the Alaska pipeline and haul road, but we hear little of the similar developments in the Soviet Arctic now opening up the northern fringes of that large and rich area. Settlement and development of the lands continues throughout the Arctic today, although under somewhat different conditions.

Conservation and concern for the environment are for the first time being considered as this development takes place. The controversy surrounding Arctic oil and gas field development and the associated pipelines and terminal facilities in both the Alaskan and Canadian Arctic are well known. Similar concerns are being expressed in other Arctic areas, and steps are being taken to minimize the impact of the development and to attempt to manage the resources in some meaningful way. Restriction on development have been initiated by several nations, and the pace of development and exploitation has been slowed to some extent.

Science in the Arctic regions has been a part of its history. The early explorers generally had scientific personnel as party members and considerable knowledge of the fringes of arctic lands was accumulated. These early reconnaissance studies were followed by more specialized studies, a pattern evolving in the Antarctic today. However, there was no organized effort on the part of any of the nations to conduct research in the Arctic. The efforts were largely the result of individual effort to obtain funding and logistic support, often from private sources.

Hickock (1977) notes the close relationship between resource development and research activities in the Arctic. The discovery of oil on the North Slope triggered the present surge of environmental research while past activities were related to whaling, fisheries, gold, agriculture, and military activities.

The scientific activities of the various U.S. federal agencies in the Arctic appears to be representative of the mode of operation of most of the other major nations. Fourteen agencies reported a total expenditure of $53,000,000 in the Arctic during fiscal year 1976, the majority of these funds spent in Alaska. A broad spectrum of activity was represented, not all of which would fall under the generally accepted definition of either research or the Arctic. Mission-oriented activities of the various agencies dominate, with the environmental baseline studies of the Alaskan continental shelf represented as the single largest program. Basic research is but a small percentage of the total expenditure.

The lack of a general "policy" and only a casual attempt at coordination by the various federal agencies through the Inter-Agency Arctic Research Coordinating

Committee results in continuing problems. Similar coordination problems exist in other nations. It is encouraging to
note increased efforts by the federal agencies to provide
advance notice and to attempt to coordinate activities,
especially in the area of environmental research.

The conduct of science in the Arctic has been and
continues to be largely a collection of independent national
efforts, although there has been, and hopefully will continue to be, some international activity. I think I am
safe in saying that the bilateral arrangements between
nations have served well in a limited way; there have been
good personal contacts established with information exchange,
but truly joint international efforts to work on specific
problems of the Arctic have been quite limited. Informal
interaction may well be more useful than the formalized
arrangements between the various nations.

One must realize that the Arctic basin is surrounded by
countries all of whom have their eyes on the north. The
Soviets have opened their Arctic sea routes and these form
an important link in the movement of goods and people into
and out of the north. The development of those sea routes
in the North American Arctic lags well behind. The area
has significant military importance to nations adjacent to
the Arctic ocean. The ability to conduct international
scientific efforts in this area is often subject to both
political and/or military approval. The prospect of joint
ventures in the Arctic remain uncertain. The increasing
potential for resource development in the Arctic basin is
rousing strong nationalistic feelings that certainly will
impact on future attempts to launch major international
scientific efforts.

The recent settlement of the native land claims in
Alaska and the recognition of the natives' interest in
their lands is now and will in the future play an increasing
role in the conduct of science in the Arctic. The interest
of the native peoples is not to be taken lightly, and
their attitude towards science activities on their lands is
most encouraging. They, too, seek joint efforts, partnership,
and input into the decision making process. Their concerns
with conservation, quality of life, and the future of the
Arctic lands and seas is real, and they are going to be
involved.

Antarctica

In contrast to the Arctic, the Antarctic is a large land mass, 97% ice covered by glacial ice up to 4.5 km. thick, surrounded and separated from populated areas by an ocean that is characterized by foul weather, huge icebergs, and a continuous ice-cover during large parts of the year. Antarctica at present has no indigenous population, no proven mineral resources on land or on the adjacent continental shelf, and commercial activity, tourism and fishing, that is just developing. While seven nations claim portions of Antarctica, most nations do not recognize these claims, now held in abeyance by the Antarctic Treaty, a document signed by all claimants.

Antarctica came to the attention of the world for the first time during the heroic age of Shackleton, Scott, and Amundsen in the early part of this century. The Richard E. Byrd expeditions in the 1920s and 1930s increased the U. S. interest in this southern continent. Following World War II large scale mapping efforts by the United States added greatly to our knowledge of the geography of Antarctica.

While earlier expeditions conducted some scientific activities, the International Geophysical Year (IGY) 1957-58, during which twelve nations established over 60 research stations in Antarctica, marked the beginning of the major scientific activity that has continued to the present. The international working agreements reached during that effort were recognized as unique by all involved, and they became the basis for the Scientific Committee on Antarctic Research (SCAR) and the Antarctic Treaty.

SCAR, established in 1958 as a committee of the International Council of Scientific Unions, is tasked to continue the scientific and logistic cooperation begun during the IGY. The working groups and groups of specialists work in a forum of openness and candid discussions; international politics are not a part of the deliberations. The SCAR seeks to identify scientific problems of circum-Antarctic scope and significance, and the member nations work independently or jointly to bring available logistics support and scientific personnel to seek solutions to these problems. Multi-national efforts are common.

The Antarctic Treaty, drafted in 1959 and ratified by all of the signatories in 1961, also continues the spirit of cooperation achieved during the IGY, but in the political rather than scientific arena. The treaty provides that Antarctica shall be used for peaceful purposes only, that

there will be freedom of scientific investigation, exchange
of information and scientific personnel, no military bases,
fortification or weapons testing, no nuclear explosions or
disposal of radioactive waste material, there shall be the
right to inspect other nations stations and activities, and
all shall work toward preservation and conservation of
Antarctic living resources. Science became the entree to
Antarctica.

Questions concerning territorial claims are deferred
and new claims or enlargement of existing claims are pro-
hibited. The treaty is silent on the question of mineral
resource explorations and/or exploitation.

Thus, there came into existence two international groups,
SCAR, the non-political scientific body, and the treaty
mechanism on the political side. The two groups meet
biennially in alternate years by mutual agreement between
the two organizations.

In the decade following ratification of the treaty,
the treaty consultative meetings drafted recommendations for
their governments for conduct of affairs in Antarctica.
Some of the recommendations dealt with conservation of
Antarctic fauna and flora in recognition of the delicate
nature of the ecosystem and the wish to protect it from
misuse and abuse. In 1964 these conservationist recommendations culminated in recommendation III-8, entitled
"Agreed Measures for the Conservation of Antarctic Fauna and
Flora." Other recommendations designated areas of historical interest, specially protected areas, and sites of special
scientific interest, specifying areas which are protected
more stringently than the rest of the Antarctic. Although
not all the treaty nations have ratified these measures,
they have accepted them in principle and have implemented
and enforced them; this is a reflection of the spirit of
the treaty itself.

In 1972 a convention for the conservation of Antarctic
seals that limits the number of seals that can be harvested
and prohibits the capture of some species was adopted.
Many recommendations adopted at the consultative meetings
originated from within the SCAR working groups or groups of
specialists.

Concurrent with the increased awareness of environmental
protection elsewhere came the same interests in Antarctica.
A SCAR symposium on ecology in 1968 devoted one session to
conservation. In 1971 a colloquium was held on environmental
problems in Antarctica, and a volume was published. In 1972

SCAR established a group of specialists to deal specifically
with environmental problems in Antarctica. The United States
has become the leader in this effort, having written environmental impact statements for two major projects, the Dry
Valley Drilling Project and the Ross Ice Shelf Project. An
environmental impact statement for the entire U.S. Antarctic
Program is in preparation.

The last decade has seen considerable change in world
interests in the Antarctic. In the 1960s the treaty consultative meetings dealt with matters of little apparent
interest or importance to any except those either working in
Antarctica or designated by their governments to attend
treaty meetings. In the early 1970s with the first hint of
hydrocarbons, the increase in tourism, and the increasing
harvest of fish and krill the Antarctic began to attract
the attention of other groups within the treaty nations and
also nations not signators of the treaty or members of SCAR.

Today at the treaty consultative meetings the delegates
consider issues of broader scope and greater difficulty than
they have in the past. The Law of the Sea conferences have
had an impact; although the subject of Antarctica has been
excluded from these conferences, some nations have informally
pressed for inclusion. In addition to the procedural issues
focusing on the admission to consultative status of nations
now active in Antarctic research and acceding to the treaty,
the matters of both living and mineral resources are topics
of deliberation. SCAR has been asked to give scientific
input to assist in the resolution of the political questions.
Antarctica's time as a refuge from international tension and
commercial considerations appears to be drawing to a close;
the honeymoon is over.

The two decades of international cooperation in
scientific research that began with the IGY have contributed
to the present interests in the resource potential of
Antarctica. Geologists and geophysicists have established
the position of Antarctica in the former supercontinent,
Gondwanaland, in which Antarctica was adjacent to South
Africa, India, and Australia. The sections of these
countries that formerly were adjacent to Antarctica contain
rich mineral resources, and suggest that Antarctica also
contains such resources.

Biologists have learned enough to estimate populations of
some species of the living resources of the southern ocean
and adjacent coastal zone of Antarctica. Speculation as to
population characteristics, management of the resource
should exploitation increase, and the ability of the ecosys-

tem to survive have been discussed in the literature and report of this symposium.

Even glaciologists have contributed to the economic assessment of Antarctic resources through calculations showing the tonnage of icebergs that calve from Antarctic ice shelves each year. Several studies have shown that Antarctic icebergs, towed to arid areas, might provide a fresh water source.

Commercial exploitation of the Antarctic has begun. At least five nations are engaged catching fish or krill in the waters adjacent to Antarctica. Tourism is expanding rapidly. The impact of cruise ships and passengers is rapidly becoming a problem in the Antarctic Peninsula area, and at least one nation has limited visits by cruise ships to their bases. Overflights of large commercial aircraft from Australia and New Zealand began this year and requests to land at stations will undoubtedly soon follow.

The unique scientific enclave of Antarctica is an endangered species. The international cooperation in all aspects of science and logistics that has characterized the Antarctic since IGY is threatened by the reality that Antarctica cannot remain isolated from the political and economic stresses of the rest of the world forever.

We stand at a time of major decision. Discussions being held both within and outside the context of the Antarctic Treaty will have a lasting impact on the ability to conduct science in Antarctica. The freedom of movement and the exchange of scientists and data that has made Antarctic science unique is threatened by the growth of nationalistic feelings among the nations as the resource questions are considered.

The single agency management of the U.S. Antarctic Program allows for close coordination between scientists from all disciplines, and there are numerous examples of a synergism that has resulted from the close proximity of those involved. The U.S. science programs have made many significant contributions to science, some discussed in this volume but also in other disciplines not discussed at the symposium.

However, there is a divergency of opinion within the United States on the question of the future of the Antarctic. Will it follow the course set in the Arctic with exploitation overcoming most other considerations, or should we take this opportunity to carefully manage this unique and still relatively pristine part of the globe? Should a limit be placed on development, or should, in fact, the continent be set aside as an "international park?"

In the Arctic the major decisions have been made. The input from scientists, engineers, and others will have some effect, but the system is in place and working; little can be done to change it. Science will continue to be supported by agencies as part of their mission, but many of the kinds of basic studies necessary for intelligent decision making will languish for lack of financial support or will be overcome by the speed and the course of events. National interests and goals will continue to dominate, and it is unlikely that truly international scientific efforts will be possible.

In contrast the Antarctic offers the opportunity for enlightened management. The existing treaty provides a framework within which to work. The pattern of problem identification and scientific assessment established by SCAR provides the basis upon which a scheme might be developed. The community of Antarctic scientists must emerge from their isolated world and get involved in the process of decision making that will determine the fate of Antarctica as an international scientific refuge.

It is my belief that the nations of the world recognize the necessity for an expansion of knowledge relating to the Antarctic ecosystem, and that the living resource question can be resolved before permanent damage is done. Input from the scientists must be considered by the assembly of international lawyers and foreign service officers. It is also my belief that the spirit of the Antarctic treaty is strong enough to survive the stresses being placed upon it by the resource questions, and that out of this will come an international agreement that will continue the concept of international scientific cooperation.

One final point must be made regarding polar science. By the simple fact that it is carried out at great distances from the sources of manpower and supplies, it is expensive. Even in the Arctic where commercial logistics support is available, there is a long logistics pipeline that greatly increases costs. Operations in Antarctica are even more expensive, and the logistics costs greatly exceed the actual science costs. The increasing costs for energy will result in increased logistics costs to support science.

The question is continually asked, does the end justify the means? Those of us who call ourselves polar scientists are prejudiced and cannot answer that question objectively. It is incumbent upon us, however, to utilize every means available to point out not only to the scientific world,

but also to the policy and decision makers who provide the
funds to support the majority of polar research, that the
scientific payoff is high enough to justify the costs associated with it. We might well learn from our associates in
space science who have done an excellent job of keeping
space science at the forefront both within the public and
scientific arenas.

The status of polar science today is good. The pros-
pectus is clouded by the potential impact of events outside
the normal venue of the scientific community. Only by a
concerted effort and involvement in the decision making
process will the voice of the scientists be heard. The
treaty mechanism and SCAR provide the arena in which the
decisions will be made. The decisions made will be political
and economic, but the scientific community will and must be
involved if they hope to maintain and improve the role of
science in the polar regions.

References

Bulletin of the Atomic Scientists (1970), Vol. XXVI, No. 10
    (Antarctica Since the IGY, Philip M. Smith, Special
    Editor), Chicago, Illinois.

Hickok, David M. (1977), Storage, Transfer, and Usage of
    Alaskan Environmental Information, Arctic Bulletin,
    Vol. 2, No. 10, pp. 189-193.

Quam, Louis O. (1971), Editor, Research in the Antarctic,
    AAAS, Washington, D. C., 768 pp.

12

Major International
Polar Research Programs

Mary A. McWhinnie and Duwayne M. Anderson

This volume is of necessity limited in scope,
since it is impossible to include the many polar
research programs whose objectives do not relate
directly to investigations of polar biota. These
programs are multidisciplinary and, in keeping
with principles of cooperation and freedom in exchange of knowledge, they are international. Some
of these are briefly described below.

As in south circumpolar seas, the relatively
circumscribed Bering Sea in the Arctic is characterized by a high biomass with an apparent high
efficiency of energy transfer. Study of the
Processes and Resources Of the Bering Sea Shelf
(PROBES) is a multidisciplinary program now being
implemented. It is directed to discovery of the
mechanisms of energy transfer from primary producers to diverse consumers with particular
emphasis on a biological tracer, the Alaskan pollock (Theragra chalcogramma). Through a systems
analysis of secondary production, this study of
the food-web dynamics of the continental shelf
community of the Bering Sea, will consider the
coupling of meteorological forcing of physical circulation, availability of nutrients, phytoplankton
size fractionation, zooplankton production, and
developmental stages of pollock. The goal of this
program is to understand intermediate mechanisms
and forces within a coastal food-web by study from
phytoplankton to higher trophic levels. The
dynamics of secondary production in any marine food
chain is little known and stands as an impediment
to further understanding of the ecology of continental shelves. A high latitude ecosystem such

as the Bering Sea has a relatively clear pulse of
initial energy transfer into the food-web after
the spring breakup of ice. PROBES is designed to
follow the course of this well defined pulse from
algae to larval and adult nekton. Study of secondary productivity will be made in the context of
understanding the quantitative linkage between the
natural oscillation of meteorological variables
and the abundance of higher trophic levels. Because of possible overfishing and oil development
in the Bering Sea, the results of PROBES will also
be of value in providing an ecological basis for
management aspects of the resources of this continental shelf.

Field work was initiated in spring, 1977, in
the Golden Triangle area of the Bering Sea. The
major work was to determine the distribution of
pollock eggs and early larval stages in association with the biological, chemical, and physical
environment in which they are found. Subsequent
seasons will continue the same general theme at
later stages in the pollock life cycle until adult
fish are the principal study. From these data a
simulation model of the secondary production regime of the Bering Sea Shelf will be constructed.

While comprehensive inventories of living resources and their temporal and spatial variations
are being developed in arctic Alaskan waters, the
ultimate goal of conservation can only be realized
by understanding the mechanisms and processes
operating within ecosystems. Attainment of this
goal also requires understanding of oceanographic
and climatological features which provide the matrix for ecosystem dynamics. The Bering Sea
offers a discrete system amenable to study of
these interactions.

With a similar goal, a comprehensive program
has been designed for Biological Investigations
Of Marine Antarctic Systems and Stocks (BIOMASS);
it is multidisciplinary in perspective and international in undertaking. The objective of this
program is deeper understanding of the structure
and dynamic functioning of the antarctic marine
ecosystem, and it will focus primarily on the
biotically rich areas of the Scotia-Weddell Sea.
As in the Bering Sea, this region is uncommonly

high in biomass and defines the once-rich whaling
and sealing grounds of decades past. However, in
contrast to the Bering Sea, the single most significant component of this ecosystem is at the
level of zooplankton. Among these are the
herbivorous euphausiid crustacea which occupy the
unique position of direct or indirect support of
all higher trophic levels including fish, squid,
birds, seals, and whales. The simplicity and
success of this ecosystem are sufficient reason
for its comprehensive study; its potential for
providing a new source of protein make it compel-
ling as commercial utilization of krill becomes
imminent.

Unique to high southern latitudes characterized by a high biotic density is a series of
oceanic currents distinguished by the eastward
flowing Antarctic Circumpolar Current (West Wind
Drift) and the westward flowing Antarctic Coastal
Current (East Wind Drift). Between these two
systems is a series of eddies and gyres with the
largest occurring in the Atlantic Sector. The
western boundary of the Weddell gyre is defined by
the Antarctic Peninsula, whereas to the east the
circulation turns south between $30^\circ E$ and the
Kerguelen Plateau, subsequently westward, and
again northward. This area also defines the region of highest known density of Euphausia superba.
A proposed international Weddell GYRE project is
being designed to investigate the current systems
of this area (both marine and atmospheric), to
examine the role and influence of sea-ice cover,
and to disclose the link between these currents
and the life history and populational success of
the euphausiids and their dependent consumers.
Another part of this program is being designed to
extend our present understanding of the formation
of Antarctic Bottom Water which flows northward
and underlies nearly three-fourths of the world's
ocean. The role of sea-ice formation, its con-
sequent salt rejection resulting in high salinity
water, and the response of ocean currents to atmospheric circulation can only be clarified through
concurrent study of chemical and physical oceanography, ice dynamics, and meteorology. Here, in
a manner similar to the Bering Sea, the interplay
of phenomena identified in the domain of biology,
chemistry, geology, glaciology, meteorology, and
physical oceanography are so reflexive and inter-

connected as to require a multidisciplinary
approach; the dimensions of such investigations in
space and time require international participation
and cooperation. The proposed Weddell GYRE project
arises as a natural extension of the International
Weddell Sea Oceanographic Expedition (IWSOE) conceived in 1966, initiated in 1968, and continuing
to the present. With new knowledge derived from
these studies, the concept of the more broadly
based multidisciplinary Weddell GYRE program has
emerged.

Similar gyres exist in other polar regions.
Indeed, since the historical journey of Fridtjof
Nansen, from 1893 to 1896, during which the ship,
FRAM, drifted with polar ice in the high Arctic
from the Laptev Sea to Spitsbergen, there have
been research stations on drifting arctic pack-ice.
The Arctic Ice Dynamics Joint Experiment (AIDJEX),
concluded in May, 1976, took advantage of this
natural floating platform as its investigations
sought to clarify the mechanics of perennial sea-
ice cover. Through five years of study, it was
planned to model the interactions of arctic air,
sea, and ice on world climate. When the model is
validated, forecasting of ice movements is expected
to improve. The Nimbus G satellite collected data
on pressure, temperature, and position from automatic data buoys placed on sea ice, thus extending
information gathering beyond that possible from
manned, ice-based stations alone. Though the
program is formally completed, these buoys continue to collect data reporting to the satellite
Nimbus G; in accord with their longevity, information gathering will continue contributing to
validation of the model.

Taking advantage of capabilities in polar air
support and automated data acquisition, repetition
of the northern circumpolar course taken by Nansen
has been proposed as a multidisciplinary and
multinational Nansen Drift Station project (NDS).
The objectives are to investigate climatology and
paleoclimatology, resource geology, marine geophysics and tectonics, acoustics, ice mechanics
and engineering, air-ice-sea interactions, upper
atmosphere and ionospheric physics, physical
oceanography, and adaptational biology and biochemistry. By locking into the arctic ice a
multipurpose research ship, an accessible and

durable platform could be available for long-term
study. The complementarity of the NDS and Weddell
GYRE projects portends a new level of understanding
of unique polar oceanographic and atmospheric
phenomena. Their discoveries should, in time,
yield the understanding required to interrelate
global phenomena whose syntheses still remain
fragmentary.

If it is approved and implemented the NDS program will provide the platform for other studies,
as well, extending investigations of other lower-
latitude programs into the north polar area.
Information gained from its marine geology and
paleoclimatology programs can provide data on the
climatic history of the Arctic and a basis for
understanding and projecting possible climatic
change. These investigations could couple with
those of Climate: Long-range Investigation,
Mapping and Prediction Study, CLIMAP, a sub-
program of the International Decade of Oceanographic Exploration (IDOE, the 1970's). In the
same manner it could extend the data, and their
interpretation, from an International Magneto-
spheric Study and the first Global Atmospheric
Research Program (GARP) through its regional
Polar Sub-Experiment on atmospheres (POLEX). The
latter are either under way or in an advanced
state of planning.

GARP is an international program representing
the largest global experiment thus far conducted
toward the understanding of climate, the role of
ice in climate dynamics, of stratus and katabatic
winds, of oceanic transport, and of upper ocean
exchange processes. The goal is to improve weather prediction. In a global network of automatic
data collecting stations, atmospheric and oceanic
processes, including air-mass transport and exchange, will be measured. The Polar-Sub-Experi-
ment is a first step toward critical tests of the
role of ice in climate dynamics.

As atmospheric-meteorological studies reach to
the upper stratosphere, the boundary of the earth's
atmospheric layer that mediates solar phenomena
with respect to earth, solar-terrestrial physics
investigations extend beyond the earth's atmosphere
into interplanetary space. The region from approximately 80 kilometers to 6 to 10 earth radii above

the earth is being intensively probed. These investigations may be said to provide a window into
the universe and an inquiry into the forces and
phenomena that affect, and interact with terrestrial phenomena. The capability to investigate
space and its physical characteristics and influences on earth are largely the result of the space
program. The vantage point of space vehicles and
their capabilities represent a powerful new in-
vestigative tool. Through these, radiation belts
and solar wind have been discovered, global weather
analysis now exists as a result of satellites, as
does intercontinental communication and geodetic,
navigational, and planetary and interplanetary
research.

Solar-terrestrial studies include the upper
atmosphere and ionosphere, including particles and
fields in the radiation belts of the magnetosphere
(500 km to ca. 10 earth radii). An objective of
upper atmospheric (and beyond) investigations is
to understand the influences of ionospheric particles and radiation belts on earth systems and, in
the long-term, to control them. There appear to
be man-made influences on the upper atmosphere as
well as the trophosphere although these remain to
be fully elucidated. As some of the conjugate
points of the earth's radiation belts are at high
latitudes, experimental investigations are being
conducted at Siple Station, Antarctica (75°56'S;
85°15'W) and Roberval, Canada (48°30'N;72°15'W).
The effects of introduction of low frequency
radio waves from a 21 km transmitter at Siple
Station are being monitored at Roberval. Through
this and other approaches scientists expect to
improve understanding of the role of the ionosphere in regulating earth phenomena, as well as
the ionosphere's interrelations with the magnetosphere, with radio communications, with particle
precipitation, and with celestial aurora. In
addition, correlations between solar variation and
weather will become better understood.

Many nations are engaged in solar-terrestrial
investigations. New Zealand conducts studies at
the U.S. Siple Station and their own Scott Base,
as does Russia at Vostok Station. Japanese,
British, and U.S. scientists work at Roberval,
Canada. The USSR and France are cooperating in
conjugate point studies, but to the present have

not used very low frequency transmitters for experimental modification of the ionosphere.

Perhaps in no other geophysical program is
there a closer relation between basic and applied
science than in investigations of solar-terrestrial
physics. The magnitude of engineering and technology required to develop such space programs is
well known; the use of knowledge gained through
them can translate directly to improved global
communication, to a grid of space power stations,
and to defining the potential for weather modification and its role in climate control. The outcome of the latter has profound implications for
humanity. Also, not to be overlooked is the potential for understanding the all-pervading cycles
and rhythms which characterize all levels of
biological organization from cells to organisms,
populations, and ecosystems. The causal factors
which will account for the complex subtilties of
predictable and periodic oscillations in living
systems, may be extraterrestrial but these remain
to be demonstrated unequivocally, though the
probability is high.

A major global thrust against the unknowns of
the world's oceans and atmospheres has been initiated through the broad-based, 10-year, multidisciplinary IDOE program which includes 47
Nations. Among these is the International Southern Ocean Studies (ISOS), a long-term physical
oceanographic program with a goal to understand
the relationships between circumpolar dynamic
processes and their interactions with atmospheric
and oceanic circulation. The circumpolar current
and its transport, as well as the dynamics and
mixing processes of the Polar Front (Antarctic
Convergence), are under study. These have focused
on the Drake Passage and the western Scotia Sea
region, and will complement information gained
from the proposed Weddell GYRE program. A limited
field study was conducted near McMurdo Sound
(1974) but sea-ice and corresponding logistic
constraints presently direct the program to somewhat lower latitudes. Completed data will include
nutrient relations, bathymetry, hydrography,
temperature and oxygen profiles, tidal flux, and
horizontal and vertical current movements. With
comprehensive world ocean studies, the many IDOE
programs are investigating all latitudes north and

south, while the ISOS sub-program is directed to
southern circumpolar ocean dynamics, ocean circulation, and correlations with world weather and
climate. In relatively brief real time a significantly higher level of understanding of global
marine phenomena and forces can be expected to
contribute also to understanding weather and climate as well as the physical milieu of earth's
biosphere.

The climatic influences of polar ice arise
from major ice sheets on land masses as well as
from perennial (arctic) and annual (antarctic) sea-
ice. The largest ice sheet on earth covers nearly
95 per cent of Antarctica, a continent with an
area of approximately 5.5 million square miles.
The only major glacial ice sheet in the northern
hemisphere covers Greenland. The Greenland Ice
Sheet Program (GISP) has been active for the last
five years. Related studies by Swiss, Danish, and
American scientists have been underway since before 1971. This international study was designed
to determine the geophysical and geochemical
characteristics of the major physiographic, environmental, thermal, and dynamic zones of the ice
sheet. Factors controlling present and past mass
balance, atmospheric processes, and the response
to climatic change should be disclosed through
these northern studies.

The Ross Ice Shelf Geophysical and Glaciological Survey (RIGGS) is a southpolar study of an
entire ice shelf on a 55 kilometer (1/2 degree
of latitude) grid. Measurements include ice
thickness, depth to the ocean floor, velocity of
ice shelf movement, surface strain rates, gravity,
and somewhat more detailed geophysical investigations of the properties of the ice. The program
is aimed at understanding the current state and
the past and future changes of the ice shelf, of
the physical configuration and submarine geology
of the Ross Sea floor underneath the shelf, and
the state of isostatic balance as determined by
gravity measurements. The RIGGS investigations
have already yielded results suggesting, (1)
that there is very little remaining isostatic depression of the area, implying that there has not
been a full-fledged ice sheet grounded within the
last few thousand years; (2) that the ice shelf is
thickening, and the grounding line between the

West Antarctic ice sheet and the ice shelf is advancing rather rapidly, at least in the southeast
corner, and (3) that there may be some striking
differences in electrical resistivity properties
of the ice between ice streams and sheet-flow-ice
as extended out into the shelf.

The foregoing programs are coupled with the
International Antarctic Glaciological Project
(IAGP) which was created in 1969, as a long-term
program of glaciological research in East Antarctica. It represents the coordinated research
efforts of Australia, France, United Kingdom,
U.S.A., and U.S.S.R. to study the ice sheet of
East Antarctica from about $60^{\circ}E$ through Wilkes
Land to the edge of the Ross Sea. The region of
primary concentration is between $90^{\circ}E$ and $145^{\circ}E$,
with current study in the vicinity of Dome C
(Charlie) and lines radiating therefrom to the
various coastal stations. Extensive programs are
being carried out by inland traverses toward the
summit of the ice sheet from Mirnyy and Vostok
(USSR), and from Casey (Australia) and Dumont
d'Urville (France) Stations. Drilling to several
hundred meters depth (950 m. at Vostok), surface
traverses with measurement of snow accumulation
rates, strain, movement, and ice thickness, as
well as radio-echo sounding from the air will all
combine to achieve understanding of this region
of Antarctica's massive ice sheet. The radio-echo
sounding program, conducted by the U.K. and U.S.,
has defined the detailed topography and ice thickness of the eastern half of the IAGP area. The
major aim is to determine the glaciological regime and processes, and to deduce at least some of
the history and the future of a sizeable part of
the East Antarctic Ice Sheet. Other goals of the
project are to clarify relationships among the
size, shape, and glaciological regime of the ice
sheet; to reconstruct stages of its development,
their causes, and the effects on the atmosphere
and the world oceans; to assess relationships between the ice sheet and changes in climate; to determine any changes in size and content taking
place at the present time; and, finally, to trace
events of human and natural origin recorded in
the ice.

Computer modeling of the thermodynamics and
dynamics of the East Antarctic Ice Sheet has

achieved the first reconstruction of its changes
over the past several hundred thousand years and
has provided predictions of current ice temperature, using isotope profiles as well as ice flow
velocities and strain rates. A primary objective
of IAGP is deep drilling to the base of the ice
sheet on or near one of the central high points
or summits of the East Antarctic Ice Sheet.
Reconnaissance of a possible site for coring this
first deep hole, required to reach the oldest ice
in Antarctica, has been made at the location
designated Dome C.

    A complementary glaciological program, the
West Antarctic Ice Sheet Project (WISP), is in the
planning phase. Its purpose is to organize a
concentrated study of the dynamics, and the state
of growth or shrinkage of the West Antarctic Ice
Sheet between its summit, in central West Antarctica, and the Ross Ice Shelf. The general nature
of the program is similar to IAGP, except that
there will be a strong concentration of investigation on one of the major ice streams which forms
the principal ice discharge from West Antarctica
into the Ross Ice Shelf and thence out to sea.
Presently the project awaits further results from
the Ross Ice Shelf Project and, more importantly,
the imminent unveiling of a radio-echo sounding
map of ice thickness, and the contour of the
continental surface throughout western West
Antarctica.

    The Ross Ice Shelf Project (RISP) had its
first field season in 1976-77, following the
seismic and flow-strain surveys which had been
conducted for three years through RIGGS. RISP is
a study of the 560,000 sq. km. floating Ross Ice
Shelf to determine its present dynamic behavior
and past fluctuations, as well as to investigate
the unique environment beneath the shelf. A drill
hole through the ice shelf will provide access to
the relatively thin water layer (the Ross Sea)
beneath the floating ice. Scientists from nine
nations will conduct investigations of the biological and oceanographic conditions beneath the
shelf. Sub-bottom sampling will provide details
of the geological history of this region.

    This project evolved from the interest of sci-
entists who believe that a number of scientific

questions could be answered if a hole were drilled
through the largest ice shelf in the world, to
sample the ice, the underlying water column and
biome, and the bottom sediments. The program to
drill through the Ross Ice Shelf began in the 1976-
77 season at a location known as J-9 (82°22'S,
168°40'W), where the ice thickness is about 425
meters, the water depth is about 240 meters, and
the northward ice surface movement is about one
meter per day. As originally conceived, a series
of holes was scheduled to be drilled at J-9 using
a wireline drilling system. About 50 to 60 investigators from nine countries were to conduct 22
individual studies. As a result of technical and
other problems, drilling of the access hole was
terminated at a depth of 330 meters when the bit
became locked in place due to rapid closing of the
ice hole. Plans for the 1977-78 season include
resumption of drilling activities at J-9, with
ultimate penetration of the ice shelf and the conduct of the carefully structured and scheduled
scientific investigations.

As the Greenland ice sheet influences the
climate of the northern hemisphere, so the vast
antarctic ice sheet must be expected to have a
profound influence on the Southern Hemisphere.
Global weather may be accounted for by the combined discoveries of the influences of both.

Preserved in ice sheets are recent as well as
ancient climatic records providing evidence of
change. Our understanding of glacial chronology
is clearly proportionate to the depth to which an
ice-core is recovered. Spectacular results were
obtained from study of a 1,387 meter core taken in
Greenland which indicated the age of the basal ice
to be about 120,000 years B.P. Strategraphic
analysis and determination of absolute age by study
of isotopes, variations in elemental composition,
atmospheric pollutants (including nuclear test
fall-out products), and volcanic eruptions, as well
as any natural or technologically-derived atmospheric changes, appear to be faithfully recorded
in these climatic records. With reconstruction of
past paleoclimates and onward into the present
there will be better understanding of what is climatically probable in the future. The importance
of such a capability can hardly be overestimated
as one contemplates cooling and warming trends,

floods, changes in sea level, and the impact of
these on populations, population centers, and
world agricultural production.

The history of an expansive south circumpolar
continent as well as its origin and past location
have long challenged curious men. The apparent
absence of an indigenous population and land animals in Antarctica, coupled with its cover by
earth's largest ice sheet, still evades comprehensive understanding. The discovery of coal deposits
and fossils of Jurassic fish and Triassic amphibia
and reptiles clearly disclose a past tropical
period, but its geological history remains obscure
in important details. In contrast to a vast area
of this continent under the ice sheet extending
across West and East Antarctica, there is a relatively small range within the Transantarctic
Mountains in East Antarctica which is essentially
free of glaciers, ice, and snow. While glaciers
may rest on the summits of the mountains, they
terminate abruptly above barren and deep-cut, ice-
free valleys below. The stark contrast of this
area, confluent within the range of glaciated and
ice covered mountains and valleys both north and
south, has attracted geologists seeking an explanation for their origin and unique characteristics.

The Dry Valley Drilling Project (DVDP) was
initiated in 1973 with the objective to understand
tectonics, paleoclimate, and the geological history
of Antarctica through a wide range of scientific
analyses. These investigations and field drilling
programs were jointly conducted and supported by
New Zealand, Japan, and the United States. The
final phase of DVDP's field work was completed in
November, 1975 with the 15th borehole having successfully produced the last core. Throughout its
three years a total of 2,231 meters of penetration
were achieved. Sediments, rocks, and all deeper
strata cored are being studied in many research
laboratories. Cores were taken from Wright Valley
(4), Victoria Valley (1), Taylor Valley (6), the
sea floor of McMurdo Sound (1) through ice near the
seaward extension of Taylor Valley, and from Ross
Island (3) yielding a total of 2,074 meters of
core recovered (93 percent recovery rate).

The Scotia Arc-Antarctica Peninsula Tectonics
Program, being conducted in West Antarctica, has

been underway for about a decade and has as its
most important goal the understanding of relationships between Antarctica and South America. Study
of the Scotia Arc, which consists of islands and
submarine ridges, involves the Southern Andes
Mountain range and its elements confluent with the
rise to the Transantarctic Mountain range on the
Peninsula. This program, with sub-programs conducted by scientists from a number of U.S. academic
institutions, is one of the comprehensive geological studies which has contributed to development
of the concepts and science of plate tectonics.
Scientists from Chile, Argentina, and the United
Kingdom are continuing investigations of the
structure of the area, its tectonic evolution, and
the sedimentary environment, mostly of the paleozoic and mesozoic age. As all geology is unified
through plate tectonics, this concept of geological
change has become the most persuasive contemporary
theory with the promise to explicate land mass
origins, and their change with time.

The understanding of past and present environments, their climates and change, are of high significance to a comprehensive understanding of the
biosphere, its history, its successes and failures,
and the principles of adaptational biology.

Research programs addressed to every component
of the lithosphere, the atmosphere, the stratosphere and beyond, and the hydrosphere, as well as
the dependent and responding biosphere, represent a
synthesis of man's efforts to understand his
planet. These are most distinctly evident in the
comprehensive interdigitating studies being conducted in polar regions which have taken their perspective and momentum from the IGY of 20 years ago.

(The foregoing brief summary of polar scientific
programs has been derived from many contributions,
including reports to the U.S. National Academy of
Sciences-National Research Council, Polar Research
Board, reports in the Arctic Bulletin, and the
Antarctic Journal of the United States, publica-
tions of the International Scientific Committee on
Antarctic Research, numerous working documents of

Committees of the Polar Research Board, and informal communications from program directors, conven-
ors, and Chief Scientists involved in many of the
programs described.)

Index

Aagaard, K., 117, 129, 131, 138
ablation, 213
Acarina, 31
accessory pigment, 212
acclimation, 203, 204
Achromobacter parvulum, 213
acoustics, 233, 276
adaptation, 203–217, 233; arctic, 21; chromatic, 212; to cold, 53; cold, in antarctic fish, 53, 55; to low temperature, 6; mechanism, 207, 209; organismic, 7; to high ultraviolet radiation fluxes, 211
adaptational biology, 276, 285
Adelaide geosyncline, 79
Adelaide orogens, 76
Adineta grandis, 213
Aditya, S., 82
aerial: photogrammetric work, 35; photographs, 235
aerosols, 112
Africa, 63, 68, 69, 73, 75–82 *passim*, 84
"Agreed Measures for the Conservation of Antarctic Fauna and Flora," 268
Agreement on the Conservation of Polar Bears (1974), 163

agricultural production, world, 284
aircraft, 234, 239, 251, 256, 257; Air Force C-141 Starlifter, 257; C-47 transport planes, 235; C-130 cargo planes, 255; commercial, 270; Hercules, 251, 255; LC-130, 251, 256, 257; seaplanes, 235
airdrops, 255
air-mass: exchange, 277; transport, 277
airplanes, ski-equipped, 255
air transportation, 37
alanine, 187, 189
Alaska, 5, 33, 73; arctic winter in, 34; coastal regions of, 41; northern, 4, 34; pipeline, 264; prehistory of, 35
Alaska Boundary Commission, 35
Alaska Cooperative Wildlife Research Unit, 41, 43
Alaskan: biology, 37; coast, 32; continental shelf, 265; geography, 35; marine environmental studies, 45; population, 5; research, 43
Alaskan Arctic, 265
Alaskan Eskimo Group, 34
Alaskan North Slope, 5
albatross, 34

British: explorer, 233;
  naval expedition, 32;
  scientists, 278
Broken Ridge, 82
Brooks Range, 207
Brown, J., 39
Bryant, B.M., 49
Bunger Hills, 205, 207
Bunt, J.S., 150
Bureau of Biological Sur-
  vey Department of,
  Agriculture, 33, 35
Bureau of Commercial
  Fisheries, Interior,
  33
Burkholder, P.R., 142, 145
Burrell, J., 84
Burton Island, 235
Buxton, M.G., 34
Byrd, Richard E., 9, 16, 64,
  232, 234, 235, 237, 239,
  243, 267
Byrd's Second Antarctic
  Expedition (1933-1935),
  234
Byrd Station, 235, 239, 243,
  245, 251, 255

Camp Century, 243
Canada, 3
Canadian Archipelago, 122
Canadian Arctic, 265
Canadian Basin, 123, 131
Cape Adare, 63
Cape fold belt, 73, 76
Cape granites, 80
Cape Horn, 11, 234
Cape orogen, 71, 76, 80
captive ballon, 251
carbon dioxide, 109
caribou, 34, 207
Carlucci, A.F., 151
Carmack, E.C., 133, 135
carotenoid pigment, 212
Carpenter, 149
Carter, R.M., 84
cartographic data, 7
Casey Station (Australia),
  281

Casshyap, S.M., 82
celestial aurora, 278
Ceylon, 63, 68, 78
Challenger expedition, 14
char, arctic, 29
Char Lake, 214
charnockite, 68
chemical: oceanography, 275;
  properties of permafrost,
  6
chemistry, 275
Chile, 257, 285; Antarctic
  Program, 15, 18
Chile Ridge, 88
chill-coma, 214
Christchurch, New Zealand,
  239, 247, 260
Chukchi Sea, 41, 231
Chukchi Sea Coast, 35
circadian rhythm studies,
  56
circular dichorism, 190
circulation, physical,
  meteorological forcing of,
  273
circumantarctic waters, 142
circumarctic activities, 45
circum-Pacific mobile belt,
  74
circumpolar: current, 279;
  ocean dynamics, 280
clay, 209
Clifford, T.N., 78
climate, 7, 276, 277, 280,
  281; changes, 97, 105;
  control, 279; dynamics,
  277; machine, 97
Climate: Long-range Investigation, Mapping and
  Prediction Study
  (CLIMAP), 277
climates, 285
climatic: boundary, 29;
  lever, 108; variables,
  165; variations, 108
climatology, 98, 276
Coachman, L.K., 117, 131,
  138
coal deposits, 284
Coast Guard, 34, 237, 251

lichens, 29, 31, 49, 207;
 growth, 48
life sciences: antarctic,
 47, 50; polar, 51
*The Life Sciences in Ant-
arctica,* 50
life systems, 51
light intensity, 150
limnology, 217
Lin, Y., 189, 193
Lindsey, A.A., 48
lipid depots, 195
lipids, 195
lithosphere, 285
Little America, 234
Little America IV, 235
Little America V, 235, 243,
 251
Little Diomede, 35
Littlepage, J.L., 177
Little Rockford, 245
liverworts, 29
Llano, George A., 2, 50
Lockhart, E.E., 49
Longwire Station, 245
Longyearbyen (Svalbard),
 264
Luyendyk, B.P., 82
Lystrosaurus, 71

Mc Cracken, F.D., 182
Mc Elhinny, M.W., 76, 77,
 78, 81, 82, 83
MacGinitie, George, 38
Mc Illhenny, E.A., 34
MacMillian, D.B., 32
McMurdo Sound, 177, 178,
 183, 191, 245, 260, 279,
 284
McMurdo Sound study, 166,
 167, 171
McMurdo Station, 50, 51,
 171, 177, 205, 207, 235,
 239, 245, 246, 247, 249,
 251, 255, 256, 257, 260
McMurdo Weather Center, 261
macromolecules, 183
McWhinnie, M.A., 179, 195
Madagascar, 63, 69, 76, 78
magnetic anomaly belts, 74

magnetic station, 32
magnetosphere, 278
mammals, 3, 31, 205, 214,
 215, 216, 233; Alaskan
 fur, 33; arctic, 3, 39;
 fur thickness, 216
mammals, marine, 7, 29, 33,
 56, 161-172; aboriginal
 hunting, 171; aesthetics
 and recreational considerations, 161, 171; age-
 specific reproductive
 rates, 170; censusing,
 166; carnivore, 41; con-
 servation, 161; density
 dependence phenomena, 168,
 169, 170; exploitation,
 161, 167, 168; extinction,
 161; habitat destruction,
 162; management problems,
 161; modeling, 161; mor-
 tality rates, 169; "optimal" population levels,
 167; population abundance,
 166; population dynamics,
 53, 167; population dynamics, Lotka equations,
 170; population growth
 curves, 167; population
 parameters, 164, 165;
 population regulation,
 167, 168, 169; population
 research, 161; renewable
 resource, 161; reproduc-
 tive rates, 161
Mandell, E.F., 142, 145,
 149, 152
Man in the Arctic Program,
 5, 40
Marble Point, 260
Marie Byrd Land, 16, 49,
 234
marine: animals, 47, 53;
 biological studies, 51;
 coastal areas, 6; cur-
 rents, 7; environment, 6,
 7; geology, 277; geo-
 physics, 276; living re-
 sources, 43. *See also*
 mammals, marine

regulatory" mechanism,
167
seals, 3, 31, 164, 275;
antarctic, 167, census of,
in the pack ice, 57; ant-
arctic fur, fisheries,
33; crabeater (*Lobodon
carcinophagus*), 166, so-
cial structure of, 57;
fur, 143, 168, 171; harp
(*Pagophilus groenlandi-
cus*), 164, 166, 169, 170;
hooded (*Cystophore cris-
tata*), 166; leopard, predation by, 57; northern
fur (*Callorhinus ursinus*),
164; ringed (*Phoca hispida*), 162; Weddell (*Lep-
tonychotes weddelli*), 56,
166, 167, 171, demographic
characteristics of, 57,
life history pattern of,
57, observation and
branding of, 48, skele-
tons and embryos of, 49
sea otters, 41
sea phenomena, 47
Seasat I, 7
seasonal: anomalies, 108;
changes, in ice, 7; vari-
ation, 6
sea urchin, 179
sea water, freezing point
of, 182
secondary: production, 273;
productivity, 274
Second Byrd Antarctic Ex-
pedition (1935-1937), 48
sedges, 267
seismic: soundings, 259;
surveys, 6
serine, 190
Seward, W.H., 33
Seward Peninsula, 33
Shackleton, E., 9, 16, 64,
245, 251, 267
Shelf Water, 135
shields, 67, 76, 77, 78, 81,
84
ship-to-shore transports, 256

shrews, 207
shrubs, 207
Siberian coastline, 6
Sierra orogen, 80
Signy Islands, 145, 213
silico flagellates, 143
Simon Lake, 232
Sinha, 82
Siple, Paul A., 48
Siple Station, 235, 239,
247, 249, 278
Siwalik beds, 84
size fractionation, 273
SKATE, 232, 233
skiways, 255
skuas, 215; predatory,
feeding territory of, 56
Sky Hi, 255
Smith, R.N., 182
Smithsonian Institution, 35
snow melter, 246
Snyder, W.E., 34
social structure, 53
sodium chloride, 192
soil microorganisms, 207,
211
soils, 209, 211
solar: phenomena, 277; radi-
ation, 103, 123, 150,
209; wind, 277
solar, terrestrial: physics,
279; studies, 278
Solomons, 11
Somero, G.N., 179, 193,
196, 197
Sondrestromfjord (Green-
land), 264
S. Africa, 69, 71, 269;
Antarctic Program, 15, 18
S. America, 63, 69, 75, 77,
78, 79, 80, 81, 82, 84,
88, 239, 285
South Atlantic Ocean, 131
South circumpolar conti-
nent, 284
South circumpolar seas, 273
South circumpolar waters, 6
Southeast Pacific Basin, 85
Southern Andes Mountain
range, 285